"MORAL ORDER" AND THE CRIMINAL LAW:
REFORM EFFORTS IN THE UNITED STATES AND
WEST GERMANY

"MORAL ORDER" AND THE CRIMINAL LAW:

REFORM EFFORTS IN THE UNITED STATES AND WEST GERMANY

by

ORLAN LEE
Washington University

and

T.A. ROBERTSON

with a foreword

by

TH. WÜRTENBERGER
Director of the Institute for Criminology and Penology
of the University of Freiburg im Breisgau

MARTINUS NIJHOFF/THE HAGUE/1973

PRINTED IN BELGIUM

To the Jurisprudence
of Our Parents' Traditions

"*...therefore keep my statutes and my judgements: which if a man do, he shall live in them....*" (*Lev.* 18,5)

ACKNOWLEDGEMENTS

The authors are indebted to Professor Max Rheinstein, Max Pam Professor of Comparative Law Emeritus at the University of Chicago, and to Professor Th. Würtenberger, Director of the Institute for Criminology and Penology of the University of Freiburg im Breisgau, who read the early drafts of the manuscript and offered many suggestions on organization and treatment of the materials. We are especially grateful for Professor Würtenberger's Foreword. It is a great honor when a scholar of often quite different philosophical persuasion can read one's work with such understanding. We are very grateful for their advice and suggestions in the preparation of the final draft to Professor Albert Ehrenzweig, of the School of Law of the University of California at Berkeley, and Professor Walter Weyrauch, of the Law School of the University of Florida. Professor Herbert J. Spiro, of the University of Pennsylvania, was also kind enough to offer suggestions in response to an abstract prepared for the 2nd Plenary Meeting of AMINTAPHIL, the American Section of the International Association for the Philosophy of Law and Social Philosophy. The text owes much for its clarity to Ulrich Ruge, judge of the administrative court in Düsseldorf, who read the section on German law in manuscript, for his certainty of expression in English as well as in German. Finally, for his very useful advice and helpful suggestions, both before our embarking on this project and during the course of its completion, we are indebted to Dr. Ulrich von Burski, judge of the administrative court in Freiburg im Breisgau.

For their support and cooperation in preparing the manuscript, we would like to thank the Department of History of the State University of New York at Buffalo and the Division of Special Interdisciplinary Studies of Case Western Reserve University. We would especially like to thank Mrs. Frank Isaly who typed the manuscript and the various revisions.

CONTENTS

CRIMINAL LAW AND REFORM IN THE
UNITED STATES

CRIMINAL LAW AND REFORM IN
WEST GERMANY

FOREWORD:
IMPRESSIONS AND REMARKS

A. *General*

This is a book concerned with the problems of criminal law reform in the United States and in Germany. The section on Germany gives the English-speaking reader a good and comprehensive introduction into the historical and on-going development of German criminal law reform and the results which have been achieved thus far.

As is suggested in the title, this presentation attempts to make clear the role of the various political, social ethical, philosophical, and religious ideas which have competed to influence criminal law reform and continue to influence further development of the law. In the course of these discussions, the authors' own fundamental attitudes to political theory become apparent. Very simply, they are based upon the importance of the ideal of the limitation of the power of the state over the individual. This is consistent with the liberal democratic tradition, as it is especially characteristic of Anglo-American thinking, perhaps; but the tradition is alive not only in that cultural sphere.

In the first chapter the authors consider some of the sociological and political developments of recent years and how these historical events are treated in various social perspectives. Among other things, the revolution of sexual permissiveness and of forms of political resistance (as for example the anti-war movement) in the United States, are considered. Similar developments are also to be observed in Germany, although in German criminal law reform these have not played as decisive a role. Yet the general liberalizing of sexual attitudes has had a certain influence on the section of the German criminal law governing sexual offenses. Political demonstrations which have occurred in Germany, too, in recent years have, furthermore, led to a government bill to reform the regulations governing what constitutes disturbing internal security.[1]

---

[1] This bill is discussed by Müller-Emmert: in *Zeitschrift für Rechtspolitik* (ZRP) 1970, fasc. 1, pp. 1ff. The bill is printed on p. 21 of the same issue.

Seen as a whole, however, I regard the work before us to be especially noteworthy precisely because of its illumination of both the social contexts surrounding the law and the ideas which underlie the efforts towards criminal law reform. An analysis of this kind has not appeared until now, to my knowledge, even in the German literature on the subject, so that this book is of great value to the German reader as well as the American.

B. *Particulars*

In Chapter IV: A the authors give a general introduction into the development of the German criminal law reform. In that connection they recognize the special role of the Christian Democratic (CDU), Socialist (SPD) coalition in the political situation [leading to passage of the reform law]. The authors emphasize the importance of the introduction of a uniform prison sentence [that is to say the termination of the distinction between kinds of prison sentences] and the elimination of short term prison sentences, as the main points of the reform in the "general part" of the code. They remark (pages 170; 192) that a uniform concept of the goal of punishment is still lacking, although, when all is said, there is a general agreement on the principle of resocialization. The absence of such a common concept is attributable, in my opinion, to the same underlying political problem as the authors previously described, namely that in earlier years no single party government and no "small coalition" [i.e. the earlier Christian Democratic (CDU), Free Democratic (FDP) coalition] was in a position to bring about criminal law reform by itself. The reasons are clear: The legislators were always attempting to base criminal law reform on very broad support, so that it could be sure of not only the approval of all political parties and religious denominations, but, more than that, of the support of all the people. If one holds fast to this goal—and one definitely should— it is naturally not possible to reduce all the divergent theories of what the penal goal should be to one common denominator.

In giving a general survey of the situation in the law pertaining to the protection of the state (page 170f.), the authors consider the importance of surrounding political circumstances in Germany, such as the attitudes of the cold-war days, the mistrust of a pure liberal democracy as practised in the Weimar Republic, and of the later stronger drive toward resuming contacts with the East. Here another central concern of the book becomes clear, namely the relationship between law and ethics. The authors

emphasize the susceptibility especially of the criminal law to the attempts
to design law according to political, philosophical, or religious ethics
(page 171). In this manner they come to address themselves to the moral-
ethical question so often raised in the debates leading to the German
criminal law reform: the contention surrounding the claim that there
should be "no guilt without moral guilt" (page 174f.).

Arthur Kaufmann defended this idea more than anyone else, and I
would like to refer on this point to his dissertation for admission to
university faculty rank, *Das Schuldprinzip* [*The Principle of Guilt*],
Heidelberg, 1961,[2] where he indicates that: "What one describes as
legal guilt is either a phenomenon of morals or it is no guilt at all...".
It is very interesting, here, how the present authors point to the other
side to that argument, namely the danger of reading-in a moral guilt,
even to ethically indifferent violations (as for example of simple administrative regulations). Where all legal guilt becomes moral guilt, a moralizing
state, untenable to a pluralistic democracy, arises.

When the authors criticize the all too self-assured invocation of the
Federal Supreme Court (for civil and criminal law) of the "absolute
moral law" in the famous decision BGHSt 6, 46 (cf. page 176f.) perhaps
even then too "moralistic" a picture of German jurisprudence arises for
the English-speaking reader. That decision was after all repeatedly
criticized, and it is very interesting to observe in this connection how
in its recognition of the validity of wills which married men had set up
in favor of their mistresses, the Federal Court has taken a surely cautious
but still clearly more liberal attitude in recent years.

On page 179 the authors remark that law without a moral-ethical
content would be only an empty collection of rules of behavior and
administration. As obvious as these words may be, I still consider it
important to emphasize them in today's technical age in which a kind
of data determinism over broad areas of life conceals the danger that
the law can forfeit its relevance to man, its humanity. Without an ethical
content in the law it would not be possible, either, for the individual
to feel bound in his *conscience* to the obligation imposed in the law.
That this is especially necessary today I have explained more closely
in my paper "On the Lawmaking Conscience." [3]

---

[2] Arthur Kaufmann: *Das Schuldprinzip*, Winter, Heidelberg, 1961, esp. Ch. 4:
"The Idea of Guilt as an Absolute Moral Principle" (*"Das Schuldprinzip als
absoluter sittlicher Grundsatz"*).
[3] Th. Würtenberger: "Vom rechtschaffenen Gewissen," in Th. Würtenberger:

Here too the authors point to the other side of the problem: the attempt to insure the moral-ethical content of the law can turn into an over-moralizing in the law (page 179). In my opinion this danger can be met insofar as we limit the criminal law to the so-called "ethical minimum" (Jellinek). This is the ambition of the plan, either to drop all minor violations from the German criminal code by 1973, or to redesignate them as simple breeches of regulations. This ambition was already realized in part by the law regarding violations of public order of 1968.[4] In this "de-criminalization" one can at the same time catch sight of a "de-moralization" in the criminal law.

Where the authors take up the difficulties one encounters in the attempt to eliminate the strictly moralizing criminal law provisions (cf. page 179) they consider the often repeated argument that the public might misunderstand the lifting of the prohibitions to mean not simply that thereafter these things would not be prohibited by law, but would infer that society no longer considered these things morally unacceptable. The authors do not regard it as a primary legislative concern to have a law for the purpose of lifting public morals, if for no other reason, than because the currently increasing rate of violent criminality confronts us with more important enforcement priorities. They critize as misleading the argument [frequently employed towards attaining the same goal] that the actual source of severe violent crime lies in open immorality (cf. page 180, n. 19). I believe that a reform must unquestionably extend to the elimination of out of date morals laws, if only to legitimate [the claim of] the criminal code to be the law not only for a moral elite but for all the people. So far as severe criminality is concerned, on the other hand, I think not so much a reform of substantive prohibitions as much more a reform of criminal procedure and penology is necessary.

In Chapter IV: A. (2), the authors consider the history of the ideas and politics behind the present reform of the German criminal code. On page 182, they conclude from a quotation from Jescheck [one of the leading German criminal law professors active on the criminal law commission appointed in 1954 to prepare what later became the government's draft code of 1960 and of 1962], which rejects the purely value-free ideal of the state, that according to his position the law

---

W. Maihofer; A. Hollerbach (eds.): *Existenz und Ordnung, Festschrift fur Erik Wolf zum 60. Geburtstag*, V. Klostermann, Frankfurt a.M., 1962, pp. 337-56.

[4] *Gesetz über Ordnungswidrigkeiten* (OWiG) of 24 May, 1968. [See also page 173, n.7, below.)

becomes an instrument of a kind of "moral rearmament". This logical consequence may be supportable from the perspective that Jescheck actually is an advocate of the thesis that there is a "morals-strengthening" power in the law. One should distinguish between two different things here, however. A form of government that wants to implement certain values does not really have to write the legislative enforcement of good morals into its platform. A declaration of adherence to ethical values in government, as for example in the list of fundamental rights contained in the Basic Law of the Federal Republic [or the American Bill of Rights] is not something primarily concerned with questions of public morals.[5]

The authors consider the tension between the penal goals of retribution and resocialization (cf. page 184f.) and try to relate these concepts to the political standpoints of the conservatives, social democrats, and social liberals. This discussion in terms of concepts and political philosophy is clearly meant only to contribute an abstract basis of reference. In practice, or when it comes to describing the attitude of any particular criminal lawyer, these points are not so easily distinguishable. The authors suggest the same thing later themselves: "Even the most hardened legal moralist adherent of retributive justice is more or less prepared to accept the resocialization theory to some extent today" (page 193). In any case it is accurate to say that political, social philosophical, even ideological questions are involved here (cf. page 185).

Whether it is a question of a choice between the rights of the individual on one hand and the rights of the collective on the other, the authors' observations following from the above discussion are very revealing especially for the German reader (cf. page 185f.). While in England and America there was always something of the debate between individualism

---

[5] [Liberal minded people in the English speaking world would probably consider the Bill of Rights (and the same provisions in the German Basic Law) to be primarily a set of legal and political guarantees, not of ethical values. Naturally it puts the matter into a much different perspective if one feels himself compelled to justify philosophically or ideologically why these guarantees should exist. In the one case we accept that these are already a part of our cultural historical heritage. In the other we have first to be able to say why we should enjoy these rights and what society itself should and should not be.

In Continental political theory—and nowadays in ideological circles in America—ultimate questions are asked before the pragmatists practical ones. But if the differences our point of departure makes are not clear from the start, the rest of our discussion will never be mutually intelligible, Auth.]

and collective interests (or between the individual and the government or "the system"), in Germany this dichotomy has never played the same role. Even German liberalism was more an economic liberalism not so much democratic, individualistic liberalism. Therefore, in Germany the debate was not formulated as often as individualism *vs.* the common good, but rather more as the good of society-conservative *vs.* the good of society-social democratic, or something else.

This view is by and large correct, although an incisive characterization such as this must always accept some degree of over-simplification. One should expand upon this impression of German political life for the English-speaking reader, however. For in Germany too, at least in the post-war years, and as a reaction to the National Socialist reign of force, a strong liberal democratic, individualistic tendency has dominated all the major parties, and has been clearly expressed in the Basic Law of the Federal Republic. Even then it is not to be denied that this wholesome recognition of the importance of the individual has in the meantime faded a little again; and since the 50's the Federal Constitutional Court has repeatedly given stronger emphasis to the obligation of the individual to his society.

If one examines the very newest development of the dominant ideas in the criminal law in the Federal Republic, one can detect that the social ideal is more strongly brought out. This is shown above all in that to the concept of "rule of law" which arose in the 19th Century (i.e. to a concept implying among other things freedom from the state) inferences are now drawn which more properly have their origin in the principle of the social state [and hence emphasize obligation to society and thus to the state]. For a further discussion on this development see my recently published collection of articles, *Criminal Law Policy in a Social Liberal Democracy.*[6]

On page 186 the authors observe (in reference to the example of the alternative draft penal code) that in Germany new ideas have first of all to be taken up in the program of one of the political parties in order to achieve political success. The justifiable recognition that West German democracy is a party democracy underlies this position. Theoretically perhaps this is only partly true, as Article 21 of the Basic Law records: "The (political) parties cooperate in the formation of the political desires of the nation." In practice, however, the generalization is every bit the case—one can take a stand on what ought to be as one will.

[6] Th. Würtenberger: *Kriminalpolitik im sozialen Rechtsstaat*, Enke, Stuttgart, 1970.

In Chapter IV: B, the authors take up the reform of the "general part" of the German criminal code. They show (page 194) the danger of a "perfectionized" resocialization plan. Implementation of such a plan could take on just as moralizing a character as a penal system built on plain retribution, in the case where the freedom to form one's own civil and social values is taken from the inmate of such a house of correction. Significantly, in the case of Red China, for example, one speaks not of resocialization so much as re-education. This may be properly said, for that matter, for all the countries of the East Bloc, in any case according to the nature of their ambitions. In order to carry out resocialization in a reasonable manner, it is certainly wise (as the authors remark on page 194) to keep the ultimate logical consequences of the resocialization argumentation before our eyes, namely that a "perfect resocialization" can only be achieved through a total reordering of the personality of the offender. Accordingly the authors differentiate between a re-education of the prisoner and offering him the opportunity of putting himself in a position to make his way in society again (page 195). This differentiation even then affords some difficulty to apply in practice.[7] In any case the authors warn against assigning educational missions [in the area of social convictions] to the American prisons in their present state, and particularly considering the mounting incidence of violations arising from political or social moral convictions.[8] This warning may be said to apply in similar manner to Germany, too.

In Chapter IV, Section C (2), the authors give a very comprehensive overview of the German penal system. Perhaps I may add a word here on the concept of "measures of safeguarding (*Sicherung*) and resocialization (*Besserung*)". This section of the penal code in the reform version applying from 1973 is now called "Measures of Resocialization (*Besserung*)

---

[7] [The latter choice is, of course, intended only to supply vocational training or additional education to those for whom either economic deprivation, or even the lack of need, or interest in the past, to pursue this course or become self-supporting, and not personal or political convictions led to their conflict with the law. Auth.]

[8] [If there is any reason at all for the marijuana smoker to be in prison, it is for violation of the law against possession, not for his disreputable taste or personal philosophy. Similarly, the draft resister, who sees some moral reason for facing prison in the United States rather than fleeing to Canada, may be because he just likes it better in the United States, is only guilty of resisting the draft. His "moral gesture", which has pretty weak impact in the United States, anyway, is not the crime. Auth.]

and Safeguarding (*Sicherung*)". The inversion of the older usage is intended to put stronger emphasis on the resocialization ideal.

Chapter V goes on to the reform of the "special part" of the code. The authors first discuss constitutional and theoretical questions. While they see a common intellectual development and historical background in the human rights concepts of the Western World, there appear to be differing ways of life and of thinking regarding whether men's legal rights pertain to the individual as such or derive instead from his social relationships and obligations to his society. On this point I am of the opinion that the social nature of man is a natural phenomenon of mankind itself.

The authors then discuss the stipulations of the Basic Law of the Federal Republic for the protection of the liberal democratic constitution of the state (e.g. Arts. 18 and 21, which permit limitations on fundamental rights in the case of persons whom the Federal Constitutional Court decides are acting contrary to the constitutional legal order of the Federal Republic). In Germany these rulings are often characterized under the political caption: "No freedom for the enemies of freedom." How often Article 18 [for which the above caption is best applied] has been invoked, (cf. page 206) may well change before publication. Even so, I do think the reference to the decision of the Federal Constitutional Court (*Bundesverfassungsgericht*) in which it emphasized its sole responsibility for deciding questions in regard to Article 18 of the Basic Law [9] is important.

In connection with the prohibition of the neo-Nazi Socialist Reichs Party (SRP) and the Communist Party (KPD) [of the years before 1956],[10] the authors consider the difficulties of devising a positive definition of what a liberal democracy must consist of (cf. page 207) [since we are often clearer on the negative formulation, what it does not consist of]. Such positive definitions are found, moreover, in § 88 of the penal code (StGB) [which enumerates constitutional principles the contravention of which is tantamount to treason], whereby even then § 88, No. 6, "Exclusion of any rule of force or action without due process of law (*Willkürherrschaft*)" is also negatively formulated. A positively

---

[9] *Entscheidungen des Bundesverfassungsgerichts* (BVerfGE) 10, 118.

[10] [The communist party was reconstituted without opposition in 1968 employing the device of switching the order of the KPD (*Kommunistische Partei Deutschlands*) to create the DKP (*Deutsche Kommunistische Partei*). For a further account see V. A (1.), p. 208ff. below. Auth.]

formulated definition may also be seen in the list of fundamental rights of the Basic Law, however. When the authors remark (on page 209) that it is not at all correct to look for a positive, dogmatic "ideology" to express the liberal democratic standpoint because that ideal does not, for the most part, go beyond the rejection of unnecessary force, this seems to be a somewhat too Anglo-American way of looking at things. The liberal democratic form of government in the Federal Republic is not intended to embody only this kind of an individualistic liberal resistance to undue coercion. Rather it is also concerned with the preservation of certain traditional, distinctly European cultural values, which one could call the "Christian, Western cultural tradition". These separate attitudes seem to be brought together on page 204 where the authors do not hesitate to equate [the constitutional commitment of the Federal Republic to upholding] the "dignity of man" of Article 1 of the Basic Law, which certainly refers to man as a moral agent, with [the philosophical dedication of American democracy to] the "certain unalienable rights" of the American Declaration of Independence. If I am not mistaken those rights ("life, liberty, and the pursuit of happiness") amount to precisely a declaration of belief by the individualistic liberal. Beyond that I would completely agree with the authors that the Federal Constitutional Court does not have the mission of defining the "correct democratic philosophy" (cf. esp. pages 207 and 209), and furthermore, that the prohibition of the communist party (KPD) was decisively influenced by the political climate of the cold-war (cf. page 209). In a broader sense one could also picture this latter decision as a moralistic intrusion into the legal sphere.

In Section A, Part (2), the authors go on to the reform of political justice and concern themselves especially with the problems of state secrets. On pages 215f., there is a very interesting argument for a legal means for revealing "illegal state secrets" [a concept originally introduced by the alternative draft penal code and which has been embodied in the reform law to the extent that § 93.II of the criminal code now recognizes that certain constitutional or treaty violations "are no state secrets"] which would not fall under the provisions of § 97a [a provision prohibiting informing a foreign power of a secret, which although "no state secret" according to § 93.II, could contribute to a "severe disadvantage for the external security of the Federal Republic"]. In this [pursuit] positively formulated inferences are drawn from the negative formulation of § 97b [a provision detailing what one should consider before concluding that he has knowledge of what ought to be "no state secret" under § 93.II and which he feels ought, therefore, to be released].

It is very understandable from a liberal standpoint when the authors criticize the whole new ordering of the political justice section as stemming from a "the King can do no wrong" mentality (cf. page 215). In any case it is a question here of a clear value judgment within the polarity between a democratic liberalism on the one hand and a strongly protective attitude toward the state on the other.

The criticism that the old § 100.III StGB [the provision protecting members of the parliament from prosecution for revealing what they considered to be unconstitutional state secrets] was stricken without a replacement offering equal guarantees is surely well taken. I would, however, still see an adequate protection in Article 46.I.1 of the Basic Law.

In Chapter V, Section B the authors come to speak of the reform of offenses against the religious peace. I can completely agree with the critical remarks about the "Germanic drive" for perfectionism (cf. pages 218ff.). In the pages 220ff., the political and religious denominational tendencies which have played a role in the reform in this area are very clearly shown.

In Chapter V, Section C, the authors take up the reform of the morals laws, under the title "Offenses Against Public Morality". It seems to me that the discussion of abortion under this heading does not fit very well, since it is a matter here, as the authors themselves say (on page 224), of an offense against life. On the other hand this part of the matter is pretty hard to separate from the discussion of birth control and the description of the economic exploitation of sex.

The authors give a comprehensive account of the problems which arise in the medical grounds for abortion, and especially in the religious background. On page 229 they see the connection between the so-called ethical grounds and medical grounds and establish the danger of suicide as a connecting link. On pages 230ff. they go on to discuss the Swedish regulations concerning the interruption of pregnancy.

The opinion of the Federal Supreme Court for civil and criminal matters cited on page 233 regarding pandering (and indecency) should not be too easily regarded as "judicial opinion" today, sixteen years later. In this sub-section one may wonder whether there has been some influence of the pill on the number of abortions. One might also mention here the reduction in penalty for performing an abortion on someone else (§ 218.III of the old version, II of the new version StGB).

In Chapters III: D and V: C (2), the authors consider the prohibition of homosexuality, and it is surely correct for them to have compared the crassly conflicting judgments and opinions in this matter in their full scope (cf. pages 164ff.; 240ff.). On page 244 they show themselves very circumspect regarding German legal perfectionism and the thesis of the "morals-strengthening power" of the law. I would also share this attitude. I believe that the law, particularly the criminal law, cannot make and form morality, but rather it can only reflect a morality which is already there and has been nurtured from other sources; but this is something that the criminal law should also do. Finally the last sentence on page 245 is written completely from the view of a pragmatic liberal but could be very useful in promoting the self-recognition of many a German, even though it shows that the "principle" represents a completely impregnable fortress in the German mind.[11]

In the discussion of adultery (Chapter V: C (3)) the authors show that here the dogma of the "morals-strengthening" power of the criminal law was of special importance in the discussion of the elimination of this prohibition. On page 249 they also come to speak of the problem of artificial insemination. The question arises in this connection how it is that the Catholic authorities resisted the idea of homologous insemination, although lust is a sin according to Catholic doctrine. This may be explainable insofar as sexual relations without the desire for progeny is held to be contrary to natural law in the same manner as artificial insemination.

In Chapter VI, the authors draw the logical inferences from these investigations. Properly they reach the conclusion that legislation is not the product of only objective needs, but rather also of the outlooks of the particular legislators (cf. page 252), and that one cannot really speak of an "end of ideology" [in the law]. One can also agree with the contention (page 253), that there is always a temptation in the making of a law not only to satisfy public needs but also to realize cultural and moral ambitions. The authors contend that the criminal law must contain a "social ethical minimum" [of what is our obligation to find in order to convict]. However, this use of the expression "social ethical minimum" seems to me a little misleading. In this inversion of meaning, the social responsibility is not so much the obligation of the individual to uphold the social values of his society as it is primarily a democratic liberal limitation upon the use of the criminal law by the public.

[11] [Not only the German! Auth.]

The authors consider briefly the theory of Popitz that there is a general preventive function in the number of undiscovered offenses. There is surely much that can be said about this interesting theory, and at least this, that it does not fit all categories of offenses, and perhaps only very few, as for example morals offenses and traffic offenses. The authors say as much themselves (on page 254).

In conclusion the authors bring their central ideas together: the law is neither solely the product of objective needs ("the shoe to the foot of necessity") nor is it an easily tractable medium for moral-ethical ambitions or even for political philosophical purposes. It contains something from all of these including apparently irrational impulses, and even completely unsound arguments. The best intentions and principles of morally committed or rational liberal lawmakers offer no guarantee against dilution and ineffectiveness because of an already prevailing practice or because of the momentum of the tried and true ("the instinctive logic of business as usual"). The solution for these inescapable complications which arise for the best legal regulations may be only to legislate for what is absolutely necessary: in this way laws are a medium for the protection of our lives, interests, and property. Philosophy, ethics, and politics are surely bound up with the laws, but their true role is to recognize the proper function of the law and to apply it with justice. The proper function of the law as seen here lies in the pragmatic Biblical sense that we may "live by them".

I consider these observations to be both valuable and illuminating. I too believe that philosophy and ethics cannot be codified and positivized, or, one may say, decreed according to law; rather, the positive law, including the criminal law, ought primarily to serve a specific purpose. Here lies the task of a pragmatic politics. But, at the same time ethics and philosophy ought not to be excluded from the sphere of the law, they must rather provide the indispensable guidelines for the *application* of the law, which men are able to be true to in their own consciences. In this manner the ethical heart of the law can be preserved, without the danger that the private life of man would become the object of an all-confining, moralizing government regulation. With that I come to speak again of the liberal point of departure of the authors.

Th. Würtenberger

Institute for Criminology and Penology
University of Freiburg im Breisgau

CHAPTER I

CRIME, THE CRIMINAL LAW, AND THE ETHICS OF CRIMINALIZATION

The following is a study of attitudes in the formulation and enforcement of the criminal law. It is not so much concerned with the problems of criminology or of the technicalities of the criminal law as such. Rather, the study is much more directed toward the question of the nature of the relationship between legal order and moral order in the area of criminal law. The nature of this relationship becomes clear, we believe, in the decisions which lead to criminalization of certain acts and the pattern of enforcement of the law once it is enacted.

To many, public morality is the ultimate basis for the prohibitions and injunctions in the law. To others, it is more practical considerations and social needs, which lead to the formulation of the will of the lawmaker in the law. There is no reason why one should not say that both of these attitudes are correct in some measure. But there may be many distinct, if unspoken, consequences in the attitudes of citizens, and the (often selective) enforcement of the law, depending on the weight attached to the one or the other of these assumptions.

In contradistinction to modern Western legal usage, historical traditional societies in various parts of the world have depended for keeping order—or conformity with the accepted norm—not so much upon law or legal sanction as upon custom and social or moral sanction, or, in other words, a unity of purpose between social and moral order. A unity of this character is not unknown or unadmired in the West. Indeed it is very much a part of the aspirations of religious communities and modern political ideological movements. But, even in Western antiquity the formalization of legal sanction was well established. And the growth of legal institutions has made a whole different order of state and civilization arise. The ideal of a moral basis for the law, and of moral reinforcement for society in the law, persists, however, in its appeal among religious-minded persons and both social radicals and patriotic conservatives, because of the sense of unity of dedication and purpose it conveys. But the unity of social and moral order of the traditional societies is not in the same sense the basis for modern Western legal systems, least of all in American constitutional history, where a distinctive Anglo-American liberal legal tradition has developed under different historical circumstances from even the most closely parallel European counterpart system. Therefore, in the Anglo-American legal tradition, the ideals of "rule of law" and "liberty under law" have special historical and conceptual meaning, which even the comparable European legal traditions do not convey in the same way.

This liberal democratic tradition has its roots in resistance to the idea of the rule of government according to its own sovereign will and not as government is defined and restricted under law. Coke best expressed this spirit when, on the authority of Bracton, he declared that, "the King must not be under any man, but God and the law...." If we may read this today to mean that we do not subscribe to a system of government of men alone, but to the ideal of liberty under law and good conscience, then there are both legal and moral values we adhere to, but a mixture of the two is not what we mean by adherence to both separately. For conditions have changed substantially from the traditional order of the past. Legal sanctions are not of the same order as moral sanctions. A real unity of social and moral order may do without legal sanctions; but a legal enforcement of moral order cannot. A legislated religious, or political social morality is never quite as estimable as the intentions of the legislators. They, we may presume, were moral men. We, alas, have to be made moral. But regretfully while such laws may command, they are not the best educators to moral decision. And yet how tiresome it is for those traditional and social moralists if we should think that we have to decide these things, when they already know what is moral.

A modern unity of legal and moral order would work somewhat differently from tradition. For, where traditional society may not have admired dissent, and may even have risen as one to put down some offenses to its sensibilities, a society of law invokes sanctions, which wield much more power. The society of tradition may not have known any other cohesion than its adherence to its social and moral norms. The unity of a society of law rests as much upon its dedication to legal institutions. But if it sees itself equally dependent upon common moral or social persuasion, it can repress dissent with much more power.

The demands of good conscience, it seems, however, ought to be embodied in the law of a society which believes in legal justice. But this is a long way from the law's being itself the embodiment of moral order—whatever any of us may mean by that according to his own religious, ethical, or political persuasion. Procedural guarantees are an injunction upon ourselves, upon society, to enforce the law with justice. But there is no limit to the prohibitions a society may impose upon itself. So long as that society believes in—or normally upholds—these sanctions, there is no problem. But if the law becomes the vehicle of defense of religious moral or social moral propositions that a significant segment of society does not uphold, another principle altogether is involved: the question of the extent of the authority of society over the individual, and the authority of the majority over substantial minorities.

Simply put, we in our system of law contribute to a political choice between law which prefers the rights of the individual or the supposed interests of society as a whole. Any of us may vacillate on such issues as to whether it is this, or that, right we want to reserve to ourselves, or whether we would agree that society requires all of these, or those, rights only to make us secure as individuals. It seems thus an obligation, too, for students of legal and social history and philosophy to make these distinctions and consequences clear. For often enough our inclinations on this, or that, issue would lead us first to one pattern, and then to the other. As a modern, literate society with institutions which supposedly guarantee some measure of democratic responsiveness we have a right to learn the consequences of what we decide, and in fact to decide, not to be called upon to react solely out of instinctive logic or inculcated commitment.

Any consistent theory of social ethics may explain these things more or less logically to us. But if we want our decisions to reflect our own considered convictions, we will have to learn to explore the logical consequences of expressions and systems of social ethics whether our own or those of others. It may seem to some that it is too much to expect of every man that he develop a reasoned system of his own. But it is not too much, we think, to learn to beware of ideas and associations which, once suggested to us, begin to think themselves, and then bequeath to us the consequences which the logic of their language alone has produced as if they were the results of our own efforts.

A society of law has an institutional strength that societies of tradition had never hoped for. An informed society of law can, therefore, afford honest divisions which might have ruined a society based solely on common purpose. A democratic society of law requires some consensus on tolerance, however. Otherwise, while a powerful society of law may secure conformity and purpose by force and repression, it can only be at the cost of the guarantees of the protection of the law.

A.   THE EXTENT OF THE PROBLEM OF CRIME,
AND MAKING THE CRIMINAL LAW

Crime has always been a major social problem, if we judge by either collected national statistics, or the historical accounts of travelers and social commentators. In the United States, national crime statistics have been maintained only since 1930, but tales of crime and lawlessness, or of the coming of law and order, have enjoyed long standing popularity in American literary and social history. Westerns and gangster movies have, for example, been a basic source of income to the film industry since its early beginnings, and make the violence and lawlessness of at least these aspects of American history internationally celebrated, and have possibly contributed significantly to changing the style of public behavior and to a resignation to violence.

Political assassinations, economic and social distress (or call it the inability to cope as individuals or groups with the demands of fitting-in economically and socially in the American way of life), resistance to the war and the draft, student unrest on campuses, and a rising crime rate whose effects are now inescapable by the people of the "main stream" of American life have disturbed the American self-image of plenty and progress in recent years, and left the country almost obsessed with violence. A series of major presidential commissions were appointed to investigate these events and disorders: the President's Commission on the Assassination of President Kennedy (the Warren Commission), the President's Commission on Law Enforcement and the Administration of Justice (the National Crime Commission), the National Advisory Commission on Civil Disorders (the Kerner Commission), the National Commission on the Causes and Prevention of Violence, and the President's Commission on Campus Unrest. All of these commissions have produced volumes of staff reports, study team reports, task force reports, and their own interim and final summary reports. One should not overlook either the independent contributions to this national discussion, including books by such leaders of the American historical profession as Arthur

Schlesinger, Jr.,[1] and Richard Hofstadter.[2] From this flood of material one is almost tempted to say there is as much interest in the United States in the medium of violence as in any protest issue or social condition that may have produced it. Surely this must have become clear to the decade of protesters. And it was only one of the more moderate reactions which discovered "the right not to listen".[3]

National self-examination on what the cultural effects of violence, resignation to violence, and violence in entertainment has not all followed any single pattern, however. The recent report of the Surgeon General's Scientific Advisory Committee on Television and Social Behavior: *Television and Growing Up: The Impact of Televised Violence* [4] only concedes moderately: "We can tentatively conclude that there is a modest relationship between exposure to television violence and aggressive tendencies," although, "the causal sequence is very likely applicable only to some children who are predisposed in this direction." This was so mild a rebuke that the *New York Times'* first reaction was to report: "TV Violence Held Unharmful to Youth".[5] Nonetheless, the public news discussion surrounding this report [6] and the Senate committee hearings on it may offer some more promising prospect of more restraint than was the reaction to some social analysts of recent events who seemed to want to persuade us to look at violence differently by their choice of medical diagnostic language to describe social facts. Here we read, for example, not simply that violence is known to occur in certain circumstances, nor that it is common or usual, not that it corresponds to many people's real sense of values, nor that it is intriguing to people who want to add adventure to their lives, but that "collective violence is normal." [7] The suggestion that there are beneficial results of violence

---

[1] *Violence: America in the Sixties,* New American Library, N.Y.

[2] Richard Hofstadter and Michael Wallace (eds.): *American Violence: A Documentary History,* Knopf, N.Y., 1970.

[3] Cf. "The Right Not To Listen," A commentary on Certain Rights of Free Speech and of Property, prepared and distributed by the Virginia Commission on Constitutional Government, Richmond, 1964.

[4] U.S.G.P.O., Washington, D.C., 1972.

[5] *New York Times,* 11 Jan., 1972, p. 1:1.

[6] See e.g. "The New Violence" and "Violence Revisited" in *Newsweek,* 14 Feb., 1972, pp. 66-69; 6 Mar., 1972, pp. 55f.; "TV Violence: Government Study Yields More Evidence, No Verdict," *Science,* 11 Feb., 1972, pp. 608-11.

[7] Cf. Charles Tilly: "Collective Violence in European Perspective," in *Violence in America: Historical and Comparative Perspectives.* A Staff Report to the National

as well as bad ones [8] has the curious ring of recalling the argument that the ends justify the means. If self-defense or revolution is violent, does this allow us to isolate a moment of a complex action as if it had no antecedents, no continuity, no purpose or lack of purpose, and call it "violence" from time A to time B and call criminal violence no more than that? Whatever that might tell us about the law of survival, it would deny the heart of the legal and moral tradition which has learned to discriminate between guilt and mitigation.[9] While there may be useful purposes for such comparisons, one unfortunate result is that it can make a conceptually isolated moment of "violence" into a morally indifferent moment by robbing the sequence of events of its only moral quality, its continuity, complexity, and inter-relationships. This is not to say that one cannot also distort events by choosing favorable characterizations, like "self-defense". But the ambition is a different one: in the latter case the advantage lies in a choice of values, in the former in the evasion of responsibility for no choice of values.

Of course violence in children's programs or in broadcasts watched by teen-agers or adults is only one example of either resignation to violence or violence as entertainment. Television has taken such a central place in American home life that the promise of the networks to modify their programming [10] can be very important. But here we might give special consideration to the warning of Dr. Ira Rubenstein, Vice Chairman of the Surgeon General's committee and overall administrator of the report project that "previous criticism of violence in children's television programs has resulted in less lethal violence but more 'sanitized violence'— that is fewer people are killed, but there are more violent acts. And violence shorn of its ultimate object…might be even more harmful." [11] After years of movies, television, and children's cartoons, where the heroes emerge unscathed from devastating conflicts, one wonders whether it is really necessary to have scientific studies to prove that a generation of urban poor whose range of experience of the national culture is limited to these media would be "predisposed in this direction", led to try to live in that style to gain the only form of recognition they have learned

Commission on the Causes and Prevention of Violence, ed. by H.D. Graham and T.R. Gurr, 1969, New American Library ed., p. 5.

[8] Cf. R.M. Brown: "Historical Patterns of Violence in America," *Ibid.*, pp. 43ff.

[9] See esp. Chapter II: A. (2), below.

[10] Senate committee hearings, 23 Mar., 1972.

[11] "Study Aides Voice Misgivings About Report on TV Violence," *New York Times*, 19 Feb., 1972, p. 1:7-8.

to esteem. Describing the new dimensions of brutality and armed violence of street gangs, a New York Youth Services worker concludes simply: "I don't really think they make any connection between shooting and death." [12]

The networks seem very much aware of the matter of "good taste" in not offending us with the normal results of violence, however, and perhaps for some good citizens this style of adventure entertainment is sufficient catharsis for their more violent emotions and reveals what it is they really seek in it. The head of a "People to People Campaign" to raise money for the refugees of East Bengal recently reported television programmers' hesitation to run a 30 second film clip taken from news film outs. The film showed a refugee girl who the red cross reporter said had been bitten by rats. The programmers thought that too offensive for television at first, but agreed to run the clip later because "the scars were not visible." It is surely not irrelevant that real suffering is not entertainment. The assassination of President Kennedy aroused the compassion of millions of people many of who had never supported him in life. After the shocking live broadcast of Senator Robert Kennedy's assassination, thousands of people who had been buying guns for self-protection, turned them in to the police. In San Francisco they melted them down to put up a memorial. But the effect of real violence lasts only as long as the shock; three years later a national news broadcast reporting that a Texas bank was offering to mail a rifle as a premium to new depositors brought no significant public reaction.

Some years ago a London revue, *Beyond the Fringe,* satirized life in various parts of the United States ending every sketch with the judicious warning, "but that's not America." The moral seemed to be that whatever else Americans might like to think of themselves as, these things were America too. History has given us endless accounts of what it would be like to be free of the horrors of the ravages of human passion, greed, and conflict. The tale of the Garden of Eden, the prophecy of the Golden Age to come, or the myth of it remembered, the design for the ideal republic, the theological notion that real peace can come only in the City of God, the romantic description of untroubled nature, the utopian dreams of cooperative communities, the Marxian promise of a withering away of the state, all seem to offer some remedy for the coercion and oppression, for the dark side of human nature we know

---

[12] "The New Gangs," *Newsweek,* 8 May, 1972, p. 81.

in "these latter and degenerate days". At the same time the science of government was invented by those like Locke, who warns us against the "rogues" in the state of nature, or like Hobbes, who from bitterer experience warns of "the war of each against all", unless we live under law and government.

This much is not new. But critics of the "consensus school" of American history—they name Daniel Boorstin (*The Genius of American Politics* [13]), David Potter (*People of Plenty* [14]), and Louis Hartz (*The Liberal Tradition in America* [15])—blame them for lulling us into accepting more of an American dream than a reality that Americans could be as liberal as Locke and Jefferson. This preoccupation with the other side of life in America which has arisen out of the reflections on the domestic turmoil of the late 60's is nowhere any better demonstrated, by reputable scholars, than in *Violence in America*.[16] A recent anthology of violent episodes in American history is a good demonstration of the fashionable success of some of its ideas; tales which some time ago would have been looked upon as only fascinating recollections of remote adventurous times and places, are here represented as more typical of America in their violence than in their retelling.[17]

A special persuasive value seems intended to emerge from recent works which characterize America as not only a place where many people resort to violence freely, but where violence is "normal". Accepting that idea carries a political program with it that what works for one can work for all. There is a violence to language, too, in not infrequent confusion of violence with everything from brute force to the results of the exercise and abuse of power, position, or authority. But obviously there would not be a need for this semantic game on the part of disaffected political groups if there were always adequate means of effective expression through the "democratic process". Probably never before have so many felt themselves individually so well equipped to speak out on national problems. But the social recognition that only the possession of a source of power evokes satisfactory results calls for collective not individual spokesmanship, and this in turn puts a premium on the conviction of collective solidarity.

[13] University of Chicago Pr., Chicago, 1953.
[14] University of Chicago Pr., Chicago/London, 1954.
[15] Harcourt, Brace, Jovanovich, N.Y., 1955.
[16] *Op.cit.*
[17] Cf. R.M. Brown (ed.): *American Violence,* Prentice-Hall, Englewood Cliffs, N.J., 1970.

In practical terms, the United States has a higher rate of violent crime than Canada, Britain, or the countries of the European Continent.[18] In many ways, and particularly in neglected parts of the country—including the urban slums—the more comfortable Americans have come to accept this condition of violence and criminality as a fact of life without looking it in the face all too often, or simply doing their best to avoid getting involved in it. But we may suppose that even these less fortunate people left prey to violence are frequently moved by other ideas and values that are also part of life in America.

The question of why crime and violence occurs is always a central concern in disputes over the proper function of the law, and all penal codes, therefore, reflect some measure of the particular concepts of society the lawmakers exhibited. When it comes to dealing with the concrete issues of crime, however, the fact that there has always been crime and violence or that it is considered to have specific social or moral origins (depending upon the particular concept of society one adheres to, or the current status of national self-examination on the subject) tells us very little about the present crime rate, its variation from place to place or time to time. And the discussion of these things alone gives us no good idea about the adequacy or effectiveness of existing laws or their enforcement.

Tables compiled by the National Crime Commission utilizing previously unpublished data from the FBI Uniform Crime Reports (UCR) Section show distinct upward trends in the crime rates for several major kinds of offenses in the years from 1933 to 1965.[19] Restricted as this data may be [20] for actual crime rates,[21] it shows a marked rise in the index

---

[18] These statistics are compared in Wolf Middendorff: *Die Gewaltkriminalität in den USA,* Walter de Gruyter, Berlin, 1970; also 81 *Zeitschrift für die gesamte Strafrechtswissenschaft* 2; 4.

[19] U.S., President's Commission on Law Enforcement and Administration of Justice (National Crime Commission): *The Challenge of Crime in a Free Society: A Report by the...,* U.S.G.P.O., Washington, D.C., Feb., 1967, p. 22f.

[20] Cf. *Ibid.,* p. 23: "Because the rural areas were slow in coming into the system and reported poorly when they did, it was not until 1958, when other major changes were made in the UCR, that reporting of rural crimes was sufficient to allow a total national estimate without special adjustments. Changes in overall estimating procedures and two offense categories—rape and larceny—were also made in 1958. Because of these problems figures prior to 1958 and particularly those prior to 1940 must be viewed as neither fully comparable with nor nearly so reliable as later figures."

[21] Cf. *Ibid.,* p. 21: Surveys made by the National Opinion Research Center

for reported crimes compiled in the United States since the end of the second World War, with the notable exception of willful homicide, which far exceeds the rate of the increase of the population during these years.

Obviously the crimes which should cause us the most concern in our day to day lives are violent or serious crimes against persons or property.[22] But in fact the full range of what we call "crime" includes in addition the whole spectrum of prohibitions of physically dangerous acts or violations contrary to announced public morality in the law, and ultimately, abuses to other persons' civil rights in the course of law enforcement. In enumerating the great variety and diversity of crimes, the National Crime Commission recounts:

There are more than 2800 federal crimes and a much larger number of state and local ones. Some involve serious bodily harm, some stealing, some public morals or public order, some governmental revenues, some the creation of hazardous conditions, some the regulation of the economy. Some are perpetrated ruthlessly and systematically; others are spontaneous derelictions. Gambling and prostitution are willingly undertaken by both buyer and seller; murder and rape are violently imposed upon their victims. Vandalism is predominantly a crime of the young; driving while intoxicated, a crime of the adult.[23]

The whole point of this enumeration is very simply to make clear the fact that, whatever the social or moral origins of such acts may be, the full range of kinds of behavior covered by official designation as "crimes" makes comparison of many of the acts involved extremely difficult, either from the perspective of severity of consequences or injury

---

(NORC) of the University of Chicago and the Bureau of Social Science Research (BSSR) of Washington, D.C., indicate: "that the actual amount of crime in the United States today is several times that reported in the UCR.... The amount of personal injury crime reported to NORC is almost twice the UCR rate and the amount of property crime more than twice as much as the UCR rate for individuals. Forcible rapes were more than 3 1/2 times the reported rate, burglaries 3 times, aggravated assaults and larcenies of $50 and over more than double, and robbery 50 per cent greater than the reported rate. Only vehicle theft was lower then by a small amount."

[22] Surveys showed that 43 % of respondents answered that they stay off the street at night because of their fear of crime (Ibid., p. v.). Furthermore, "one-third of Americans feel unsafe about walking alone at night in their own neighbourhoods, according to the NORC survey" (p. 50), although "the surveys uniformly show that people feel safer in their own neighbourhoods even if they actually have a higher crime rate than other areas" (p. 50).

[23] Ibid., p. 18.

involved, motive, or any other respect than prohibition by law.[24] Surely these are all still crimes if the prohibitions are violated, but it does not necessarily assist our understanding of the nature of the crime, its origins, or the danger, risk, or the costs involved to know only the fact of prohibition.

Let us not conclude too early, however, that the crimes which are ostensibly not comparable to crimes against persons or property are all in the category of youthful defiance of traditional morality. In an article on over-criminalization [25] (in which he extends his original contribution to the 1967 National Crime Commission Task Force Report on the Courts [26]) Professor Sanford Kadish describes the surprising range of jurisdictions where legislatures, aroused against various kinds of acts, omissions, and miscellaneous exceptionable behavior, have imposed criminal sanctions:

In the process of revising the California criminal law, we encountered a mass of crimes outside the Penal Code, matching the Penal Code itself in volume, and authorizing criminal convictions for such offenses as failure by a school principal to use required textbooks,[27] failure of a teacher to carry first-aid kits on field trips,[28] gambling on the result of an election,[29] giving private commercial performances by a state supported band,[30] and allowing waste of an artesian well by a landowner.[31] Then there are the criminal laws, enforced by the state police force, which have been the primary means used to deal with the death and injury toll of the automobile. [e.g., manslaughter—motor vehicle [32]; failure to render aid; hit and run, etc.[33]]

---

[24] This point is acknowledged by the National Crime Commission *Ibid.,* p. 3: "These crimes can no more be lumped together for the purposes of analysis than can measles and schizophrenia, or lung cancer and a broken ankle. As with disease, so with crime: if causes are to be understood, if risks are to be evaluated, and if preventive or remedial actions are to be taken, each kind must be looked at separately. Thinking of 'crime' as a whole is futile."

[25] Sanford H. Kadish: "The Crisis of Overcriminalization," 7 *American Criminal Law Quarterly,* 17 (1968) (Reprinted from *Annals of the American Academy of Political and Social Science,* 187 (1967).

[26] U.S., President's Commission on Law Enforcement and Administration of Justice: *Task Force Report: The Courts,* U.S.G.P.O., Washington, D.C., 1967, pp. 97-107.

[27] *California Education Code* § 9255.

[28] *Idem.,* § 11955.

[29] *Calif. Elections Code* § 29003.

[30] *Calif. Government Code* § 6650.

[31] *Calif. Water Code* § 307.

[32] *Calif. Penal Code* § 192.3.

[33] *Calif. Motor Vehicule Code* § 2001.

Indications are that this response may ultimately do more harm than good by blocking off politically harder, but more likely, remedial alternatives.[34] Problematic also has been the use of criminal sanctions to enforce economic regulatory measures [35]....[36]

Since innovation or change in the area of the criminal law depends ultimately on people's attitudes, the existence of a host of traditional offenses besides the obvious crimes against persons and property, such as homicide, assault, and larceny, reflects not only the rate of the incidence of crime but also the persistence of traditional ideas and associations. Especially in the case of criminal liabilities extended to such offenses as those noted by Kadish, criminalization reflects public reaction to a given offense or practice and the associations it arouses.

Since the end of the second World War there have been some notable achievements in the reforms of the criminal law in the United States, however. The *Model Penal Code* of the American Law Institute (A.L.I.) has provided a basis for discussion and furtherance of reform work in a number of states where it has provided a model for revising various sections of the state's criminal code.[37] Sections of it are still under consideration in other states. Simplification and reform of the criminal law is a desirable goal now because, in the past, changes in American criminal law have generally progressed by extension, to cover new types of offenses, and very often also to include penalties for many social ills which are not necessarily best controlled or alleviated simply by criminal law proscription. Kadish examines the consequences of this past procedure so far as the practical effect of achieving the social goals in question is concerned:

...American criminal law typically has extended the criminal sanction well beyond... fundamental offenses to include very different kinds which threaten far less serious harms, or else highly intangible ones about which there is no genuine consensus, or even no harms at all.[38]

There are three typical examples of over-criminalization, he suggests:

---

[34] Kadish cites Moynihan: "The War Against the Automobile," *The Public Interest*, No. 3, Spring 1966, esp. at p. 21ff.

[35] Cf. S. Kadish: "Some Observations on the Use of Criminal Sanctions in Enforcing Economic Regulations," 30 *Univ. of Chicago Law Rev.*, 423 (1963).

[36] Kadish: "The Crisis of Overcriminalization," *loc. cit.*, p. 18f.

[37] Cf. H. Wechsler: "The Challenge of the Model Penal Code," 65 *Harvard Law Rev.* 1097 (1952).

[38] Kadish: "The Crisis of Overcriminalization," *loc. cit.*, p. 17.

(1) to declare or enforce public standards of private morality, (2) as a means of providing social services in default of other public agencies, and (3) as a disingenuous means of permitting police to do indirectly what the law forbids them to do directly.[39]

In each case the law could be used to provide better remedies elsewhere, where they are needed, if they are needed at all.

Kadish goes on to mention certain morals offenses, abortion, gambling, use of narcotics, drunkenness, writing bad checks, and non-payment of support to wife and family, all of which are proscribed in one way or another by different state codes. Many of these titles may be properly described as moral offenses and many of them should be considered legal violations. The question is, however, whether all of these offenses are, properly speaking, criminal. Kadish considers this overuse of legal proscription to be a dilution of the criminal sanction on problems which would be better handled in other ways, or perhaps not under the law at all. For, he concludes:

The plain sense that the criminal law is a highly specialized tool for social control, useful for certain purposes, but not for others; that when improperly used it is capable of producing more evil than good; that decision to criminalize any particular behavior must follow only after an assessment of gains and losses—this obvious injunction of rationality has been noted widely for over 250 years, from Jeremy Bentham, to the National Crime Commission, and by the moralistic philosophers as well as the utilitarian ones. And those whose daily business is the administration of the criminal law have, on occasion, exhibited acute awareness of the folly of departing from it. The need for restraint seems to be recognized by those who deal with the criminal laws, but not by those who make them or by the general public which lives under them. One hopes that attempts to set out the facts and to particularize the perils of overcriminalization may ultimately affect the decisions of the legislatures. But past experience gives little cause for optimism.[40]

In the course of the following investigation the authors have examined this situation in the criminal law in order to explain:—what they believe are both the social historical background of this mixture of often only half conscious attitudes and responses in the law,—and what they consider to be the significance of an understanding of this, part rational, part functional development for the dilemma in society and the criminal law today. In brief outline, they find the law to be not simply a functional

[39] *Ibid.*, p. 19.
[40] *Ibid.*, p. 33. (Contrary to the impression that even many of "those who deal with the criminal laws" show the restraint Kadish misses in the public and the legislature, see note 48 below.)

development of the organization of human behavior. In the defense of what society comes to believe are its vital interests it tends to protect not only what some may look upon as basic social needs, it also seeks to defend certain values or ideas which in one way or another the law makers identify with their collective existence as a society. There are unquestionably constitutional principles without the protection of which the political character of our society would no longer exist. There are doubtlessly also moral principles without the cultivation of which the quality of human life and association will suffer. But the identification of these latter principles falls either in the realm of religion which the constitution clearly separates from the state, or personal philosophy, about which in the United States we are taught that we ought to have the protection to follow our individual consciences.

A society with a tradition of strong legal sanctions is in a position to exercise far greater control in areas where less legal-minded societies would only express displeasure, and more tolerant ones, perhaps, exhibit no interest whatsoever. Where such strong legal sanctions exist, however, the temptation to try to solve other problems than deliberate social or moral offenses with sanctions, too, is difficult to overcome. Again, where legal rulings are both social defense and social remedy, there is strong reliance on the legal system to provide guarantees against abuse of the system of law itself and insurance for the exercise of due process of law. It is in this latter charge that the remedies of the American system of law have been the most successful. But here, too, because reliance on legal rulings is only effective in the rational, intellectual atmosphere of the law and the courts, the disposition of prisoners, the conditions in which they are held, the fact of their being held at all over long periods where the courts are yet unable to act, and, of course, in the case of the social origins of crime where that is not affected by sanctions, the reliance on written law and procedure only is monstrously ineffective.

The rising standard of material well-being in the United States has made more and more of us able to pay for services we require. But the more we earn the more we find ourselves dependent upon a series of economic relationships whose demands can ruin us if we should for some reason not be in a position to pay for any length of time. For the poor, the uninformed, and the members of minority or sub-culture groups, being confronted with the problem of what to do, when one is a victim of a violation of his rights or of an abuse of due process, or, short and simple, the defendant (guilty or not) in a criminal action, can be reduced to a problem of economics: those who can afford to pay are better served.

In the years since 1914, and particularly during the years of the Warren Court in the last decade, there was a considerable development of case law concerning due process [41] (see Chapter II: C. below for a more complete discussion). It was during this time that the "exclusionary rule", which denies the prosecution the use of evidence obtained by illegal means, was developed [42] and later applied to the states as well as federal jurisdictions.[43] The right to counsel was declared to be essential if defendants were to avoid prejudicing their cases,[44] and the states were obliged to provide counsel for those who were unable to retain their own.[45] Times when the accused must have access to counsel and be informed of his rights were formally laid down.[46] And more recently release on one's own recognizance for those who could not afford bail has been legislated for federal jurisdictions.[47]

One cannot treat the importance of these developments in the theory of due process of law lightly, especially considering the shocking abuses of procedural standards which occurred in many of the cases in which these rulings were given. But to restrict our remarks on due process solely to the theory of what takes place in court, or, we hope, at least in any review of a case (and what to many people means that the courts are soft on crime [48]), would be to neglect the greater realities of the

[41] Cf. e.g. A Kenneth Pye: "The Warren Court and Criminal Procedure," 67 *Michigan Law Rev.* 249 (1968); A.T. Mason and W.M. Beany: *The Supreme Court in a Free Society,* Norton, New York, 1968, ch. XVI, "The Warren Court in the Vanguard."

[42] Cf. *Weeks v. United States,* 232 *U.S.* 398 (1914).

[43] Cf. *Mapp v. Ohio,* 367 *U.S.* 643 (1961).

[44] Cf. *Hamilton v. Alabama,* 368 *U.S.* 52 (1961).

[45] Cf. *Gideon v. Wainwright,* 372 *U.S.* 335 (1963) 344f.

[46] Cf. *Massiah v. United States,* 377 *U.S.* 201 (1963); *Escobedo v. Illinois,* 378 *U.S.* 478 (1963).

[47] Cf. 1966 *Federal Bail Reform Act.,* 18 *U.S.C.* 3146 (a.).

[48] Cf. e.g. Quinn Tamm (head of the International Assoc. of Chiefs of Police): "Police Must be More Free," and Frank J. Schira (Exec. Director of the National Police Officers Assoc. of America): "The War in America the Public Refuses to Face!" in Shalom Endleman (ed.): *Violence in the Streets,* Quadrangle Chicago, 1968, pp. 397-402; 414-16. Tamm cites Cardozo, former Attorney General Katzenbach, now Chief Justice Warren Burger, former California Governor Pat Brown, and the late Supreme Court Justice Harlan on the need for commonly understood rules of obtaining evidence so that criminals are not released because of police errors. Thus far there is no disagreement. But the key Supreme Court decisions at issue were

administration of criminal justice today. For the criminal procedure with which most people arrested and not released on bail are concerned,

> handed down as a result of abuses that can hardly be so lightly dismissed as:
> [law enforcement officers'] alleged overzealousness, possible errors in judgment, or because of lack of familiarity with the complex restrictions placed upon them. (p. 397)

Tamm approaches the real issue much better with the question:

> Could it be then that the deterrent effect of swift, sure, and just punishment has been lost because the courts and parole and probation *authorities have become more preoccupied with the rights of the individual rather than with the rights of our society?* (p. 399, emphasis added)

This division is more powerful than a mere philosophical difference, however. Because the arguments are meant ultimately for an unphilosophical public the danger is that the further we generalize the discussion away from the concrete issues and evidence of abuses, the easier it is turn this into a battle of associations. Shira talks of "small but powerful minority groups" whose "allowing civil disobedience" as "a short cut to court or legislative relief" has promoted the causes of "criminal and communistic groups". "Charges of police brutality" he says "recalls the Hitler propaganda program".

> ...officials of government on every level failed to support their officers. In turn, the officers of the law had no alternative than retreat from effective enforcement and respect for law and order. (p. 415)

Compare also such articles as: Seymour Lipset: "Why Cops Hate Liberals—and Vice Versa," *The Atlantic,* Mar., 1969, pp. 76-83. Norval Morris and Gordon Hawkins also try to answer Lipset's question and volunteer their impressions of police selectivity in their attitudes toward the law:

> Why are there no strong police voices for a retrenchment of our moralistic criminal law?...Why are they not dedicated to achieving a more modestly phrased but socially effective criminal law, aiming to protect us as far as it can from physical violence and certain serious property depredations—and little else? They do not hesitate to object to the Supreme Court's decisions on arrest, search, and interrogative procedures. But they seem to want to have it both ways. They want to be the accepting, uninquiring enforcers of morals law, because they are the law, and the critical repudiator of judicial interpretation of other law.... They say they have a duty to "uphold the community morals and enforce its system of morality" and they must not "abandon this responsibility". (p. 88f.)

(in *The Honest Politician's Guide to Crime Control,* Univ. of Chicago Pr., Chicago, 1970.) William A. Westley elicited many much stronger police defenses of use of strong arm tactics at their own discretion in a case study of a municipal police force: "Violence and the Police," 59 *American Journal of Sociology,* 34 (1953). See also Ramsey Clark: *Crime in America: Observations on its Nature, Causes, Prevention, and Control,* Simon and Schuster, New York, 1970, ch. 19, "Confessions, The Fifth Amendment, and Human Dignity".

In an article in a special issue of the *The Annals* on "Combating Crime", Jennie McIntyre analyses: "Public Attitudes toward Crime and Law Enforcement". Among

is the detention, often 4 to 6 months, before arraignment, in the dehumanizing conditions of local jails; then pre-trial detention, often several months longer and with delays both because the state defender's office is overtaxed and also often on advice of counsel taking advantage of the over-crowded court situation to test the patience of witnesses and the reliability of memories.[49] Although conditions vary there too, the state and federal prisons, where convicted felons are confined, are, particularly in the richer and more progressive states, far less outright destructive of human personality; and some few low security prisons are quite tolerable by comparison.[50] Even then many cases do not go through complete formal trial proceedings; guilty pleas are bargained for reduced

other sources she examines the results of Gallup and Harris polls and surveys conducted for the National Crime Commission by the National Opinion Research Center (NORC) and the Bureau of Social Science Research (BSSR). In her conclusion she finds a very interesting variability in people's emotional and rational reactions to crime—depending on how the question is put to them:

> Although attributing an increase in crime to lowered moral standards, most persons would depend on the police and the courts for stern treatment of offenders in order to diminish the level of crime. Not as many, but nonetheless a substantial proportion, would recommend increased employment opportunities and other improved social conditions to combat crime. Along with reliance on law-enforcement officials, there was willingness to permit the police considerable latitude in their efforts to apprehend and convict criminals. This apparent harshness toward offenders was immediately mitigated when the issue of rights of the individual was posed. (p. 46)

(Cf. 374 *The Annals*, 34 (Nov., 1967).)

[49] The right to a speedy trial was specifically re-emphasized by the Warren Court in *Klopfer v. North Carolina*, 386 *U.S.* 213 (1967) in rejecting the usage of an extraordinary device of criminal procedure known as "*nolle prosequi* with leave" which would entitle the prosecutor to discharge a defendent, but with leave to re-institute proceedings at a later date. Lawyers may ask continuances for their clients' cases for many reasons, but one should not overlook the inherent difficulty in proving a case when it is long delayed. This was brought home by the appeals court in *Ross v. United States*, 121 *U.S. App. D.C.* 233 (1965):

> The record before us is, thus, one which shows (1) a purposeful delay of seven months between offense and arrest, (2) a plausible claim of inability to recall or reconstruct the events of the day of the offense, and (3) a trial in which the case against the appellant consists of the recollection of one witness refreshed by a notebook. We are not convinced that successful police operations against narcotics in this jurisdiction depend upon proceedings of such slender dimensions.

[50] Robert Ostermann observes simply: "The nation's jails rarely come close to offering the amenities of the worst prisons" (p. 151). He offers a brief survey of the American penal system and its history in the last two sections of: *A Report*

charges or more favorable sentences,[51] thus taking some load from the courts, perhaps, but circumventing the established route of justice, if

in Depth on Crime in America, "Newsbook", The National Observer, Silver Springs, Md., 1966. Another current broad survey is Austin MacCormick's: "Adult Correctional Institutions in the United States," submitted to the President's Commission on Law Enforcement and Administration of Justice, multilith, 1967. The National Crime Commission's *Task Force Report: Corrections* summarizes their findings on the 400 or so prisons as follows:

> Some are grossly under-staffed and under-equipped conspicuous products of public indifference. Overcrowding and idleness are the salient features of some, brutality and corruption of a few others. Far too few are well organized and adequately funded. (p. 4)

The nations local jails are generally even more unsatisfactory:

> ...Not only are the great majority of these facilities old but many do not even meet the minimum standards of sanitation, living space, and segregation of different ages and types of offenders that have obtained generally in the rest of corrections for several decades. (p. 75)

[51] Plea negotiation is an established practice, and in many cases is probably the most sensible course of action. Obviously, it is also open to abuses. The National Crime Commission thinks that the procedure could be made more acceptable if its chief characteristics: "when plea negotiations are conducted, they usually are conducted informally and out of sight" (p. 333), were regulated. The Commission recommends: that the terms be "stated on the [court] record" and even "in serious ...cases reduced to writing" (p. 337f.). Their further recommendation, though a logical expansion of the first ones, calls for regularized sharing of information between prosecution and defense (p. 338f.). And, while this too has its merits, one wonders whether in the situation of a rising crime rate where "as many as 90% (of the defendants) in some jurisdictions...plead guilty..." (p. 333), this will not lead to a blurring of distinctions between prosecution and defender agencies. (Cf. *The Challenge of Crime in a Free Society, op.cit.,* pages cited from reprint by Dutton, New York, 1968.) In the Report of the Task Force on Law Enforcement to the National Commission on the Causes and Prevention of Violence (J.S. Campbell; J.R. Sahid; D.P. Stang (eds.): *Law and Order Reconsidered,* U.S.G.P.O., Washington, D.C., 1969) D.D. Ellis, Jr. quotes Justice Goldberg's enumeration of traditions and policies supporting the 5th Amendment privilege against self-incrimination in *Murphy v. Waterfront Commission,* 378 *U.S.* 52, 55 (1964). The second of these points: "our preference for an accusatorial rather than an inquisitorial system of criminal justice", Ellis says, "can be dismissed out of hand...since in recalling the Star Chamber and the Spanish Inquisition it, "elicits emotional rather than rational support for the privilege" (p. 490f.). So firmly rooted does the adversary system seem to be in the American concept of justice! However that may be, if anything like 90% of criminal cases are handled by negotiated pleas, we may be drifting into a second system of convenience, which may be best regulated as something like a parallel but distinct inquisitorial system.

that means trial in open court or trial by a jury of one's peers.[52] What it also seems to indicate, however, is an occasional agreement between courts and prosecutors that the mandatory sentences for conviction for higher degree offenses are too stringent—or if those sentences were intended to achieve a reform of the convict during his imprisonment, then the realities of prison life today may make longer detention self-defeating.[53] Yet, with all due respect for the humanity and responsibility of these officials, unless these circumstances are brought out into the open for the information of the public and study of the legislatures, no real penal reform is possible, and this device leads to circumvention of full operation of the law. This may be morally legitimate in the absence of any other recourse, perhaps, but it is a dubious kind of policy in a supposedly democratic society of law. Needless to say, those who insist on trial and are then convicted of higher order crimes are disproportionately over-penalized by comparison with those who have pleaded guilty to a lesser offense, but for what may be practically the same order of crime.

Recently the first census of city and county jails was conducted by the Census Bureau for the Law Enforcement Assistance Administration of the Department of Justice.[54] They found that as of March 15th, 1970,

---

For a table of statistics concerning guilty plea convictions, see U.S. President's Commission on Law Enforcement and the Administration of Justice: *Task Force Report: The Courts,* U.S.G.P.O., Washington, D.C., 1967, p. 9.

[52] Differing perspectives on this problem in American criminal procedure are discussed in the following: Advisory Committee on the Criminal Trial, of the American Bar Association (ABA) Project on Minimum Standards for Criminal Justice: *Standards Relating to Pleas of Guilty,* Tentative Draft, Feb., 1967; Arnold Enker: "Perspectives on Plea Bargaining," in U.S. President's Commission on Law Enforcement and Administration of Justice: *Task Force Report: The Courts,* 108, 112-14 (1967) (Appendix A.); Donald J. Newman: *Conviction: The Determination of Guilt or Innocence Without Trial.* The Report of the American Bar Foundation's Survey of the Administration of Criminal Justice in the United States, Little, Brown, Boston, 1966; "Note, Guilty Plea Bargaining: Compromises by Prosecutors to Secure Guilty Pleas, 112 *Univ. of Penna. Law Rev.* 865 (1964); Richard Quinney: *The Social Reality of Crime,* Little, Brown, Boston, 1970, pp. 143-50; Arthur Rossett: "The Negotiated Guilty Plea," 374 *The Annals* 70 (Nov., 1967).

[53] These reasons—among many others—seem to figure as motives for negotiating pleas in the studies of Donald J. Newman: *Conviction, op. cit.;* and "Pleading Guilty for Considerations: A Study of Bargain Justice," 46 *Journal of Criminal Law, Criminology, and Police* Science 780 (1956).

[54] Cf. J. Rosenthal: "Jail Census Finds 52% Not Convicted," *New York Times,* 7 Jan., 1971, p. 1:4.

there were 160,863 persons, 7800 of them juveniles, in a total of 4037 municipal or county jails. (The estimated number of inmates in state and federal prisons was 350,000.) Of those 160,863 prisoners, 83,000, or 52% had not been convicted of any crime. 35% had been arraigned but were still awaiting trial. And 17% were still awaiting arraignment. Richard W. Velde, Associate Administrator of the Department of Justice agency commented, "There are many cases where inmates—children, mental incompetents, and hardened felons—are all lumped together in less than human conditions of overcrowding and filth." Beatings—both by other inmates and guards—have been widely reported along with accounts of rackets—including drug peddling—and sexual attacks.[55] Suicides and riots are now more frequently the ultimate resort of the lost.[56]

 The right to trial within a reasonable period is also a part of due process. But extentions up to 6 months before arraignment are not uncommon, and it may take two or three times as long for the trial itself.[57] Understandably, *habeas corpus* appeals by prisoners have risen from

---

[55] Cf. e.g. the summary of incidents commonly reported, in Ramsey Clark, *op. cit.,* ch. 13, "Prisons: Factories of Crime".

[56] A number of articles concerning prison riots and suicides appeared in the *New York Times* between Aug., 1970, and Mar., 1971. Since the *New York Times* is the closest thing to a national newspaper, reports on conditions in New York City and State receive considerably more notoriety. In an article on 14 Mar. 1971, the New York City Criminal Justice Coordinating Council reported the results of the first over-all study of how the City's police, prosecutors, courts, and jails are fighting crime. The report concluded that they are :

neither efficient enough to create credible fear of punishment, nor fair enough to command sincere respect... (p. 70:1)

[57] The statistics on delays in court actions are broadly surveyed by David J. Saari in "Court Management and the Administration of Justice," ch. 21 of *Law and Order Reconsidered, op. cit.:*

Delay in civil personal injury actions in 97 selected jurisdictions in the United States averages 20.7 months. The *median* delay in felony cases in federal courts is 9.5 months in Washington, D.C., and 9.4 months in the eastern District of New York. 19% of the criminal cases in the federal courts are pending for 1 year or more. Nor is the problem of delay confined to the trial courts. In federal appellate courts in 1968, the median time for the completion of the record was 1.8 months in civil cases and 2.8 months in criminal cases. The filing of briefs took an additional 3.5 months. Another 1.5 months slipped by before the typical case was heard or submitted. After the case was heard, still another 1.5 months was required for final disposition. Since 1959, the number of cases held for extended periods after argument has increased by 500%. (p. 512)

5,819 in 1965 to 10,663 in 1970.[58] But, for appeals too, the prisoner needs counsel. Yet how efficient can counsel be when the public defender's office is overtaxed with its normal load. While the abuses of the system of criminal justice may grow from its simple inadequacy, and not class conspiracy (after all what theory of justice offers economic advantages to those who come into conflict with it), affluence still seems to be the only insurance that one can gain the access to the guarantees the system does provide. That lesson is surely not lost on the leaders of organized crime.

The crime rate has been rising alarmingly over the last decade and surely many of the people awaiting trial in the jails are likely to be found guilty and many do bargain for lesser sentences. But if the courts are inadequate to hear all the cases brought, then we must ask, when much of the violent and petty crime is handled in this off-hand manner, what cases are being heard in the courts? According to the district attorney's office of Cook County, Illinois (Chicago), for example, an average of 400 drug abuse cases are heard a day—the majority of them involving marijuana.[59] Chances are that many of those who can afford marijuana can also manage to put up bail and hire counsel—or their parents can. We have to recognize that with the growing number of youthful persons doing their own thing, or traveling across the country,

---

[58] Cf. "Justice on Trial," *Newsweek*, 8 Mar., 1971, p. 45. In reaction to overcrowding in the jails, delays up to 18 months in cases coming to trial, and riots in the jails because of conditions and delays, the Administrative Board of the Judicial Conference of the State of New York announced that beginning in May, 1972, state courts would dismiss criminal charges in all but homicide cases, if through no fault of the defendant, he had not come to trial within 6 months of the arrest. Exceptions would be allowed for "good cause". (Cf. "State Puts Limit on Trial Delays in Criminal Cases," *New York Times*, 30 Apr., 1971, p. 1:5.) In addition, if trials have not begun within 3 months of arrest, defendants will be released on bail or parole (except in homicide cases). California, Illinois, and the District of Columbia also have such rules, and Federal Courts in the 2nd Circuit (New York, Vermont, and Connecticut) planned to adopt the rule in June, 1971. This is obviously an extraordinary measure, in view of extraordinary circumstances, and extraordinary protests, to place extraordinary pressure on the legislature to provide for more support for the judicial system to enable it to overcome its crippling backlog.

[59] Cf. Charlton: "Marijuana Terms Range from Seven Days to Life," *New York Times*, 22 Mar., 1971 (p. 1:1-2), p. 25:2. According to the *Newsweek* article cited in n. 43:

Every second case on the Los Angeles criminal-court docket is a pot offense, every fourth arrest across the nation a drunk case... (p. 18)

In fact drunkenness may account for every third arrest.

today, many of these people who are largely themselves the only victims of their crimes, will be without means and spend time in jails. But, while many youthful offenders may spend time in jail, and while penalties for possession of marijuana range from seven days in jail in Nebraska, to life imprisonment in Texas, many of these cases will result in suspended sentences or probation,[60] or, where there is in fact a prison term, it will begin only after conviction.

The question one must ultimately face, in this regard, is whether society has that much benefit from its reaction to pot-heads, cavalier drug offenders, and in general offenders in crimes for which there is only theoretical social injury to tie up the already over-burdened criminal justice system even further. Although the situation has already been widely discussed,[61] no systematic reform of courts, jails, and prisons for that matter, is in sight, and it is clear that no reform could be accomplished without substantial expenditures, and in hard times these will naturally have low priority. The fact that even minor reforms, such as for example in court administration, do not make much progress seems to reflect a general lack of information and concern both on the part of the public and of their elected officials.[62]

Much more serious for many people, who lived relatively undisturbed lives in the past, is the mounting rate of violent crime, from which there is no escape, little recourse, and little compensation, except possibly in flight to the suburbs, if one has the means and the mobility. For,

---

[60] *Ibid.*

[61] In addition to the many recent works cited in these notes, and the extensive reports assembled by the presidential commissions, we would like to refer to Herbert Packer: *The Limit of the Criminal Sanction,* Stanford Univ. Pr., 1968, a study of what one may practically expect prohibition alone to accomplish.

[62] For studies of the possibilities of applying better management techniques in the criminal justice system, see: U.S. President's Commission on Law Enforcement and the Administration of Justice: *Task Force Report: Science and Technology,* U.S.G.P.O., Washington, D.C., 1967; this material has been evaluated in *The Challenge of Crime in a Free Society,* the report of the Commission *op. cit.,* ch. 11, and in a brief article by Alfred Blumstein: "Systems Analysis and the Criminal Justice System," 374 *The Annals* 92 (Nov., 1967). Brief reference to the use of these techniques in court administration is made in: *The Challenge of Crime in a Free Society,* Dutton ed., pp. 578-82; Abraham Blumberg: "The Criminal Court as Organization and Communication System," (reprinted from his: *Criminal Justice,* Quadrangle, Chicago, 1967) in Richard Quinney (ed.): *Crime and Justice in Society,* Little, Brown, Boston, 1969, pp. 267-91; U.S. President's Commission on the Causes and Prevention of Violence: *Law and Order Reconsidered, op. cit.,* ch. 21.

unless one catches an offender in the act, has very good witnesses, or has the good fortune that the police can pick up a likely suspect without much effort, minor crimes—and many very serious ones—simply do not get investigated these days.[63]

If we may choose an example from among cases reported, but not pursued, perhaps we can let the casualness with which such incidents are regarded, both by individuals and authorities, speak for itself. One of the present authors recently found himself taking a statement from some students, who could not get satisfaction from the police, from our university area patrol, nor from the university authorities, after they had been attacked in their apartment near the campus.

A working student: sturdy, blond, blue-eyed, more blue collar than "hip" looking, and apparently capable of taking care of himself, was threatened before witnesses in a polling place when he went to vote in the outwardly respectable, working-class, Italian-American neighborhood where he lived near campus. His accoster, a large man wearing a jacket with identification of a union local, which the student recognized from the brewery where he was himself employed, warned him to "move by the end of the week" or he would "be killed". The next day, however, a girl student with whom he shared the apartment (out of convenience, they say, both being otherwise attached), and two guests visiting there at that time, were attacked in the apartment by about 10 men armed with crowbars. The students were beaten and driven out, and their car windows were smashed as they fled. The apartment was subsequently looted in shifts, being broken into between checks by the precinct police. The students drove to the university area police patrol

---

[63] In 1966, the National Opinion Research Center (NORC) conducted a survey (of 10,000 households), and the Bureau of Social Science Research (BSSR) conducted more detailed surveys in certain precincts of Washington, Boston, and Chicago to provide the National Crime Commission with an estimate of the extent of unreported crime in the United States. See: *The Challenge of Crime in a Free Society,* Dutton ed., pp. 96-100; and Albert D. Biderman: "Surveys of Population Samples for Estimating Crime Incidence," 374 *The Annals* 16 (Nov., 1967). Biderman concludes:

Respondents...report being victimized by crime more than twice as frequently as would be expected on the basis of the UCR "Crime Index". (p. 32)

Abraham Blumberg; *loc. cit.,* adds:

The FBI reports on a rather consistent basis that only about 25% of all crimes reported are actually cleared by arrest. (p. 275)

station (like many large American cities today, the university area is obliged to have its own private force). But here they were given the precise advice that they might have been assisted, but the site of the attack was just outside of area jurisdiction; and, besides, all but one of the students were from the downtown, state university. The precinct police were notified, however, and the students were taken to the university hospital for first aid and x-rays. The precinct police arrived at the hospital where they questioned the students. The police informed the students that they "should know better than to live in that area", but escorted them back to the apartment, "to get what they needed for the night", then drove them to the station where they could "take a cab". The next day the police were to meet them at the apartment again so that they could pack their things. In the meantime the apartment, which had been locked when the students had returned and left with the police, was broken into; this was established by the first student, who returned home late from his job, after the others had come back and gone away again with the police.

None of the neighbors came to their assistance. But the landlady later claimed that she thought she knew who the ring-leader and members of the gang of assailants must be and where they lived because they apparently had used that same tactic on other residents before. Although this report would appear to offer adequate leads to pursue, no investigation was conducted. At first the students were under the impression that they had given a statement to the university police, and that that had been relayed to the police precinct. Later no record was found and a second report was made. Still later it was discovered that the second statement did not include the mention of stolen goods. University officials had "too much to do regarding thefts on campus" to press the matter with the police. The students, products of an eroa of belief in American efficiency, expected something to be done at once. Their idealism shattered, they had already moved; now they resigned themselves to their losses (quite substantial for the one student on his own and obliged to work a 40 hour week on top of a full course of studies). They may now be counted among that part of their generation disaffected with "law and order". In America, incidents of this kind always seem a little bit unreal—both to those who hear about them and to the victims. One has to ask himself, however, would it have been different for the victims if they had been "your average citizen" (dependent of course on the community); or if they had been rich.

When "minding your own business" while the neighbors in your building are threatened, attacked, and looted is thinkable; when the victims accept gang assault with deadly weapons, breaking and entering, and burglarly, without exhausting all recourse among public officials; when the police come to see their job as reporting crime "so that we will know whether the rate of crime has gone up or down in our area" and not investigating it; then in that society who will worry about persons arrested for being careless enough to be picked up, even if they do not come to trial in a reasonable period? The authors do not claim that the incidents described above from the account of the attacked students are either all the facts, or are even completely reliable as reported. Investigation and collection of testimony is not within our power. But it seems to us that when charges of this magnitude are brought, we have the right to expect a police investigation. We do not charge negligence; and we recognize the fact that the police may be overburdened with calls. But what order of priorities of law enforcement is there in a society where crimes of violence go uninvestigated and crimes without victims require at least 25% of courtroom time, in times when only about 10-15% of those convicted of crimes go through full trial proceedings, at all.

The extent of the change in the way of life in America today as the result of crime that has followed upon social changes and dislocations is perhaps best demonstrated by the fact that there is practically no public reaction to incidents which even 10 years ago most people would only have heard of in gangster movies or wild West films. Today: "That's the way it is now!" This is by no means to belittle the strength of the political cause of "law and order". But the disturbances to law and order that have been significant enough to arouse this concern have been primarily "ghetto" riots, protest marches, or the much more purposeless "trashing" episodes. In short, where only the life, liberty, and property of individual persons is involved, one is fortunate to get fleeting notice from his fellow citizens, the news media, and, more important, but perhaps the consequence of the preceding, from the police and public officials. The great symbolic demonstrations do arouse reaction and anxiety. And the political response is directed toward those. In the public eye and in the outlook of many elected officials, certain kinds of political activity and bizarre manners and dress have become suspect. And those seem to receive a disproportionate notoriety and public attention.

Ultimately, however, it is just those extraordinary events and appearances which are the real subject matter of an investigation of the nature and discussion of social ethics in the criminal law. For that is the direction in which public attention is drawn. Under these circumstances reform is not very much in the public discussion at all except for example in critical commentary on the more liberal decisions of the Supreme Court which has been the only really effective center of reform in the area of criminal law in the United States (see Chapter II: B. and C. below). The liberal Court of recent years has thus had far more effect in simply interpreting the essentially liberal ideals of the Bill of Rights than any legislature responsible to a far less liberal-minded public.

Let us make no mistake in this matter, however. It is not so much the rate of crime which is at stake in the issue of criminal law reform, except insofar as perhaps certain abuses in the course of selective law enforcement can be curtailed. Crime is not ordinarily the result of not enough things being against the law, although the prohibition of behavior that is somehow associated with crime may provide an easier target than hard crime itself. Liberal reform is far more an issue of the realization of the political ideal of democratic control over what has often seemed to be the unbridled use of public power by the authorities (although frequently with outward public approval), and of the re-direction of the authority of society towards the protection of the rights and interests of its members. The only *legal* reform that may hopefully exercise some influence on the rate of crime is perhaps social reform, reforms in the area of the administration of justice, and reform of the penal institutions themselves. (On this point we fully concur with Professor Würtenberger's opinion expressed in the Foreword, page XVI.) The source of inspiration towards the pursuit of those reforms in the democratic state, we believe, however, to lie in the greater appreciation of the rights and dignity of the individual. A state may be entirely within its prerogatives and traditions in emphasizing our collective obligations to the greater interests of society as a whole. But success in suppression of crime, with no proper regard for its origins or the guarantees of due process, can easily become the rationale for the suppression of dissent, and the enforcement of conformity.

The limitations a society imposes upon itself, even in pursuit of its acknowledged collective interests, are proportional, we believe, to that society's depth of understanding of the issues of the relationships between individual rights and collective responsibilities. This kind of understanding is promoted, we believe, by a study of the role of social attitudes and values in the development of our own criminal law structure. But the comparison of ideas and developments in the course of the debates of recent years which have led to the reform of the German criminal law, for example, are another source for the examination of social and intellectual forces at work in our own system. Only in this case, because of the distance that many of those developments seem to have from the realities of American experience, it may be easier to examine the historical development of attitudes—many of which have their counterparts in the United States—with greater detachment and hopefully a sharper eye for their logical consequences.

The authors do not pretend to be presenting a complete picture of recent changes in American or German criminal law. Treatment is focused on only a few highly controversial areas. In general, these are the areas in which comparable changes have occurred or have been discussed in the debates over criminal law reform both in Germany and the United States. It is hoped that by examining the more hotly contended issues such as these that the process of change in criminal law will be made clearer, and that the main thesis of this study, that the law often emerges from attitudes and ideas whose origins and logical consequences are little known and little examined in public discussion, can be illustrated.[64]

The purpose of this study, is, therefore, to demonstrate the operation of social ethical, social political ideas in action in the making, or reform, of the law. One particular object of investigation is the often mistaken concept of reform by liberalization. According to what "liberalization" means to its proponents, it can serve many purposes, some of which may be distinctly non-liberal, if one examines them for their effects as opposed to their ambitions. The theoretical result of the ambition of a law to provide a design for society, makes social democratic or social

---

[64] A discussion of the psychological implications in the criminal law, and of the dynamics of its reform, would require a more extensive treatment of another kind than is attempted in this study. Our concern here is with the public discussion of privately held opinions and attitudes which may be unwittingly played upon in the influence game of political process. For a treatment of the psychology of how such attitudes may emerge at all we refer the reader to Albert A. Ehrenzweig: *A Psychoanalytic Jurisprudence*, Sijthoff, Leiden; Oceana, Dobbs Ferry N.Y., 1971. An older article on the proposed German *Draft Criminal Code* of 1958 employs a similar method: Hochheimer: "Zur Psychologie der strafenden Gesellschaft," *Kritische Justiz* 27 (1969). See also the discussion of the psychological implications of the criminal law in Reiwald: *Society and its Criminals*.

liberal purposes and methods very similar to social or moral conservative ones—regardless of whether the supposed "conservative" values or theoretically "more democratic" ones are ideological, class, economic, or religious values. No one is to say that societies and legislatures shall not design for themselves. But it is the obligation of the critics and interpreters of legal and social theory and philosophy and the students of the social sciences and systems of social analysis to make clear to their readers and audiences what may indeed be taking place. Lawmakers and citizens may choose to reform and restructure their laws consciously and according to plan and theory, but hopefully will not be misled into far different social legal structures through ignorance of the consequences of the social and legal ideas they adopt and pursue.

B.   INDIVIDUAL FREEDOM AND SOCIAL ORDER

Kadish refers cautiously to the use of the criminal law as a tool for social control. Surely, there is a definite political element in the making of the criminal law, just as there is in all other areas of the law. But, where the legislator turns to the task of shaping society as well as controlling abuses within it, the question necessarily arises as to whether the moral of such laws should not be debated publicly, and whether it is the criminal law which is the proper means for legislating this kind of social design.

If we were always conscious of the general goals of prospective legislators, we might insist that their general programs be the subject of national debate. But in fact in the United States we are barely aware of the political and philosophical ramifications of our various attitudes on specific issues. The result is often the mixture of the Constitution's libertarian ideals with quite different social or moral political attitudes in the law, and especially in the criminal law.

In the non-philosophical world of Anglo-American politics and law, the criminal law is usually not bound by any one general theory, though various theories about correction and social control may be called upon to support what already exists.[65] For the most part, the criminal law

---

[65] In a recent article for the German criminal lawyer: "Strafwürdigkeit und Moral in der Angelsächsischen Rechtsphilosophie," 82 *Zeitschrift für die gesamte Strafrechtswissenschaft* 538 (1970), Norbert Hoerster has attempted to discover a basis in social theory for Anglo-American moral attitudes in the criminal law. The article contains a broad survey of the literature, especially that bearing on morals

does not stem from any grand design or theory, but is either a matter of practical convenience or is the result of causes which stir public sentiment or moral concern. Although theoretical debate may have far-reaching consequences for the manner in which the criminal law touches the lives of individuals, the public is generally far more concerned about various specific offenses. And when a change is made in the nature and requirements of the law in this area, it is probably far more a reflection of legislative interpretation of the public will, or what the public will stand for, than an expression of criminological theory.

Yet what the public appears to want, or will stand for, does seem to reflect tacit political attitudes or inclinations, unphilosophical as the English-speaking public may be. And from time to time these ideals become the real subject of discussion in the debate over any given issue. Perhaps a paradigm example of such an instance occurred several years ago when England discussed reforming the prohibitions against acts of male homosexuality, a subject always surrounded by emotion and anxiety. In September, 1957, the *Wolfenden Report* [66] had appeared, recommending ending of the prohibition for private homosexual acts between consenting adults. Some months later, Sir Patrick Devlin (since, Lord Devlin), who as a leading jurist had concurred in the ultimate recommendations of the Wolfenden Committee, attacked the language and logic of the *Report* itself in a lecture to the British Academy. That lecture was later included in a book which is an extended treatment of the subject of enforcement of morals. [67] The lecture aroused extensive reaction itself, [68] and remains at the center of popular discussion in this area. Neither the *Wolfenden Report* nor Devlin's reaction to it make any pretentions of being a complete philosophical exposition, and in

laws. Hoerster also emphasizes the importance of the Hart/Devlin debates discussed here. His interpretation is, however, more in terms of theory than many an Anglo-American lawyer would attempt. In what follows we do not want to suggest so much that the moralist argument in particular is based upon theory, as that its even untheoretical fundamental principles involve logical consequences which are little different from those of more elaborate theoretical systems.

[66] Great Britain, Home Office/Scottish Home Dept., Committee on Homosexual Offenses and Prostitution: *Report of the Committee...*, H.M.S.O., London, 1957 (reprinted 1962), Cmnd. 247. (Cited hereafter as *Wolfenden Report*.)

[67] Patrick Devlin: *The Enforcement of Morals*, O.U.P., London, 1965.

[68] A bibliography of these is included in Devlin's book at p. xiiif. See also a review of the book itself by Glanville Williams: "Authoritarian Morals and the Criminal Law," *Criminal Law Rev.* 132 (1966).

fact the debate revolves more or less around two general positions which reflect again simply the conservative and liberal attitudes.

After consideration of arguments specifically bearing on the practice of homosexual acts themselves the *Wolfenden Report* concludes the Committee's examination of the problem by confronting a general proposition which could as easily be applied to all sorts of similar prohibitions based exclusively on moral objections where no outward harm to other persons is involved:

...We have outlined the arguments against a change in the law, and we recognise their weight. We believe, however, that they have been met by the counter-arguments we have already advanced. There remains one additional counter-argument which we believe to be decisive, namely, the importance which society and the law ought to give to individual freedom of choice and action in matters of private morality. Unless a deliberate attempt is to be made by society, acting through the agency of the law, to equate the sphere of crime with that of sin, there must remain a realm of private morality and immorality which is, in brief and crude terms, not the law's business. To say this is not to condone or encourage private immorality. On the contrary, to emphasise the personal and private nature of moral and immoral conduct is to emphasise the personal and private responsibility of the individual for his own actions, and that is a responsibility which a mature agent can properly be expected to carry for himself without the threat of punishment from the law.[69]

The criterion of no objective harm is rarely seen the same by the moralistic traditionalist (or modern day moralistic ideologist for that matter), however, for he may see the basic structure of society threatened by the disregard of traditional morals and observances. The idea that the structure of society is simply the work of tradition is, moreover, a very old and widespread conviction. In the Analects of Confucius, for example, a follower more zealously traditionalist than Confucius himself defends just that idea. A high officer of the ancient Chinese state of Wei said:

For a man of high character to be natural is quite sufficient; what need is there for art [i.e. culture] to make him such? (*Analects* XII.8.1)

Upon which the zealous Confucian defended:

Culture [or form] is just as important as inborn qualities [or substance]; and inborn qualities no less important than culture. The hide of a tiger or a leopard stripped of its hair, is like the hide of a dog or a goat stripped of its hair.[70]

---

[69] *Wolfenden Report*, p. 24, para. 61.
[70] (*Analects* XII.8.1)=W. E. Soothill: *The Analects of Confucius*, Yokohama, 1910, p. 575; (XII.8.3)=Arthur Waley: *The Analects of Confucius*, Vintage, New

This idea would seem to have much to say for it in those Oriental societies where the state power was distant and often inaccessible for the needs of the common man. There, customary usage bound the small society together with bonds of mutual deference and form. Difficulties or disputes which arose in those societies were settled preferably by mediation. Resort to law, where it was possible, was frowned upon, both because it meant invoking the authority of a distant or uninterested magistrate to meddle in the internal affairs of the local community, and because it meant literally rejecting principles of customary morality or equity for the mere chance that a magistrate, armed with a law designed to maintain order and not principally to adjudicate disputes, would act justly. And even if he did, or wanted to, the magistrate had no investigative apparatus, and frequently no police power to speak of, either to protect person or property, or to enforce peace between parties over a long period. He could only manage to compromise himself, therefore, if he became entangled in a local affair far from his base, which he could not settle promptly.[71] In the context of the self-controlled local community of an Oriental empire, where representational power was used for other purposes than constant police protection and recourse to law, tradition, customary usages, the rites and ceremonies, politeness, and accepted *mores,* taken as a whole, gave the world of this little society a sense of order it might otherwise not have had.

Any given member of the community might enjoy his particular moral standing in the community according to whether he derived the abstract principles of his behavior from the tradition and *mores* of his society. This attitude is perhaps not too distant from what Lord Devlin means when he says:

York, p. 165f.; James Legge: *The Four Books, Confucian Analects,* etc., Paragon Reprint, New York, 1966, p. 163. Literal translation leaves much to be desired for English style; good style often is too free a translation, hence the reference to three translations.

[71] In recent years the study of the customary law of traditional societies has been fairly extensive. See e.g.: Laura Nader; K. F. Koch; B. Cox: "The Ethnography of Law: A Bibliographic Survey," 7 *Current Anthropology,* 267 (1966). A further discussion of this point will be contained in: O. Lee: *Legal and Moral Systems in Asian Customary Law,* forthcoming.

One of the most illuminating single examinations of the mediation system of customary law compared with mediation in Western legal matters is: F.S.C. Northrop: "The Mediational Approval Theory in American Legal Realism," 44 *Virginia Law Rev.* 358 (1958).

Most men take their morality as a whole and in fact derive it, though this is irrelevant, from some religious doctrine. To destroy the belief in one part of it will probably result in weakening the belief in the whole.[72]

The Judaeo-Christian doctrine of sin, which even the Indian religious concept of violation of *dharma* does not approach, and a tradition of exact theology, gives a whole new dimension of reinforcement to the Eastern notion of the unity of moral law and social order,[73] which, in China at least, is simply an expression of moral outlook and philosophical tradition. To describe Lord Devlin's world view, we should perhaps speak in terms of the social teachings of the Church of Rome and a late Archbischop of Canterbury,[74] of the unity of Christianity and social order.[75] In contrast not only to the individualistic liberal, but also to the individualistic Protestant conceptions of man, in the conservative and Catholic tradition, man's role as primarily a social being is emphasized. Professor F.S.C. Northrop describes this conservative conception of man's social role which is derived from early Christian theology. He contrasts what he calls the elements of Lockean and Protestant non-conformist individualism in American democracy with the philosophy of British conservatives which he describes as "theologically grounded, anti-laissez-faire, organic, hierarchical conception of the good state and the good individual." [76] He traces the origins of this social trait in England to the historical consolidation of national feeling under Queen Elizabeth I and the articulation of a tolerant religious compromise in Anglicanism which combined the social doctrines of the Roman Church

[72] Devlin: *Op. cit.*, p. 115. This notion is criticized by H.L.A. Hart: *Law, Liberty, and Morality*, Vintage, New York (c. 1963), esp. pp. 51, 72; and Williams: *loc. cit.*, p. 140f.

[73] For a sociological analysis of the function of the unity of moral law and social order in the traditional societies of South and East Asia, see Paul Mus in *Annuaire du Collège de France.* 56 (1956) pp. 272-79, 57 (1957) pp. 333-44, 58 (1958) pp. 372-74, 59 (1959) pp. 413-25, 60 (1960) pp. 307-08.

[74] Cf. William Temple: *Christianity and Social Order*, Penguin, New York, 1942, p. 34. For an older statement which seems to have represented the same general thesis to the idealistically minded conservatives of the last century see: Coleridge: *Church and State.*

[75] A very efficient and compact digest of the Catholic social teachings is contained in: Union Internacional de Estudios Sociales: *Codigos de Malinas, social, familiar, moral internacional, moral politica*, 2nd ed., Editorial Sal Tarrae, Santander, 1959.

[76] F.S.C. Northrop: *The Meeting of East and West: An Inquiry Concerning World Understanding*, Macmillan, New York, 1950, p. 170. See also George Trevelyan: *English Social History*, Longmans, Green, New York, 1942, pp. 179-81.

with the demands of reformers. But above all he sees this kind of social consciousness in England as the historical result of a social theory set down by Richard Hooker in his *Ecclesiatical Polity*.[77]

The Western liberal democracies' ideal of rule of law has, however, created legal institutions and recourse, not available to the members of traditional Oriental or Medieval or even Elizabethan society. This is not to say that liberal democratic society has dispensed with the need for or the value of traditional *mores*. But it does mean that moral, religious, and political pluralism is possible in a society of law guaranteed under legal rights and legal institutions. The violation of the rites and ceremonies which could upset the lives of a traditional Chinese or Indian village, or Medieval, Christian, European village, or American small town, for that matter, is hardly of the same order of disruption for modern legal society as it may once have been, and in some cases may still be for societies governed primarily by tradition. Again, this is not to say that the traditionalist or fundamentalist in our present legal society might not be offended or outraged if he knew we were somehow disdainful of his rites, ceremonies, or beliefs. The point is, however, that democratic pluralism establishes legal tolerances within which we think we can at least stop short of legal liability, and still do no lasting injury to the fabric of society.

For Lord Devlin, however, an act of private behavior which if known could serve to subvert public morality is to be regarded with the same concern as under conservative Confucian identification of form and substance:

All sexual immorality involves the exploitation of human weaknesses. The prostitute exploits the lust of her customers and the customer the moral weakness of the prostitute. If the exploitation of human weaknesses is considered to create a special circumstance, there is virtually no field of morality which can be defined in such a way as to exclude the law. I think, therefore, that it is not possible to set theoretical limits to the power of the State to legislate against immorality.... . Society is entitled by means of its laws to protect itself from dangers, whether from within or without. Here again I think that the political parallel is legitimate. The law of treason is directed against aiding the king's enemies and against sedition from within.... . an established morality is as necessary as good government to the welfare of society. Societies disintegrate from within more frequently than they are broken up by external pressures. This is disintegration when no common morality is observed and history shows that the loosening of moral bonds is often the first stage of disintegration, so that society is justified in taking the same steps to preserve its moral code as it does to preserve its government and other essential

---

[77] Richard Hooker: *The Works of...*, Vincent, Oxford, 1843.

institutions. The suppression of vice is as much the law's business as the suppression of subversive activities; it is no more possible to define a sphere of private morality than it is to define one of private subversive activity.[78]

It would appear then that Lord Devlin is also aware of and not averse to the apparent identification of society and its morality in his line of thought. Professor Hart has made the same point regarding what one can infer from Devlin's philosophy:

> There seems...to be central to Lord Devlin's thought something more interesting, though no more convincing, than the conception of social morality as a seamless web. For he appears to move from the acceptable proposition that *some* shared morality is essential to the existence of any society to the unacceptable proposition that a society is identical with its morality as that is at any given moment of its history, so that a change in its morality is tantamount to the destruction of a society. The former proposition might be even accepted as a necessary rather than an empirical truth depending on a quite plausible definition of society as a body of men who hold certain moral views in common. But the latter proposition is absurd. Taken strictly, it would prevent us saying that the morality of a given society had changed, and would compel us instead to say that one society had disappeared and another one taken its place.[79]

In reply Lord Devlin indicates that he does not conceive of morality—or society—being frozen at one stage of development any more than a contract would be precluded from amendment, or that the "inclusion of a penal section into a statute prohibiting certain acts freezes the whole statute into immobility and prevents the prohibitions from ever being modified." [80] It seems, at least, that Lord Devlin does not want to preclude change, although he has certainly not provided for it so far as morality goes. What is more important for our understanding of his position is, however, his identification of society with its established morality, for as he says: "I would venture to assert, for example, that you cannot have a game without rules and that if there were no rules there would be no game." [81]

With that it should be clear, if it were not before, that Lord Devlin is convinced that modern Western society is as much dependent on its moral order as on the law. In the abstract this may still sound inoffensive. The problems arise—as Professor Hart suggests—when morality changes,

---

[78] Devlin: *op. cit.,* pp. 12f.

[79] Hart: *op. cit.,* p. 51f. See also Richard Wollheim: "Crime, Sin, and Mr. Justice Devlin," *Encounter,* Nov., 1959, p. 34.

[80] Devlin: *op. cit.,* p. 13f., n.l.

[81] *Ibid.,* p. 13, n.l.

or when a pluralistic society with perhaps non-conflicting but also non-congruent moralities exists. Because we are, ostensibly, dedicated to the continuity of our particular society, we are, according to Lord Devlin, committed to the preservation of its "morality":

A man who concedes that morality is necessary to society must support the use of those instruments without which morality cannot be maintained. The two instruments are those of teaching, which is doctrine, and of enforcement, which is the law.... . No society has yet solved the problem of how to teach morality without religion. So the law must base itself on Christian morals and to the limit of its ability enforce them, not simply because they are the morals of most of us, nor simply because they are morals which are taught by the established Church—on these points the law recognizes the right to dissent—but for the compelling reason that without the help of Christian teaching the law will fail.[82]

The question of pluralism aside, a vital issue is settled here in the abstract consideration of the rationale for enforcement of morals. For Locke [83] and Mill [84] society existed as a historical structure guaranteeing our civil, legal rights; to that extent our rights were our primary legal consideration. For the moralistic traditionalist—if he expresses himself like Lord Devlin—morality may and should be enforced to preserve society, and, without it, society cannot exist. Society is in turn obliged to teach and preserve established morality, which is tantamount to saying established religion or religions. The primary consideration, then, may be religion and the institutions of society, for they are each bound to the other—but clearly, though we may benefit individually from their existence, we are bound to uphold their particular established existence as primary. Lockean society promised us guarantees. In Lord Devlin's society we are participants bound to uphold the preservation of society, morality, and religion, in order that we, and others, may benefit collectively. The same argument of the traditionalist conservative holds, by the way, equally for the social democrat and the Marxist. It is merely that they have replaced traditional or Christian social teaching with rationalist social doctrines.[85]

---

[82] *Ibid.*, p. 25.

[83] John Locke: *Second Treatise of Government* (1690), many eds.

[84] John Stuart Mill: *On Liberty* (1859), many eds., esp. Ch. IV, "Of the Limits of Society Over the Individual".

[85] See esp. Gustav Radbruch: *Rechtsphilosophie*, 6th ed., E. Wolf (ed.), Koehler, Stuttgart, 1963, esp. p. 226f. F.A. Hayek: "Kinds of Rationalism," in *Studies in Philosophy, Politics, and Economics,* Univ. of Chicago Pr., 1967; J.L. Talmon: *The Origins of Totalitarian Democracy,* London, 1952.

Devlin, himself, descended from Locke and Mill, with the rest of us, has his own reservations about such apparent logical consequences of the assumption of the unity of moral law and social order:

...that authority should be a grant and liberty not a privilege, is, I think the true mark of a free society.[86]

For the more orthodox conservative or collectivist, social rationalist or radical who might be an adherent of the kind of system which Lord Devlin seems to have described, with the exception of the above reservation, the benefits of society are to be enjoyed collectively in order to be enjoyed at all, or, enjoyed genuinely. To the conservative or collectivist the individualistic liberal seems to advocate a selfish personalism. For that liberal, on the other hand, if liberties cannot be enjoyed separately and individually there is no collective benefit, for the collective benefit is only the possibility of our separate individual benefits. For individualistic liberalism, collectivism is the annihilation of the collective benefit, by pre-emption of the rights of the individual.

In all fairness, one must, however, interject that without the "spirit" of legal, liberal democracy its guarantees can be easily frustrated too. For there are both those who go to lengths to get all they can within the law, and those, too, who use the limit of the law to fight for another system. That is a weakness of libertarian democracy, but one it will have to bear if it is to survive as an ideal. The German constitutional lawyers talk about "self-destructive democracy":[87] the fact that the enemies, or even the friends, of government under liberal democratic principles can manage to bring it down as long as it cannot act to curb the action of those who exercise their freedom of action in a liberal democratic society in a manner calculated to confound and defy the institutions which guarantee legal rights to them. Success of that liberal democratic system, perhaps far more than any other, requires adherence to its forms, but above all mutual tolerance and deference often beyond the common practice, but hopefully not beyond the common endurance,

---

[86] Devlin: *op. cit.*, p. 102.

[87] This point is discussed more fully in the context of German constitutional theory in Chapter V: A. (1) below. See also: Theodor Maunz; G. Dürig; R. Herzog: *Grundgesetz Kommentar*, Beck, Munich, 1968, Vol. I, pp. 18, 4-5; and H. von Mangoldt; F. Klein: *Das Bonner Grundgesetz*, 2nd ed., Vahlen, Berlin, 1955, pp. 113-16.

if it is to accomplish what it was organized to do. But, tolerance, however desirable or necessary, is not identical with the system of rule of law itself.

C. "THE RIGHT-MINDED" AND "THE REASONABLE MAN"

For someone so often represented in terms such as the advocate of "authoritarian morals" (Williams),[88] it is all the more interesting to observe where Lord Devlin looks to find what the moral judgment of society may be, that he contends ought to be enforced as law. It is curious that the man who, in Hart's words describes morality—not the law— as "a seamless web",[89] who in our words above describes "the unity of the moral and the social order", has no one established ideology or church doctrine, to support as the arbiter of morality, nor any personal conception of his own to put forward, for all societies. For British society, true enough, he says, "So the law must base itself on Christian morals...." [90] But in Britain church and state are still bound together in law. "Outside Christendom," he says, "other standards derive from other religions." [91] (Whether one can be "outside Christendom" but inside British, or American, society will be a proper question for some of us.) Essentially, however, the morality Lord Devlin is talking about belongs democratically to the common man: "It is the viewpoint of the man in the street," "or...the man in the Clapham omnibus."

How is the law-maker to ascertain the moral judgments of society? It is surely not enough that they should be reached by the opinion of the majority; it would be too much to require the individual assent of every citizen. English law has evolved and regularly uses a standard which does not depend on the counting of heads. It is that of the reasonable man. He is not to be confused with the rational man. He is not expected to reason about anything and his judgment may be largely a matter of feeling. It is the viewpoint of the man in the street—or to use an archaism familiar to all lawyers—the man in the Clapham omnibus. He might also be called the right-minded man. For my purpose I should like to call him the man in the jury box, for the moral judgment of society must be something

---

[88] Cf. Glanville Williams: "Authoritarian Morals and the Criminal Law," *Criminal Law Rev.* 132 (1966).

[89] Cf. H.L.A. Hart: *Law, Liberty, and Morality*, Vintage, New York, c. 1963, p. 51.

[90] Cf. Patrick Devlin: *The Enforcement of Morals*, O.U.P., London, 1965, p. 25.

[91] *Ibid.*, p. 4.

about which any twelve men or women drawn at random might after discussion be expected to be unanimous.[92]

The point has already been made earlier that Lord Devlin, like most educated men in the English speaking world is also heir to the liberal democratic theories of Locke and Mill and others, who have all contributed to the evolution of our political way of life. Though it may be difficult to understand on the basis of the arguments for enforcement of morals he presents us with, he is known to have testified before the Wolfenden Committee in favor of the reform of the prohibition against homosexual acts done in private between consenting adults because: "Punishment will not cure and because it is haphazard in its incidence I doubt if it deters." [93] Glanville Williams reminds us too

...in one or two instances Lord Devlin would come down on the side of the libertarians for practical reasons. He has publicly supported the Wolfenden proposals on homosexuality. He evidently thinks that the law of abortion is too disputatious to be maintained in its present state. Devlin, as a judge, left his humane and intelligent mark upon the criminal law; and in *Adams* he came closer than anyone else has done to legalising voluntary euthanasia by medical men.[94]

It is unfortunate, therefore, that a reasonable and responsible judge should become something of an authoritarian straw man for liberal writers to demolish periodically for having dared to say aloud what many people are obviously thinking, and what many a less forthright soul would not have uttered in face of the inevitable onslaught of popular liberal rejoinders. This is not to say that Devlin has written any more cogently. But his thesis does merit this much consideration, we believe, precisely because it is the not infrequent—if by no means universal—reaction of many people who see themselves as pretty much the common man. But, here, an often badly expressed popular position is expounded by an articulate and highly accomplished member of the English judiciary.

It is something of a standard Anglo-Saxon turn of phrase to speak of oneself and of the common man. But this democratic gesture is not known for its distinguishing neatly between what attitudes or behavior is, properly speaking, one's own and what legitimately can be said of others. What is more the impression conveyed by the description the "common man" is perhaps somewhat more elevated that the designation the "average man". Hence in thinking abstractly it may be easier to

[92] *Ibid.*, p. 15.
[93] *Ibid.*, p. v.; see also p. 97.
[94] Williams, *loc. cit.*, p. 145.

assume that the common man (or Englishman) in the jury box would endeavor to decide or report matters of public morality as fairly and judiciously as one would endeavor to do himself, and not as we are sometimes led to believe, say the average (white) man in a jury box in Mississippi might, in the case of a trial of a local Ku Klux Klansman accused of murdering a Northern civil rights worker, or in the case of a grand jury hearing for police and highway patrolmen accused of having fired on Negro students, without provocation (we are told) killing two of them.

There is a fundamental difference in the character of the decisions one asks of a juryman in even controversial cases and the kinds of decisions as to the very nature of social and moral order we understand Devlin's thesis to entail. A juryman is asked at most to reach a decision as to fact according to evidence. To ask a jury to decide whether in fact an act of murder, larceny, assault, or even an act of incest, sodomy, fornication, adultery, or what have you, has been committed, is a far different request from asking them to decide what is "the moral judgment of society" on incest, sodomy, fornication, adultery, prostitution, bigamy, obscenity, drug abuse, etc. It is one thing to reach a conclusion on a question of fact on the basis of evidence and under the guide rules of the law, custom, and the traditions of the English speaking peoples. It seems quite another matter to ask a member of a jury to reach a conclusion when he is supposed to have all the evidence already innate in him, or, at least: "He is not expected to reason about anything and his judgment may be largely a matter of feeling." Even granting that there are some issues where we have innate moral judgments, let us suppose that a juryman who had such a moral judgment against the practice of abortion was prompted under some circumstances to procure one. Are we to conclude that he acted contrary to his better moral judgment? That his moral judgment changed? Or that his moral judgment was, after due deliberation with himself, to do that which he felt morally compelled to do? Who is to say that all of these conclusions are not correct, or even that that is not what we mean by moral judgment? Unless one in fact begs the question, by assuming that the nature of religion, tradition, Constitution, or our laws is such that we would not be who we are if we did not make certain specific established moral judgments—or did not hesitate to say so openly, if we should in fact disagree—it is probably as likely we would find with Plato, "There are as many forms of Constitution as there are men."

This is not to say that the doctrine of the reasonable man is not or should not be employed by juries and judges in making decisions as to fact. In the concept of negligence, for example, there is the implicit assumption that there is a pattern of behavior which would not have been negligent. It has been the ambition of the courts to establish what one might reasonably have expected from an ordinary average individual of such and such accomplishments or limitations, in given circumstances. Prosser summarizes the doctrine in this matter from representative cases in the law of torts:

The courts have dealt with this very difficult problem by creating a fictitious person, who never has existed on land or sea: the "reasonable man of ordinary prudence".[95] Sometimes he is described as a reasonable man, or a prudent man, or a man of average prudence, or a man of ordinary sense using ordinary care and skill. It is evident that all such phrases are intended to mean very much the same thing. The actor is required to do what such an ideal individual would be supposed to do in his place. A model of all proper qualities, with only those human shortcomings and weaknesses which the community will tolerate on the occasion, "this excellent but odious character stands like a monument in our Courts of Justice, vainly appealing to his fellow-citizens to order their lives after his own example." [96, 97]

It is hard to believe that Lord Devlin would ask the jury to go beyond the context of the law to legislate even a common moral judgment. Since he first suggested employment of "the reasonable man" doctrine for establishing the moral judgments of society, however, an unusually moralistic decision in the House of Lords has provided a device whereby the kind of moral judgment by a jury envisaged by Lord Devlin becomes conceivable, with the judgment being properly a determination of fact under the law. In *Shaw v. Director of Public Prosecutions* (1961) [98] the Lords affirmed the conviction of Shaw for publishing an obscene article, living on the earnings of prostitutes, who paid for advertisements in his *Ladies Directory,* and conspiring to corrupt public morals. In pressing the final charge, the prosecution invoked a dictum of Lord Mansfield from 1774:

---

[95] Prosser refers to the first mention in *Vaughan v. Menlove* (1738) 3 *Bing. N.C.* 468, 132 *Eng. Rep.* 490.

[96] Cf. A.P. Herbert: *Misleading Cases in the Common Law,* 1930, pp. 12-16.

[97] William L. Prosser: *Handbook of the Law of Torts,* 3rd ed., West, St. Paul, Minn., 1964, p. 153f.

[98] *Shaw v. Director of Public Prosecutions* (1961) 2 *A.E.R.* 446; (1962) *A.C.* 223. The case is discussed by Hart: *op. cit.,* pp. 6-12, and by Devlin, *op. cit.,* pp. 91-101.

Whatever is *contra bonos mores et decorum* the principles of our laws prohibit and the King's Court as the general censor and guardian of the public morals is bound to restrain and punish.[99]

Their Lordships (one dissenting) appear to have subscribed to Lord Simonds' fears:

...since no one can foresee every way in which the wickedness of man may disrupt the order of society. Let me take a single instance.... . Let it be supposed that at some future, perhaps early, date homosexual practices between adult consenting males are no longer a crime. Would it not be an offense if even without obscenity such practices were publicly advocated and encouraged by pamphlet and advertisement? Or must we wait till Parliament finds time to deal with such conduct? I say, my Lords, that if the common law is powerless in such an event then we should no longer do her reverence. But I say that her hand is still powerful and that it is for Her Majesty's judges to play the part which Lord Mansfield pointed out to them.[100]

Lord Devlin welcomes this decision affirming Lord Simonds' dictum that "the purpose of the law is to conserve the moral welfare of the State" adding:

What makes a society is a community of ideas, not political ideas alone but also ideas about the way its members should behave and govern their lives.[101]

Is is not entirely clear what may have befallen the "moral Welfare of the State" in Britain since the recent realization of the Wolfenden Committee's recommendations (1967). But if Britain has its counterpart of the underground press in America, where there has been no *Wolfenden Report,* then papers and advertisements with more bizarre things than Lord Simonds foresaw have become current. But it is a credit to Anglo-American regard for security of law, the reservation against prosecution of behavior which is not explicitly prohibited by law, that there has not been a flood of litigation under the resurrected dictum of Lord Mansfield or existing dead letter statutes in America. Of course the most sweeping changes have come in the wake of liberalized obscenity rulings both in Britain and America, but these have not been followed by charges of *contra bonos mores.*

It is true that with the formula of offense against public morals and decorum there is theoretically the fact of public offensiveness that the jury could decide, and not whether such and such ought to be a crime.

---

[99] *Jones v. Randall* (1774). *Lafft.* at p. 385.

[100] *Shaw* (1961) 2 *A.E.R.* at pp. 452f.; (1962) *A.C.* at p. 268; see also Hart: *op. cit.,* p. 9.

[101] Devlin, *op. cit.,* p. 89.

Yet if such and such behavior offends, it would seem incumbent upon the legislature, if the offense warrants, to prohibit such behavior specifically. In Shaw's case, he was convicted both of publishing an obscene article and of living on the earnings of prostitutes. Under the circumstances the addition of the further charge (and conviction) of conspiring to corrupt public morals seems purely gratuitous, and merely typical of the prosecuting attorney's custom of pursuing multiple violations charges in order to be sure of obtaining a conviction for something, and perhaps also out of pure vindictiveness for the trouble. But, with the host of existing recognized legal charges one can make, it is questionable whether any judge in Britain or America would admit a charge that could not be more specific, than that something was contrary to good morals and decorum; of course, if the offense falls under any existing title, then it is also limited by the established definition. Otherwise a serious constitutional question would arise in both countries: whether conviction occurred for a crime that did not exist (there being no specific prohibition); and if it did in fact exist, by virtue of a decision (that there had been an offense to good morals and decorum), whether it had not become a crime *ex post facto*.

In another sense, however, Devlin seems quite right about the action of juries, that they already give a moral judgment in some cases, and that is a known and accepted practice in the operation of the law:

> Their province of course is fact and not law, and I do not mean that they often deliberately disregard the law. But if it is too stringent, they sometimes take a very merciful view of the facts.[102]

The law is blind and cannot tell, as in the case Devlin cites, that, for example, to a man under 24, a girl may look over 16. But a jury may find that to them either her person or her character seems that mature. A jury may also be more generous with damages when they construe that it is an insurance company and not an individual who pays.[103] But if these are moral judgments as well as determinations as to fact, then they are moral judgments as to how the law is to be applied and whether mercifully and with equity. They are not moral judgments as to what the law should be, and not judgments as to what is moral. And there are times and places, as already observed, when we may suspect

---

[102] *Ibid.,* p. 21; see also p. 90f.
[103] Cf. e.g. Harry Kalven, Jr., and Hans Zeisel: *The American Jury,* Little Brown, Boston, 1966.

that it was not a jury's best moral judgment which led them to let some go free.

Lord Devlin's faith in the moral judgment of the jury demonstrates the good experience of a learned and fair dealing jurist. And, there is, despite appearances to those who reject legislating for morality, a curious kind of positivism in Lord Devlin's call for enforcement of morals. For, as was said at the outset, Devlin does not advocate any exclusive system to be observed everywhere, because it represents true or scientific morality, or the morality of the only true religion. He does say for England that it is ultimately Christian morals that should be enforced. But it is with the understanding that Christian morals are the morals of the Englishman or of the common man in Britain. It is not because these standards are Christian that they should be enforced. But because they are the standards held in common, the "practical morality" of the people:

It is what Pollock called "practical morality", which is based not on theological or philosophical foundations but in the mass of continuous experience half-consciously or unconsciously accumulated and embodied in the morality of common sense.[104]

And that morality must be upheld because the survival of the society is tied to it:

Immorality then, for the purpose of the law, is what every right-minded person is presumed to consider to be immoral. Any immorality is capable of affecting society injuriously and in effect to a greater or lesser extent it usually does.[105]

Here is a further defense of the notion of the unity of moral and social order which we have discussed above. The point here, however, is that because there is a readily identifiable "practical morality" it can and should be resorted to, to reach judgments which will be in harmony with what is "the moral judgment of society". And the principles which one ought to be able to say reflects "the moral judgment of society" "must be something about which any 12 men or women drawn at random might after discussion be expected to be unanimous."

This final provision that they "might be expected to be unanimous" could in fact put a stricter limitation on the number of principles one might expect to issue from such juries. And we might also hope that

---

[104] Devlin, *op. cit.*, p. 15.

[105] *Ibid.*, p. 15; cf. also Pitrim Sorokin: *Crrisis of Our Age*, Dutton, N.Y., 1942, esp. ch. IV, "The Crisis in Ethics and Law".

such principles remained within the bounds of what Pollock called the "morality of common sense".[106] The reason for suggesting this unique method of letting the jury ascertain the moral judgment of the people is very simply because the legislator is too easily persuaded, Devlin believes, that:

> In deciding whether or not take the initiative the relevant question nearly always is not what popular morality is but whether it should be enforced by the criminal law.[107]

In adopting Pollock's description of "practical morality", however, Devlin seems to have made it do far different work. Pollock's "right-minded man" acting also on the basis of "practical morality" or "common sense morality", seems comparable enough to the "reasonable man" referred to in the torts lawyer's pleas of negligence. But for Pollock the "right-minded man" acts just as the "reasonable man of ordinary prudence" would to live according to "experience...embodied in the morality of common sense". He does not legislate or determine anything for anyone else. He does not determine, what Devlin suggests the criminal law should: "the minimum standards of human conduct".[108] For himself, however, he may aspire to much more, since "right-minded", to Pollock seems to be one's having been conscious of higher moral goals, as well as practical ones.

Speaking of some misconceptions of what the function of the law is, Pollock says elsewhere, "The most fruitful of these fallacies, if indeed it be not the common root of them all, is the assumption that the law of the land purports to be a general guide for the conduct of life." [109] That is rather the job for "practical morality", which makes it unnecessary for us to rest exclusively upon a fixed system of higher morality or scientific ethics:

> It is by no means an uncommon belief that a system of ethics resting on either theological or philosophical foundations is needful for the security of practical morality. And this belief, though not exactly in its commonest form, is adopted

---

[106] Sir Frederick Pollock: *Essays in Jurisprudence and Ethics,* Macmillan, London, 1882, p. 353.

[107] Devlin, *op. cit.,* p. 95.

[108] *Ibid.,* p. 23.

[109] Sir Frederick Pollock: "Lay Fallacies in The Law," in *Celebration Legal Essays to Mark the 25th Year of Service of John H. Wigmore as Professor of Law in Northwestern University* (ed. by A. Kocourek), Northwestern Univ. Pr., Chicago, 1919, (pp. 5-17) p. 6.

by Mr. Herbert Spencer, who affirms that the establishment of rules of right conduct on a scientific basis is a pressing need. We cannot help thinking this statement too broad and positive. It seems to imply that nations are made moral by systems of ethics; whereas people make ethical systems (as we submit) because they are already moral. A theory of ethics is an attempt, which may or may not be successful, to make explicit that which is implicit in practical morality. Its failure, if it fails, does not affect the worth of practical morality or ordinary men's conviction of it. The scientific basis of working morals is not in any formulated rules or propositions, but in the mass of continuous experience half-consciously or unconsciously accumulated and embodied in the morality of common sense.[110]

D. "THE COMMUNITY" AND "THE PEOPLE"

Even in a pluralistic society there is sometimes a natural offensiveness, about what goes beyond what we are ready to admit is arguable. In the United States, we often reach that point when we come to issues that question the principle of the two party system. Patriotism, morals, God, and family, and in their own ways the rights of liberty, equality and the pursuit of happiness, are put in a special position by many of us. But, as often happens where principles are honored, there is very little discussion of what they actually mean. It is unfortunate, therefore, that everyday political questions are allowed to become issues where, instead of practical considerations, unimpeachable principles are at stake.

So bitter can some debates over rights and mutually exclusive ideals become that it is sometimes a serious question whether the Constitution of the United States, let alone the Bill of Rights, the principal source of our private rights in law, would succeed in getting the approval of a decisive majority of Americans today if it were not for the prestige of the document as such apart from its content. A proposal by the late Senator Dirksen to call a new constitutional convention was, therefore, greeted with alarm by many liberal-minded people. The late senior Senator from Illinois wanted the convention in order to institute formally constitutional provisions which would guarantee the right to continue old state and local practices which had been excluded by the Supreme Court's decision forcing certain states to reapportion congressional districts on the basis of the interpretative doctrine of "one man, one vote", and banning the use of prayers in official functions in public schools, to uphold the separation of church and state. The petition started by

---

[110] Pollock: *Essays,* p. 353.

the Senator came at one time within one state of the necessary two thirds to call the convention.[111]

For the Senator, as indeed for many others, the idea of the school prayer was intimately associated with those moral values which for him were fundamental to the American way of life. Just as for Lord Devlin, it seemed improper to Senator Dirksen to accept passively what looked to him like trading moral foundations for a libertarian principle. The appeal in a case like that is not to individual liberty, which the attitude protective of moral foundations tends to see deriving from those foundations, if it is good; it is not so much really an appeal to the people, for there is no willingness to submit moral principle to majority rule. The appeal is, it seems, to the nobler sense of right or "moral judgment" of the people—which ought, they believe, to be embodied in the positive law. Morality ought to be protected in the law, the argument goes on (if somewhat curiously paradoxical with the reasoning which discovered this higher principle in the people in the first place) because otherwise this moral nature in the people would be undermined.

It is not to majority rule that he is appealing, Lord Devlin maintains when he refers to "the moral judgment of society".[112] But neither are those educated and liberal men who deny the place for enforcement of morals in the law, for basically they do not believe in entrusting questions of right or liberty to a popular mass decision of "the people" either.[113] There may be some hesitation about this challenge for liberal

---

[111] For a brief review of the history of the Dirksen call for a constitutional convention, see: "Dirksen's Ghost," *The New Republic,* 25 July, 1970, p. 8f. The fate of Dirksen's proposals for constitutional amendments dealing with state reapportionment and voluntary participation in school prayers is discussed in J.H. Laubach: *School Prayers: Congress, the Courts, and the Public,* Public Affairs Press, Washington, D.C., 1969, pp. 141-54. A brief history of the issue over prayers and Bible readings in public schools is given by Robert G. McCloskey in the introduction to: *The Bible in the Public Schools:* Arguments before the Superior Court of Cincinnati in the case of *Minor v. Board of Education of Cincinnati* (1870) with the opinions of the Court and the opinion on appeal of the Supreme Court of Ohio, DaCapo Pr., New York, 1967, pp. vii-xvii.

The recently approved State Constitution in Illinois demonstrates that, despite the fears echoed by these authors, astute politicians may succeed in making the fundamental laws, of even a conservative state, more liberal. See "Illinois Votes New Constitution; Bill of Rights Clauses Widened," *New York Times,* Thurs., 17 Dec., 1970, p. 35: 1-2.

[112] Patrick Devlin: *The Enforcement of Morals,* O.U.P., London, 1965, p. 15.

[113] Cf. Devlin's essay "Mill on Liberty in Morals," *Ibid.,* pp. 102ff.: Regarding Mill's unwillingness to yield liberty to majority rule, Devlin observes, "The Articles

thinking people, since there is something of the appearance of adhering to one of those inviolable principles of assent to majority rule in a democracy involved. But let us be careful to say that in a liberal democracy that principle is not intended to mean majority rule without liberty. For it is just as impossible for anyone who believes in liberal democracy to accept any possible or eventual termination of basic rights and liberties, as it is for a religious person to accept any move to deny him the right to practise his own religion.[114] And in the latter case, if one does not have, or want, the choice of a political system connected directly with his religion, then a political system which protects his rights, even if it does not grant special privileges to promote his religious moral ideas, would seem desirable.

It is difficult to miss a certain parallel between the kind of reasoning recommended by Devlin for the enforcement of morals (by which he means, he says, "the moral judgment of society") and a sympathy widespread at present for such ideas as the ultimate moral (and political) wisdom of "the people" as a self-generated force arising out of "community". This comparison is not intended as a new criticism of Lord Devlin, who is certainly aware of all libertarian reservations regarding his thesis. Our concern here is rather with the contention that either a self-realizing moral or social spirit in the community is a better political foundation than law, or that the law should reflect the single interest of "community" rather than individualistic particularity.

The roots of such contentions are quite diverse and arise out of cultural and religious, philosophical elements as well as the results of scientific social analysis. The chief difficulty with these idealistic social philosophical claims is precisely that one can only rarely separate their philosophical or ideological content from the sociological or "scientific" evidence which is supposed to support them. The problem is by no means a new one for the social sciences, however. And Leopold

---

of the [U.S.] Constitution were made difficult to alter, but Mill dealt in immutabilities. No society, he said, in which the liberties which he prescribed were not on the whole respected was free, whatever might be its form of government..." (p. 103).

[114] The most eloquent statement of this principle is still John Stuart Mill's in: *On Liberty*. Cf. chapter IV: "Of the Limits to the Authority of Society over the Individual." In the Appleton-Century-Crofts edition (New York, 1947), pp. 75ff. An interesting study of the literature in this field, and its implications for constitutional law, is: Horst Ehmke: *Grenzen der Verfassungsänderung*, Duncker & Humblot, Berlin, 1953.

von Wiese described it very aptly in his discussion of the early history of sociological analysis:

Early sociology...combined two dissimilar ambitions, which failed because of their improper relationship to one another: on one hand they wanted to interpret history and demonstrate the progress of the intellect [*Geist*] through the centuries, and, where possible, prophesy its future course. On the other hand they wanted to point out the real interrelationships of mankind. This second goal, which seems to us to be the proper one for sociology, came in too short against the pressing priority of philosophical interpretation of history.[115]

The social sciences have come a long way in the meantime, but the same fundamental problem persists, wherever the goal of social investigation remains as much consciously, or subconsciously, the promotion of social philosophy or political philosophy as anything else. Again, this is not to say that the observations are, therefore, wrong, for both social philosophy and social science have come a long way since the mid-nineteenth century. It is rather that even among the most accomplished social scientists, jurists, and social and political philosophers there are those who, in enthusiasm for their results, fail to make their own social philosophical predispositions clear even to themselves, or if they do, fail to give representatives of other positions credit for being equally honest or sincere.

Given a particular set of moral or social values it seems entirely within the realm of academic propriety to demonstrate the relationship between one's philosophical outlook and his social ambitions or to describe the consequences of a social structure which promotes a contrary way of thinking. Should one fail to point out exactly what one is doing in this regard, however, he leaves himself open to the challenge of deliberate misrepresentation. In our own unphilosophical society, perhaps more than others, there is still no assurance that one will be understood the way he wants to be. At a recent joint session of the American Academy of Religion and the Society for the Scientific Study of Religion, for example, Professor Werner Stark delivered an address on the social contexts of the humanistic and the scientific study of religion and the contrast between their two divergent approaches. Professor Stark attempted to make it clear from the outset that he was discussing the idea that:

---

[115] Leopold von Wiese: *Soziologie: Geschichte und Hauptprobleme,* Sammlung Göschen, Vol. 101, de Gruyter, Berlin, 1960, p. 126.

...the style of thought of a society depends on its mode of action...and it acts in accordance with the valuations and value preferences characteristic of it.[116]

Still, in failing to indicate the extent to which his claims represented the traditional social historical attitudes of both Western, and tribal, religious communities rather than the results of purely empirical analysis, he left himself open to severe criticism.[117] Professor Stark spoke in the terms of Ferdinand Tönnies [118] of two kinds of society: "community" ("*Gemeinschaft*") and "association" ("*Gesellschaft*") and of the extent to which either form supported religious life:

The descent group which looms so large in the early history of humankind, whether it is called clan or sib or *genos* or any other name, is a typical community in the sense which Tönnies has given to the word. In a descent group the mind of men is immediately and quasi-automatically carried back to the origin of things. If I feel myself to be, not so much Jacob as Isaac's son...etc., then I raise my eyes towards the founder of my family, then I peer into the dim and distant past. But whether I like it or not, this brings me up against the mystery of being, and I must develop some attitude towards it.... Not only the Judaeo-Christian tradition is in this way one of the mental products of clan-society or community, but all the many primitive cults which we call totemic have also sprung from the same root. In one word, the social form of life which we call community is favorable to the development, and therefore also to the appreciation of religious phenomena. It is different with associational societies of which our own is one. In such societies the individual does not consider himself the product of antecedent forces, of the parent society from which he has come, but he thinks of himself as an independent will which acts in and on the future and is more especially the creator of coming social forces and forms. Social contract theories are characteristic of associational societies; society is something that is made by man, not man something that is made by society. The reference is always forward, as it were, never backward-looking as in communities. This alone militates against a religious or even a metaphysical world-view.[119]

Unless we are greatly mistaken, however, these social observations

---

[116] Werner Stark: "Humanistic and Scientific Knowledge of Religion: Their Social Context and Contrast," 38 *Journal of the American Academy of Religion*, 168 (1970), p. 168.

[117] See comment by Kurt H. Wolff which accompanies the preceding in *loc. cit.*, pp. 173-75.

[118] Ferdinand Tönnies: *Fundamental Concepts of Sociology (Gemeinschaft und Gesellschaft)*, transl. by C.P. Loomis, American Book Company, New York, 1940. The concept of "community" has been examined in regard to many of its historical and legal applications in an interesting series of discussions in II *Nomos: Yearbook of the American Society of Political and Social Philosophy, Community*, ed. by Carl J. Friedrich, Liberal Arts Pr., New York, 1959.

[119] Stark: *loc. cit.*, p. 171.

include a good part of the "valuations and value preferences" of specific religious communities in them, if not from the religious community itself, then perhaps through the cultural background of both Tönnies and Stark.

At a time when the social and political problems of our own society seem, especially for the young and the disaffected, so little susceptible of adequate response through the traditional resort to individual and contractual efforts, the collective strength, which the idea of a dichotomy between community and association is said to offer, can make programs based on the prospect of institutional change to communal forms theoretically more attractive. Until such social political ideas are studied together with regard for their origins, their sociological importance in any given functional context, and the theoretical implications of their introduction or application, there is little hope of separating the deliberate social moral choice of a design for society from the reliability of these terms for functional historical analysis. Often the community of belief which unreflective acceptance of a style, or outlook, conveys may be worth as much to the believer as, either any historical truth it may represent, or any practical social results it may accomplish. And if their elders already act out of unreflective identification with a community of belief, the young meet the challenge of one "community" with another. It can hardly be expected then that substantive understanding can be conveyed from one group to the other, if each understands itself more by group identification than systematic representation of an intellectual position.

No civilization has yet survived that could not convey its ideas and institutions to its succeeding generations. But there is also no reason to believe that any radically new civilization would come in the place of one which did not. On the contrary a generation born into a world which it learns to understand through the cultural language of its elders may pick and choose among the aspects of its cultural heritage for what it is willing to accept. But, again, an unreflective acceptance of old ideas may bring with it the benefit of the experience imitated, but can also result in the repetition of some historical misadventure. This is not to argue that peoples can not exchange their pasts for a new social form, but this cannot be taken all too seriously unless they are willing to accept at least a comparable break with their old surroundings as emigrés of the past had to do. Otherwise a society may accept a new theoretical description in words, or even carry out a revolution, and still find themselves living by old habits in new dress.

It is interesting to examine the concept of community from the point of view of religion, as Stark suggests, as much as from the perspective of any strictly social economic theory. In fact the preference for the idea of community probably characterizes the American New Left as descending at least as much from Christian social ethics as from Marxian. Community in the sense of the Church is not the parish or the local community, but the whole greater community of the faithful. The state, from the point of view of the revived natural law school, as well as the medieval scholastics, is the temporal organ of the community, or, that is to say, the people, for perpetuation of the values of the community, which is essentially coextensive, though not identical, with the community of the Church.[120] The institutions of the state thereby receive a distinctive social purposiveness, to educate the young and perpetuate the values and unity of the community, that is society as a community. The liberal democratic state, by contrast, is only that which its citizens make it. It has no higher purposiveness than to serve the functions assigned to it, to facilitate the convenience and protection of the citizens who have, theoretically, delegated power to it.

Easily the former idea is more conducive to the identification of the individual with the whole people, indeed the institutions are structured so as not to let him forget it. But the spirit of identity with a whole community of the faithful by no means dies when one becomes the citizen of a liberal democracy. One simply receives instruction in both ideals. And the conservative, therefore, by continuing to extend the moral values of the Church community to society at large sees no objection to the imposition of his moral values upon a democratic society. On the contrary he sees a definite threat to the perpetuation of his traditional sense of community if he does not, and if he identifies the origins of what he values in democratic society as arising out of the

---

[120] In an eloquent and modern restatement A.P. d'Entreves has concluded that natural law is the "point where values and norms coincide, which is the ultimate origin of law and at the same time the beginning of moral life proper" (*Natural Law: An Introduction to Legal Philosophy*, Hutchinson, London, 1951-64, p. 122). We may well be able to discover such points where values and norms coincide for any given civilization. But surely there are issues, perhaps larger areas, of the law, where norms, and even values, have little to do with moral choice. And, even where the association of norm and value and moral life is a proper one, it may still be a matter of continuing search and reevaluation. Accepting the definition as the description of a real point, rather than a figurative analogy, must imply the purpose of temporal law to be to recognize and enact what already exists.

moral virtues of the traditional or religious community, he may see the apparent re-ordering of moral values as a threat to democracy as well. The social reformer who borrows the idea of community may introduce new or reinterpreted social moral ideas, but the ideal of social purposiveness is much the same for the social radical as for the traditional conservative.

The concept of "the people" has had a somewhat different but parallel history in our social philosophical development. Ultimately, however, the liberal democrat looks at his society as a collection of individual people who enjoy specific guaranteed rights and have their own peculiar interests. For him the national government is an institution for measuring the benefits of one group or interest against those of another for the greatest benefit to the society collectively and to its members individually. In the "people's democracies" the individual is expected rather to look at himself as primarily a member of his society. Emphasis on individual rights is considered bourgeois and divisive; the good citizen should rather think first of the whole people, and their collective interests. The doctrine of "class struggle" also entails the apparent desertion of what is regarded as the inherently collective working class economic, class interests if the individual elects to pursue essentially "bourgeois" guarantees of private rights. From this perspective, not only does the state take on the aura of a higher purpose in the name of promoting the welfare of society, collectively, but the individual is educated to his role, which is to dedicate himself to the service of his society. Society is again personified as "the people", but not any specific individual people, nor even people in our own time, but "the people", functionally speaking, as they exist collectively and in all times. It should not be overlooked, however, that the working man particularly is honored in the socialist state and is given certain privileges or priorities, rather than many bourgeois rights which he might enjoy only theoretically in liberal democratic society unless he has developed an attachment for these rights—usually by thinking of himself as an individual. In liberal democratic societies, on the other hand, we tend to hold a little more of those bourgeois rights, and do not concede that because of these guarantees the society is any the less able to provide the social benefits that we also aspire to have.

One does not need special training to recognize that he may have certain legal rights in liberal democratic societies that do not necessarily bring him material well being; but that is not their purpose. Liberal democratic reservations about socialist law are plainly addressed to that same issue. Organization of the state on socialist principles may secure social material benefits for those who may have been inherently, or historically, disadvantaged in a system which protects accumulated property and capital. But the beneficiary of the new legal protection, which the ideal of rule of law has historically promoted against the domination of the governing system, becomes rather the system itself, which is then in turn protected against the particularistic interests of its citizens.[121]

There are socialist legal systems of all degrees of liberality of course. And it should be no comfort to conservatives that another system should also have become the target for liberal reservations against the power of the center. What is more properly of interest to us here is rather the mechanism through which a system designed specifically to procure common benefits and social well being should become the instrument for the concentration of power abusive to the rights and safety of individuals and the ideal of rule of law. For political power, even when it provides benefits, but is not constrained by law, becomes a system which designs law for its own purposes.

The historical development in the common law which made the sovereign rule according to law and not his own will furnished the basis for the growth of liberalism in the English speaking countries. The roots of that development lay in a tradition very wide spread both in Europe and the East, that the sovereign ruled according to the laws and customs of the people.[122] But Jacob Talman has shown in *The Origins of Totalita-*

---

[121] Interesting to consider in this respect is the shift in emphasis of legal protections from the individual to the state in the recent reform of the criminal law in the German Democratic Republic. See a general summary of the comments in West Germany in "DDR Strafrecht: Gemischtes Doppel," in *Der Spiegel,* No. 53, 25 Dec., 1967, pp. 22f.

For comment from East Germany and a tentative translation of the new Code see: Heinrich Toeplitz: "The New Penal Code of the German Democratic Republic," 2 *Law and Legislation in the German Democratic Republic,* 5 (1968); "Penal Code of the GDR of January 12, 1968," pp. 15-90; "Introductory Law to the Penal Code and the Code of Criminal Procedure of the GDR of January 12, 1968," pp. 91-96. See also: Hilde Benjamin: "The New Criminal Law of the GDR," 2 *Law and Legislation in the GDR,* 5 (1967).

[122] For a very erudite study of the development of the idea that the sovereign ruled according to the laws and customs of the people in Medieval Europe see John E.E.D. Acton: "The History of Freedom in Christianity," in *Essays on Freedom and Power,* Meridian Books, New York, 1955, esp. pp. 87ff.

rian Democracy [123] how the idea of rule of the people interpreted to mean rule according to ideas such as the "general will", which often is known best by restricted circles of "leaders" or "activists", has lead to theories of government which have supported authoritarian regimes while persuading their peoples that it was actually they who ruled, and the government which only acted out the will of the people, or of its new and supposedly now democratic leading class.

The justification for the regime's or the leader's acting in the name of the general will is a kind of social moral one. They establish government on the basis of the popular will and secure the liberty of ruling, for what that is worth as a concept, to the people. For Marx and Engels there is similarly a kind of social moral self-justification in ending the alienation of the working man from the product of his labor, and the theoretical self-assertion of the working class to ownership, as a class, of the means of production.

The examples of authoritarian rule on the theory of rule of the people, are not all on the left, however. German National Socialism was another variety on the same general pattern, but here with the benefit of another supposedly scientific anthropological, biological notion, that purer races were superior to "degenerate" ones. But, the race and hero mythology aside, another theory of the spirit of the people was developed out of German idealistic philosophy and the study of national folklore and the historical development of customary law in the German nation. There was again the idea of the source of political power in the people,

---

The idea of the sovereign ruling according to the "laws" and customs of the people in the Far East must be interpreted somewhat differently. For while the Chinese emperor or the Indian prince was expected to uphold traditional ideas of moral law and usage, these did not exert "legal" restraints on him in our sense. Still the best description of the meaning and sense of law in China is Joseph Needham's paper "Human Law and the Laws of Nature in China and the West," now included in *Science and Civilization in China*, Vol. II, ch. 18. For a more recent study see Derk Bodde and Clarence Morris: *Law in Imperial China*, H.U.P., Cambridge, Mass., 1967, Pt. I: "Preliminary Essay on Concepts and Practices". J.D.M. Derrett has written extensively on Hindu law and custom in India; several papers are collected in: *Religion, Law and the State in India*, Free Press, New York, 1968, see esp. ch. 6: "Custom and Law in Ancient India".

A very illuminating article which makes clear the King's theoretical role as the source of justice not of law in Buddhist Southeast Asia is Robert Lingat's: "Evolution of the Conception of Law in Burma and Siam," 38:1 *Journal of the Siam Society*, 9 (1950).

[123] Jacob Talmon: *The Origins of Totalitarian Democracy*, London, 1952.

exercised by the party leadership, and the source of law in the spirit of the people, recognizable in the "wholesome feelings of the people (*gesundes Volksempfinden*)" [124] again interpreted by the party leadership. A concise and apparently sincere (at least for that time) expression of this philosophy if in somewhat inflated language, is presented systematically in the 1935 edition of Karl Larenz's *Rechts- und Staatsphilosophie der Gegenwart*.[125] It may seem unfair to recall a scholar's past associations after nearly 40 years, but there is no clearer statement of the jurisprudence of the organic concept of the state and its intellectual origins: its dedication to the folk ideas—what might be called folk-prejudices—of the national community, and its fundamental rejection of liberal democratic ideals:

Just as all human creation and form arises out of the spirit of the people [*Volksgeist*] and its various concrete expressions, in the same way their precondition and goal as a living accomplishment is the community of the people [*Gemeinschaft des Volkes*]. Even the law is the creation and formulation of the national spirit [*völkischen Geistes*], and serves the community. It is neither a relationship between individuals, nor only an ought-to-be, a directive for the individual, but rather expression and formulation [*Form und Gestalt*] of the national community, and as such a concrete order. Its validity rests upon the bonds of the individual to his people, upon his membership in the community; this bond is in its essence the obligation of loyalty, it binds a man to the substance of his own being. The basic legal philosophical category is not the single person, the individual as an atom of the social world, or as a self-realizing ethically free personality, but rather the community as an organic social unity [*Lebenseinheit*] and the comrade-in-the-law [*Rechtsgenosse*] as member of the community, as compatriot, and as a member of narrower communities of family and social estate [*Stand*]. Property is then not the fundamental legal right or sphere of authority of the individual which is recognized and at most limited by the legal order, as in the opinion of the natural law and even for that matter in the "existential philosophy" of Husserl, rather it is lodged in the community and is "an assignment to personal responsibility and proper employment of an object according to its nature". The legal community is not founded by single individuals by contract or any other means, rather the national community as a legal community makes it possible through its concrete order for its members to close contracts and form legal relationships.

[124] Cf. *Reichsgesetzblatt* (RGBl) I. 70, 5 July, 1935, p. 839: The Law to Amend the Penal Code of the 28th of June, 1935, Art. 1 § 2: "Anyone who commits an act, which the law declares to be punishable, or deserves punishment according to the basic principles of one of the penal laws and according to the wholesome feelings of the people, will be punished. If no one penal law is directly applicable, the act will be punished according to the law, the underlying principle of which fits it the best."

[125] Karl Larenz: *Rechts- und Staatsphilosophie der Gegenwart*, 2nd ed., Junker und Dünnhaupt, Berlin, 1935.

While the natural law and postivist, individualist legal theory want to trace communities like marriage, and even the state, back to contractual relationships, the objective idealist is striving to the contrary to see even the contractual relationship as an, even if limited, objective natural relationship [*Ordnung*] between the parties, which can have a differentiated content and development through their subjective and common desires. Finally, while the subjective idealist always looks for the norm under which he can "subsume" a living process, and to him a relationship of this life only appears legally recognizable as a "concern of legal norm", the objective idealist finds that many a relationship of life has its (natural) order inherent in it before any norms arise; he will want to compare and individualize rather than subsume; his concepts are not empty conceptual categories, but rather concrete, i.e. meaningful and "inherent concepts" (Binder) or "concepts based on forms" requiring further concretization (Huber).[126]

Faced with the moral self-righteousness of systems which are based on what their authors consider inherently correct propositions, all discussion fails. Whether the authors make no philosophical pretentions but argue, regardless, that their logic arises out of common sense practice, or whether they base their conclusions on abstract rational principles, when their ideas or concepts are identified with "the community" or with "the people", unless we are prepared to agree, we find that—less than wrong—we are anti-social. An abstraction that was a term of convenience becomes all too easily a concrete reality in the minds of those who believe in the functional existence of all they can give a name to. It makes no difference then whether the concepts, or what might be called social or moral truths, arose self-generated from the people or through abstract reasoning, "truths" identified with the people of the community are exclusive truths and to deny them is to attack "the community" and "the people" themselves.

If they are "true", then it also follows, according to the theory, that they should be implemented. If they are true and ought to be implemented, and are still rejected and denied, then it becomes a kind of duty to implement them with radical, or dramatic, or revolutionary means. The logic of the consequences of the identification of the "true social goals" obviates the necessity of further discussion, which can only serve to delay the implementation of what is "socially necessary". This also seems to be the logic of Professor Herbert Marcuse and his associates in *The Critique of Pure Tolerance*.[127] Tolerance, far from being the very

---

[126] *Ibid.,* p. 165f.

[127] R.P. Wolff; B. Moore; H. Marcuse: *Critique of Pure Tolerance,* 1965. A critique of tolerance is still a long way from revolution, however, and is perhaps only an injunction to confrontation of well-known issues. What happens when the

basis of social cohesion in a society naturally combined of particularistic individuals, is instead looked upon as an excuse not to eliminate the inequalities which artifically fragment a naturally cohesive society.

The public is, to return now to the main line of our discussion, far more concerned with crime—or what is offensive to them—than it is with either criminal law, its niceties, or its reform. Political speeches and popular journalism probably reflect and guide the attitudes of the public far more than professional opinions or misgivings, though the words of these latter, too, become a part of the general vocabulary on the subject. General theories of deterence, correction, or rehabilitation, or propriety or impropriety of this form of social control also become a part of these discussions, but usually only insofar as they refer to specific offenses or specific measures of control.

It is the irony of American criminal law, therefore, that, while the Constitution and the Bill of Rights generally reflect the influence of Lockean liberalism and the ideal of the limitation of the authority of government over the individual, a good part of the various codes of criminal law, and the criminal penalties attached to provisions of other sections of the law, reflect more a concern for regulating behavior on the basis of far different principles.

Americans have always been ready to re-dedicate themselves to the principles of rule of law and due process. But the temptation, even for the most liberal and democratic minded people to proscribe behavior which offends, embarrasses, or distresses can also hardly be questioned.[128] The temptation to banish moral ugliness and be rid of social disturbances by prohibitions is a drive that is present in all people but especially reinforced among those with traditions of effective legal sanctions. We are, therefore, reminded that we are obliged for the sanctity of our rights to the protection of the Constitution and laws of procedure (until they become, as now appears to be the case, utterly bogged down because of inadequate court facilities), and not to the unpredictable liberality of our fellow citizens.

Without the historic champions of rule of law and security of law,

---

"confrontation" comes at a leading university is told with more humor—and perhaps more "reason"—than he actually seemed to live it at the time by Wayne C. Booth: *Now Don't Try to Reason with Me,* Univ. of Chicago Pr., Chicago, 1971.

[128] Henry Weihofen devotes a chapter to this attitude in: *The Urge to Punish: New Approaches to the Problem of Mental Irresponsibility for Crime,* Farrar, Strauss, & Cadalup, New York, 1956, esp. ch. 6.

there would of course be no tradition of legal guarantees to help to moderate between the legal interests of the individual and of society, or of groups. For the liberal democratic ideals of tolerance, equality before the law, and security of private individual rights, our greatest protection is not reliance on the momentary popular majority. "Rule of law" as we have come to understand it historically and constitutionally is not and cannot be "law and order" in the sense of the person who cries for "laws"—meaning in fact "prohibitions"—but rejects "law" including the "security of law". This limitation easily confuses and frustrates both those who believe in the unlimited rule of the majority, when they are in the majority, and those who claim the right to decide in the name of "the people" or "the community", because they have (they believe) come to realize what the real interests of "the people" are and would (they believe) in time be able to educate "the people" to recognize their real interests too. Yet under "rule of law," which is as much a system of guarantees of ("unalienable") rights and due process of law as it is of specific regulations and prohibitions, the representatives of the majority, as law makers or sovereign, are bound, so long as they claim to act according to law and not simple force, to confront the same principle of limitation upon their exercise of power which in the growth of the liberal tradition in Britain was used to restrain the unbridled exercise of power by the king.

When James I attempted to rule differently, in one major case, from Coke, then his Lord Chief Justice, he was told that although the courts ruled in the name of the King they ruled not according to his own private sense of justice but according to the laws of England and the law required some considerable professional understanding. This was to say, the King objected, that he, the Sovereign, was subject to the rule of another, and that was treason. To this Coke replied, with the authority of Bracton, that while the King was subject to no man he was not the source of law but rather ruled only according to it:

The King must not be under any man, but God and the law, because the law makes the King. Let him therefore bestow upon the law what the law bestows upon him, namely, rule and power, for there is no King where will rules and not the law.[129]

---

[129] Henry de Bracton: *De Legibus et Consuetudinibus Angliae* (f. 5b) translated as: *Bracton on the Laws and Customs of England*, ed. by Geo. E. Woodbine, transl. by Samuel E. Thorne, Harvard Univ. Pr., Cambridge, Mass., 1968, vol. II, p. 33 (f. 5b). Quoted by Coke in "Prohibitions Del Roy," 12 *Rep.* 63.

It is sad to say that, while Coke prevailed on that day, he was sent to prison (for a time), as the result of another issue, not long afterward. But the lessons of history are no poor warning of the fragility of due process of law when its exercise is entrusted to those who have little understanding of it, or little respect for it. This is not to say that the measure of due process lies simply in whether one can get a fair trial when he is charged with an offense. It is a matter of the availability of the same restraint and regard for the rights of the accused until he is proved guilty—and, for that matter, the rights of the convicted, and of society, that punishments will be exercised only by those entrusted to do so by law, and only to the limits imposed by law.

E.   LEGAL OBLIGATION AND MORAL OBLIGATION

To conclude our introductory and theoretical discussion, we would like to examine the issue of the functional differences in the subjects of legal and moral obligation. Certainly this brief concluding section is far from adequate for dealing with so central a problem in ethics and juris- prudence. Yet, in another sense, that question is the main subject matter of this whole effort, and requires rather that we attempt to demonstrate the focus of our interest in this investigation, here, and present the outline of our thinking in preparation for the treatment of the issues following.

We too believe that there is a vital relationship between legal and moral obligations and that in the relationship established between these two focuses of human concern the character of the institutions of society are determined. Indeed it was the defense of this proposition which led us into this present undertaking to examine the role of social and moral ethics embodied in the law. One of the present authors had earlier advanced a thesis, not far removed from Lord Devlin's (examined in Section B. above), which maintained that in certain traditional societies of South and Southeast Asia customary law had depended—in the absense of precisely the legal, institutional structure of modern Western countries—on a kind of identity of moral and social order, for its implementation.

One reaction to that earlier effort was a claim—which we would much more prefer to be able to make ourselves in this present offering —that not philosophy but needs proved more often to be the source of law (cf. page 251). As sound as that proposition may be for much of what is customary law, and legislation as well, we still seem to encounter substantial argument concerning the necessity for social-moral ethics in the law, both in Oriental societies, and in Western ones. In the former case, however, the dependence of the customary legal order on social sanctions, as much as, or even in place of, those of a legal or political authority, is strikingly significant.

In all due respect for the contention of what law might be if it were only the behavioral result of needs rather than reason, we seem to encounter unrelenting attempts, and certainly a share of necessity, to put reason—albeit sometimes misguided or overly sectarian or particularistic for application to a whole society—into practice as a design for the law. We have undertaken, here, to examine that course in Western setting, specifically in the case of the criminal law, because those areas where criminal law and the concerns of social-moral ethics are so strongly mixed had become such central issues of public controversy in the years leading to the recent reform laws in Germany, and have been of no small account in similar debates in England and the United States.

We also concede without reservation that our position on the relationship and separation of these subjects is and ought to be clear when it enters into the discussion at all. Very simply, that position is, politically, as Professor Würtenberger has correctly perceived in his Foreword (cf. page XIII), based upon the ideal of the limitation of the power of the state or society over the private concerns of the individual, so far as these do not come to interfere with the rights of others. In the realm of moral philosophy, we believe that the proper acknowledgement of moral obligation is to see to the carrying out of laws (arrived at, hopefully, under something defensible in terms of the ambition of the political ideal of rule of law) in pursuit of legal and moral justice. There is surely place for the exercise of moral philosophy in the legal process in order to attempt to guarantee justice under law. But the intrusion of moral philosophy into the law to the extent of designing the character of life for either the individual or society as a whole would seem to us to contradict the democratic political ideal of limitation of the exercise of undue coercion over the individual (we have expressed this view in somewhat more detail in our concluding remarks on page 254f.; cf. also Professor Würtenberger's analysis in the Foreword, page XXIV).

This is not to argue, however, that "immorality" may not be the underlying source of an offense against the legal interest of an individual or society. It is merely to acknowledge that the moral and legal issues are separate and that law enforcement is concerned only with legal obligations in dealing with the offense. Yet, even this separation of issues does not entitle anyone acting in the name of the law to disregard the standards of civility and human decency recognized in our society in order to act supposedly impartially with regard to the law. For it is, ultimately, in order to live in these standards that we argue principles of moral, social, and legal philosophy at all.

It is precisely at such a point as this that the "social" moral philosopher will tell us that the bare bones of legal obligation are nothing without the human reality of morals and civilization upon them. In his Foreword to the present discussion, Professor Würtenberger tells us that: "The liberal democratic form of government in the Federal Republic," for example, "is not intended to embody only this kind of an individualistic liberal resistance to undue coercion. Rather, it is also concerned with the preservation of certain traditional, distinctly European cultural values, which one could call the 'Christian, Western cultural tradition' " (cf. page XXI above).

In the United States we also have something of a cultural tradition. But, if there is anything specifically American in this, it is the political tradition. This political tradition surely derives from older and contemporary developments in other parts of the world. For some, surely, this system was a refuge for which they came to America. For others, however, it was economic or social opportunity which brought them. The developing individualistic liberal political tradition may have been no inducement for many who came to the United States, but a relatively (and often unduly) flexible institutional system has provided security and even local domination for them without obliging the country, with its diversity, its ethnic quarters, and religious denominational and political culture belts, to be plunged into some kind of cultural 30 Years War.

True enough, for those who did not come into those boundaries by choice: the Negro slaves and their descendants, the Mexicans brought in by annexation, the Indians, Eskimos, and island peoples, and the descendants of immigrants, who though they may have chosen to come to the United States, did not necessarily find the opportunities they had hoped for, institutions based primarily on individualistic or economic liberalism have been very slow to provide the social security to put these others on the same social footing. In those instances, the political and legal benefits of individualistic liberalism—which exist on tolerance of other people and authorities in the best of circumstances—may not even now be meaningful where these people cannot emerge from the throes of social and economic limitations which oblige them to exist in a condition always something less than the free individual personality the American philosophy hopes to cultivate. What is more, even in prosperity we are increasingly tied into a system of economic relationships where our whole economic and social existence is conditional upon our un-interrupted employment—and even advancement—in our respective fields of endeavor, whether that field is commercial, industrial, academic, bureaucratic, or something else.

When so many people in good positions are intimidated by their dependence upon the approval of some superior who disposes over human existences "in the best interest of the institution" which they serve, how much less will those without that security, fall short of the independence of self-sufficient, rugged individuals?

Very often, it seems, you have to be something on the order of a healthy corporation to exert your individual rights under the law; but, the ideal still retains its attraction. And these authors seem to find something of this even in those commune-minded individuals who try to re-capture the self-sufficiency of American frontier days; American student culture is, of course, immersed in the ideal of the development of the individual, so much so that astute New Leftist leaders have measured even their successes in the student protest movements against the heresy of the protesters' individualism.

To these authors, the center of protest of American students has been for years not contrary to American ideals but the direct result of them. The cult of individualism, which is not the legacy of universities so much as the chambers of commerce, patriotic organizations, popular journalism, and popular media of all kinds, promotes a whole saga of individualism, and then demands, on the other hand, the most abject conformity, to demonstrate acquiescence in the ideals of the myth itself. The paradox that the "rugged individual" should be "self-reliant " but not "free-thinking" long ago produced its individualistic rebels in business, the academic world, and all other walks of life. And for these few, there were always many more who thought they did the same, if in more bizarre dress. And, meanwhile the public which assents to ideals of "leadership", "competitiveness", and "rugged individualism" is sold on images which are controlled not to reflect too much that would not conform with their own group's view of their place in the world.

Yet recognizing all these limitations, we still see the political goals of individualistic liberalism as offering the promise of greatest institutional security for those citizens who aspire to be free from the prejudices of even their own communities, and free from economic and social dependence on even their own professions, institutions, and enterprises. But, just as we observed before that legal and institutional obligation alone is something short of the moral obligations which civility and human decency require in our civilization, legislating for any particularistic system of social or moral ethics gives undue preference to any single school where all seek to abide in the protection of the same legal system, although they may not be all Christian, or even—in the usual sense—all Western.

The conviction that the security of a moral social order rests upon acceptance and cultivation of a body of ethics deriving from a logically complete system of theological or philosophical foundations is well known to us from the history of moral philosophy. The principle is not much altered when one hears the claim for a scientific basis in place of a traditional theological or philosophical one. The idea is always that education in the formal system—indeed embodiment of the principles of the system in the corpus of existing law—is essential if we are to create and preserve a moral society.

If we can accept the argument that the law has a "morals-building" or "morals-strengthening" effect,[130] it is immaterial whether the kind of morality we are talking about is said to be composed of rules which reflect divine or natural, or purely rationally ascertainable principles of order. The claims are similar whether they are made by the conservative adherents of some traditional religious beliefs or the advocates of political order based upon social-minded principles, and whether the latter derive from "scientific" or ideological conviction, or merely from social or ecological concern.

Both systems of the left and of the right agree in their denunciation of the chaotic alternative of what they consider to be the purely relativistic opinions of the center.[131] The security to be won by application of systematic moral theory, its adherents claim, lies in the certainty of its

---

[130] For a relatively recent statement of this position see H.-H. Jescheck: *Das Menschenbild unserer Zeit und die Strafrechtsreform*, in the series *Recht und Staat*, Nos. 198-99, Mohr (Siebeck), Tübingen, 1959.

[131] An excellent analysis of the attitudes towards the law of many a conservative, socialist, and individualistic liberal—and an admirably objective statement from a committed partisan theorist—is Gustav Radbruch's: *Rechtsphilosophie*, Erik Wolf (ed.) Koehler, Stuttgart, 1963, esp. p. 226f.

results which, relying on what is "natural" and "true", apply the "higher purposes" of "natural order" in our social action and organization.

If it were sufficient to be moral that one had only to apply natural purposes—whether these are said to be discovered by traditional theological or revolutionary ideological means—that would seem to these authors only a rhetorical inversion of what had previously been expressed as no need for ethics or morality at all. For if in fact a moral act is merely the exclusion of the interference of the self (or even of the lesser self) from the normative workings of a logical system of behavior, there is nothing that can be called "moral decision", only the desire that the system "decide" itself, or that it realize its own norms.

Legal obligation may correspond to moral obligation. But conforming to legal obligation is no guarantee of upholding a moral one. Some traditional theological or revolutionary ideological systems would like to impose no legal obligation where there is no moral obligation and would make moral obligations into legal ones.[132] Yet this not only relieves us of some legal obligations where there is no moral one, it also tends to reinforce legal obligations with moral claims. Above all we have to consider whether in making a legal obligation of what seems today a moral one, we may not be enforcing today by legal sanction what we may tomorrow be unable to uphold morally.

It is the paradox of the moralist position (whether a traditional theological or revolutionary ideological one) that it obviates the necessity of moral decision. Instead it relies on a desire for unity of social and moral order.

The authors would let the law be content to serve a functional purpose rather than claim to embody "moral purpose". Here laws are not moral absolutes, but primarily rules of convenience in order for us to "live by them".[133]

---

[132] This was often repeated "reform" ambition of those who worked on the German *Draft Criminal Code* of 1962 (EStGB 62). An early, clear statement of this legal theory is in Arthur Kaufmann: *Das Schuldprinzip*, Winter, Heidelberg, 1961, esp. Ch. 4 *"Das Schuldprinzip als absoluter sittlicher Grundsatz."* This same position was incorporated in the theoretical justification (*Begründung*) of the *Draft Criminal Code* of 1962 (*Entwurf eines Strafgesetzbuches*—EStGB 62), esp. p. 96.

[133] This distinction relies primarily upon whether one considers the state to have been created to serve an overall purpose or whether it is not merely the executor of laws enacted to serve specific purposes. This distinction is put in terms of the different attitudes toward public and private law by Radbruch in *Rechtsphilosophie*, p. 226f.

The foregoing should not automatically be interpreted as simple preference for personal relativism either. Rather the authors would see that kind of characterization of the alternatives to the right and the left as equally misleading. For aside from the claims for an absolute moral law or a social morality, and what may perhaps legitimately be characterized as behavior measured against a personal relativism, there is also a practical morality we should not overlook. The practical morality of a people, or that is what we can say of their practical moral behavior, may be largely the result of their historical, cultural development, part of which may depend upon a system of ethics or higher teachings. But we tend to judge an action to be "right-minded" if it reflects a moral feeling although that may be understood in terms of a common cultural tradition as much as it is as the result of an individual's human reason or common decency.

We may also try to incorporate what is "right-minded" in this sense, into the body of the law. The place for morality in the law, which is designed to serve a functional purpose and not primarily to strengthen the morals of society, would seem to be to try to be "right-minded" in the use of the law and what we can establish about the degree of responsibility one has for actions under the law. We would, in other words, not only create new obligations, but put limits on our own use of the law. If our moral ambition is justice under law then that seems to imply the need for "moral decision" in the use of the law. And in this understanding of "law" and "moral decision" one cannot attribute to "law", which "decides" nothing, that it is already "moral".

It is perhaps in Pollock's terms, in the exercise of law and law enforcement by "right-minded" men that the proper role of moral obligation in support of the law can be achieved.[134] Lord Devlin, who has otherwise distinguished himself as an advocate of "the enforcement of morals"[135] has also suggested that we can preserve specific cultural values under our legal system, without *legislating* for the enforcement of these. He proposes instead to invoke the "practical morality" of the "right-minded man".[136] Devlin demonstrates a remarkable faith in the common law tradition of the jury system when he goes on to claim: "The moral judgement of society must be something about which any

---

[134] See Sir Frederick Pollock: *Essays in Jurisprudence and Ethics*, Macmillan, London, 1882, esp. p. 276.
[135] Cf. Patrick Devlin: *The Enforcement of Morals*, O.U.P., London, 1965.
[136] *Ibid.*, p. 15.

12 men or women drawn at random might after discussion be expected to be unanimous." [137] In his opinion "practical morality" would be decided as a *fact* something on the order of the way the concept of the "reasonable man of ordinary prudence" is referred to in the law of torts,[138] to establish what a reasonable precaution against causing an injury might be.

When Devlin refers to "practical morality" he refers to it as if it were *fact*. And there is no denying that in an important sense it is—as custom, or even, as in the traditional Christian theology, as the practical manifestation of absolute moral law.[139] But there is something else to "practical morality", however: the need on the occasion where custom, the law, and perhaps even theology are only a guide, to make one's own practical moral decision. One need not be unaware of the moral philosophical, moral theological dilemma surrounding this proposition. There are those who simply may not be able to decide such questions for themselves. For them, there is no reason why custom, traditional moral instruction, or religious teaching should not serve as a model. On the other hand, who can silently assent to the action of that man who invokes higher principles as the justification for his action, but when a possible human disaster unforeseen by those principles arises, closes his eyes to the results of his action and refuses to acknowledge moral responsibility for his own decision? And even if such a man were to be found guilty of no legal offense, who could say that he was also not guilty of a moral one?

---

[137] *Ibid.,* p. 15.

[138] For a concise statement of this theory in the law of torts, see the summary in William L. Prosser: *Handbook of the Law of Torts,* 3rd ed., West, St. Paul, Minn., 1964, p. 153f., quoted on page 40 above.

[139] A remarkable judicial declaration suggesting that the principles of absolute moral law are ascertainable out of the nature of things was contained in the decision of the German supreme court for civil and criminal matters: *Entscheidungen des Bundesgerichtshof in Strafsachen*—BGHSt—6, 52. The propriety of that decision was widely contested then and is perhaps better taken as a sign of traditional convictions among jurists of those times than as a lasting attitude preserved in German jurisprudence. That decision is quoted on page 177 n. 12 below. To continue with a distinction introduced at the beginning of this section: If society and the state themselves are purposive, then our laws may perhaps rightly be considered extentions of a theologically ascertainable or social-moral higher law. For the individualistic liberal conception (in Radbruch's terminology), however, it is immaterial whether the higher law exists or is ascertainable at all. For while higher laws may govern moral action, the only law in question in secular courts is the law which has been duly enacted or sanctioned by custom.

Generations of moral philosophers have been plagued by the dilemma that if we accept the responsibility of moral decision for ourselves, there are those who will act immorally and call it moral; there are those who will not know any better; and the really conscientious will not know what to do because they will constantly have to weigh first one way and then the other. Ingenious proofs have been devised which all suggest: if the moral law does not exist it has to be invented. The rationalist philosophies are no less exhorted then the religious ones. Conservative and rationalist Confucianism has given perhaps the best paradigm of this kind of reasoning, and one which in many ways reveals the logic of "whole truth" systems, which like some modern rationalist systems believe that we can grasp the nature of human condition by analysing it "scientifically", and then applying the principles, practically, that we seem to have discovered to be in operation, theoretically:

The men of old who wished to shine with the illustrious power of personality throughout the Great Society, first had to govern their own state efficiently. Wishing to do this, they first had to make an ordered harmony in their own families. Wishing to do this they first had to cultivate their individual selves. Wishing to do this, they first had to put their minds right. Wishing to do this, they first had to make their purposes genuine. Wishing to do this, they first had to extend their knowledge to the utmost. Such extention of knowledge consists in appreciating the nature of things. For with the appreciation of the nature of things knowledge reaches its height. With the completion of knowledge purposes become genuine. With purposes genuine the mind comes right. With the mind right the individual self comes into flower. With the self in flower the family becomes an ordered harmony. With the families ordered harmonies the state is efficiently governed. With the states efficiently governed the Great Society is at peace.[140]

[140] From *The Great Learning* transl. by E.R. Hughes: *The Great Learning and the Mean in Action,* Dent, London, 1942, p. 146f. In Confucion tradition *The Great Learning* is considered to be a digest of Confucius's teaching and is attributed to his grandson. However, on the basis of the *Analects,* one may find another attitude in the words of Confucius. The attempt at systematizing Confucian teaching the *Great Learning* may be a logical extention of Confucius's thought which goes beyond what his own words may have intended. In *Analects* VI. 16, Confucius says:
    It is only when nature and training [i.e. form and content] are proportionately blended that you have the higher type of man.
In VIII. 12, an overzealous follower expands the idea to be:
    Art, as it were, is nature; as nature, so to speak, is art [i.e. form and content are identical].
Once form and content are translated from a necessary balance to an identity, it is only a short way until the representation of traditional form implies the customary content. (Cf. W.E. Soothill transl.: *The Analects of Confucius,* Yokohama, 1910, reprinted Paragon, N.Y., 1968.)

How familiar are these arguments, and how persuasive that concrete social changes can follow upon changes of heart. But in the final analysis is that what we mean by "right-minded", to think "the right thoughts"? Is that what we mean by "genuine" or "sincere", to let our words show that we accept the "true religion", or that we accept "class struggle" as the true basis of human social relationships ?

This is not to deny the soundness of the values cultivated by any of these systems. Least of all is this intended to diminish the sincerity of mind of Confucian doctrine. With the study of the nature of things our knowledge reaches the utmost we can command. Consciousness of what experience and study tell us of nature, society, and history, assists the individual to cultivate the arts and insights of the world's civilizations. Out of awareness cultivated from man's civilized heritage we can face the quandary of moral decision knowing that while we may fall short of others' expectations or our own, still the danger of that for civilized man is no greater than if he could meet such situations only with a fixed rule.

The logic of systems which argue from the consistency of the totality, making the rules of the macrocosm apply to the microcosm, are not all so unfamiliar to us nor by any means the property of only ancient philosophies or of medieval Christianity. Modern mathematicians and physicists, used to the logic of closed systems, are not unknown to apply them in their personal philosophies as well.

Professor Werner Heisenberg, for example, who has reinforced our awareness that our knowledge of the physical world is based more on probability than certainty, has ended a recent contribution with what appears to be the transfer of the logic of a closed system to his social philosophy:

If harmony in a society depends on the common interpretation of the "one", of the unity behind the multitude of phenomena, the language of the poets may be more important than that of the scientists.[141]

The Wittgenstein of the *Tractatus* is of course completely explicit in this approach to the logic of our world:

---

[141] These are the closing words of Werner Heisenberg's: *Natural Law and the Structure of Matter*, Rebel Pr., London, 1970, p. 45. Heisenberg's thesis seems to be that mathematical language (i.e. the language of abstract ideas) best expresses the modern understanding of the nature of matter and energy:

I think that modern physics has definitely decided in favour of Plato. In fact these smallest units of matter are not physical objects in the ordinary sense; they

1.   The world is everything that is the case.
1.1   The world is the totality of facts, not of things.
1.11   The world is determined by the facts, and by these being *all* the facts.
1.12   For the Totality of facts determines both what is the case, and also all that is not the case.
1.13   The facts in logical space are the world.
1.2   The world divides into facts.[142]

It is further significant to notice that the world—which resolves into the sum of its facts—includes potential facts as well as already recognizable ones:

2.012   In logic nothing is accidental: if a thing *can* occur in an atomic fact the possibility of that atomic fact must already be prejudged in the thing.
2.0121 It would, so to speak, appear as an accident, when to a thing that could exist alone on its own account, subsequently a state of affairs could be made to fit.
        If things can occur in atomic facts, this possibility must already lie in them. (A logical entity cannot be merely possible. Logic treats of every possibility, and all possibilities are its facts.)

In a modern statement concerning the philosophy of natural law A.P. d'Entrèves summarizes by quoting Kant's observation that for the perfectly good will there are no imperatives:

"I ought" is here out of place, because "I will" is already of itself necessarily in harmony with the law.[143]

And here d'Entrèves finds the heart of the idea of natural law expressed as well:

are forms, ideas which can be expressed unambiguously only in mathematical language. (p. 32f.)

On the other hand the social philosophical implications of the unity of a theory of ideas and of matter is quite clear to him:

The great success of the scientific method, of trial and error, excludes in our time any definition of truth which would not withstand the sharp criteria of this method. At the same time it may be a well established fact in the social sciences that the internal equilibrium of a society depends, at least to some extent, on the common relation to the "one". Therefore the search for the "one" can scarcely be forgotten. (p. 38f.)

[142] Ludwig Wittgenstein: *Tractatus Logico-Philosophicus* with an Introduction by Bertrand Russell, Kegan Paul, Trench, Trübner, London, 1922, p. 31.

[143] Immanuel Kant: *The Moral Law, Groundwork of the Metaphysics of Morals*, transl. by H.J. Paton, p. 81, quoted by A.P. d'Entrèves (see n. 15), p. 121f.

This point where values and norms coincide, which is the ultimate origin of law and at the same time beginning of moral life proper, is, I believe, what men for over 2000 years have indicated by the name of natural law.[144]

We cannot resolve the deep seated problems of philosophy and theology here. But, we can observe that the weight of authority is not all on the side of holisms. The later Wittgenstein departs from his earlier logical analysis for linguistic analysis: and here analysis presupposes only a language game, not the whole of language.[145] P.W. Bridgman also discusses the difficulties with atomic analysis of the living world. Among other things, he notes Bohr's argument that the measuring instruments themselves would do injury to the structure and order of the system we wanted to measure before we succeeded in analysing it. He is reconciled, however, to "the inevitability of describing the world from himself as center":

...a unity is thereby restored to the world, the unity conferred by the necessity of seeing everything from a single origin. This is not the illusory unity which we formerly thought we had, but it is the only unity we can use, the only unity possible in the light of the way things are.[146]

We convey this unity in much the same way to our moral philosophical judgments. But, let us add straightaway, to see a unity is not always, or even primarily, to interject something of our own. We are in many ways the products of our civilization—and, even if we have never heard of many of its constituents that is not to say that they have not affected what went into our intellectual make-up. The fact that we recognize that the unity we see is a unity which makes what we see sensible to us, does not say that we have altered moral philosophy. It merely recognizes that we have selected and judged on the basis of how we have come to understand. But what went into our understanding is usually composed

---

[144] A.P. d'Entrèves: *Natural Law: An Introduction to Legal Philosophy,* Hutchinson, London, 1951-64, p. 122.

[145] For an analysis of Wittgenstein's later philosophy, see e.g. George Pitcher (ed.): *Wittgenstein: The Philosophical Investigations,* Anchor, Garden City, N.Y., 1966.

[146] P.W. Bridgman: *The Way Things are,* H.U.P., Cambridge, Mass., 1959-69, p. 248. For an analysis of how such a "unity" of perspective or hypothesis may sometimes be applied in the social sciences or in social philosophy as if it were a definite rather than a perceptual description, see, for example, F.A. Hayek: "The Theory of Complex Phenomena," and "The Results of Human Action but not of Human Design," in *Studies in Philosophy, Politics, and Economics,* Univ. of Chicago Pr., 1967.

of the same elements as recommended themselves to generations before us. Only in a world where we do not take our moral philosophy to be principles of a grand design in which we are only a passing observer, these principles must recommend themselves not primarily to our faith and loyalty, but to our reasoned judgment and conviction.

Not to legislate social and moral ethics does not mean that one should ignore the models of ethics which are known to us, however. For to aspire to higher ethical ideas is what "right-minded" also means:

The ethical judgments of mankind, or of the more thinking part of them, are framed not only upon the existing standard of positive morality, which alone we have hitherto considered, but also with regard to an ideal standard; so that a man who is thoughtful as well as right-minded will himself obey moral rules which differ somewhat from those commonly recognized in society, whether as being more extensive and precise or as being, in some exceptional cases, in actual conflict with them. He will often say, "Thus I ought to do, though the common voice would not blame me for leaving it undone;" and sometimes he may have to say, "Thus I ought to do, though the common voice bids me not to do it." [147]

If a man is thoughtful, as well as right-minded, and exercises common sense morality, then, according to Pollock's understanding he needs no morals legislation, but will at times do better than the law, or society, expects, and at times, may have to stand his own ground even if society would say no. Perhaps, this may be more than one can expect of the common man. This may still offer an invitation for the foolishness of some who exercise an unwarranted faith in their own powers of reason. But it would seem to justify the hope for human responsiveness better than one could expect of moral directives in the law:

Divers ingenious persons holding opinions contrary to the official ones on divers matters of faith and speculation have, in sundry times and countries, perversely and obstinately continued to be good men, good companions, and good citizens.... And, what is worst of all, these facts have been too notorious to be in any way got over.... "It is very true," say our would-be champions of morality, "that individuals who rejected our principles have been good men. But that was because they had the inestimable advantage of learning practical morality in a society where our principles were accepted.... Once let their ideas become current enough to leaven a whole generation; once let our only true and original mould be broken, and then you shall see how morality will go to pieces. A truly painful duty is ours, indeed; we would hurt nobody's feelings for the world. Our only comfort is that we have warned you in time; you may not be wicked and miserable yet, but if you go on at this rate your children will be." [148]

---

[147] Pollock: *Essays,* p. 276.
[148] *Ibid.,* p. 290f.

The right-minded man who attempts to live according to practical morality and do what he feels he ought to do, though less were required of him, makes his moral judgment, but need not impose it in the law, or in the judgments of the courts. One cannot oblige all men to be right-minded, as desirable as that might seem. But the model of right-minded men, if we cultivate that ideal, may have far more influence than laws which require right action but do nothing to produce an understanding of right. One thing more, however, it is by no means only morals we are concerned with here. For, many a social and political philosophy would urge us to accept the same arguments to legislate for a new secular, social moral conscience, and even the social ethical ambition of creating a "new man", who is unselfish and whose mind is "right".

We may any one of us have misgivings in seeing the society we know, or thought we knew, changing, or appearing to change, in a way we had not foreseen, or had thought would never occur. Changes in public morals, particularly, have aroused the dismay of moralists who see the corruption of society tied to the decline in standards of decency and decorum. There seems to be no good reason to deny, either, that the weakening of religious belief may be in direct relationship to any decline in public morals—at least among those for whom religion was the only grounds for their adherence to any such public behavior and form. The policy of preventing change—or, more precisely, preserving "revolution"—in communist China uses much the same reasoning. For, once the revolutionary man with an unselfish social conscience is created, it requires "continuous revolution" (advocates of the Cultural Revolution tell us) to keep this "revolutionary conscience" alive.[149]

---

[149] According to Stuart Schram (*The Political Thought of Mao Tse-tung*, rev. ed., Praeger, New York, 1969) it was Liu Shao-ch'i who "rehabilitated" Trotsky's theory of "permanent revolution" in 1958 (p. 98). Liu attributed the theory to Mao, however, and Schram concedes that "it bears Mao's stamp and reflects the temper of his mind" (p. 129). The theory has since become the inspiration of the Cultural Revolution. The permanent struggle appears in Mao's thought directed, among other things, at our susceptibility to succumb to "selfishness" or "liberalism". In an article in the *People's Daily* (9 May, 1966) Kao Chu summarizes:

We must always remember Chairman Mao's instructions never to disregard the enemy in the area of consciousness, never to forget the class struggle.

(Cf. Franz Schurmann and Orville Schell (eds.): *The China Reader 3, Communist China:...*. Vintage, New York, 1967, p. 616.)

If reassurance of the preservation of the "welfare of society" can be secured by enforcing morals, or if enforcing the moral judgment of society can prevent society from being undermined by preventing morals from being undermined, it seems justified, for those who see things that way, to proceed with the ambition to fix legal moral standards. We must be clear, however, that just as when moral standards are significantly altered a different kind of civilization may appear, with the alteration of legal standards the political, legal character of our society would also be seriously changed.

This is not to say that the legal system should not be moral. But it is to say that the standard of what is legal or moral cannot be fixed to any exclusively particularistic set of moral standards in a pluralistic society.

There is, in conclusion, one more aspect of legal and moral obligations which must be considered here because of the frequency of its arising in discussions which tend to link the two. This is the issue of the moral element in guilt under law. For many, unless there is a particular moral guilt, it is a spurious legalistic argument to speak of legal guilt. Contrary to the initial appeal of such a doctrine, this idea can have very serious if unforeseen consequences.

The legal doctrine of *mens rea* or the "guilty mind", establishes the essential characteristic of "intent" in any offense. In brief, the doctrine rests on the theory that it is not the act alone which establishes guilt, but the "mind" with which it was done [150].

The requirements of *mens rea* present problems in many instances. The fact that specific conditions have been recognized to establish the extent of *mens rea*, itself indicates the hardiness of the notion that guilt under law is in an important sense a reflection of a moral standard, involving basic exercise of individual choice, rather than as the purely

[150] The classic definition of *mens rea* for common law countries is that enunciated by Salmond:

The general conditions of penal law liability are indicated with sufficient accuracy in the legal maxim, *Actus non facit reum, nisi mens sit rea*—the act alone does not amount to guilt; it must be accompanied by a guilty mind. That is to say there are two conditions to be fulfilled before penal responsibility can rightly be imposed.... The material condition is the doing of some act by the person to be held liable.... The formal condition, on the other hand, is the *mens rea* or guilty mind with which the act is done.

(Cf. Sir John Salmond: *Salmond on Jurisprudence*, 11th ed., Glanville Williams (ed.), Sweet and Maxwell, London, 1957, p. 398.

objective operation of an instrument of social control, demanding adherence to certain purely legal standards. (It must be acknowledged, however, that this latter goal, too, has provided a fruitful area of controversy between distinct social philosophical and religious moral outlooks.)

Let us be clear, however, that "morality" in the sense it enters the problem of *mens rea* is a question of individual "moral choice" in the day to day affairs of individuals in their relationships with one another. Whatever may be the basis of any particular individual's "moral decision", in the expectations of a legal community it may entail a decision in the sense of established *mores* or decision according to custom, tradition, or what the community conceives of as proper in their relationships with others.

On the other hand, this notion of "moral" does not necessarily refer to any absolute or unchangeable morality, although particular individuals may unquestionably accept such a "morality" as the basis for their own "moral decisions". What is said by this discussion is briefly that the "morality" in question is the function of "moral decision", and not the application of a fixed standard, traditional, religious, or philosophical, although such standards may underlie the "moral decisions" of most individuals.

What this notion of guilt does not amount to is what has become celebrated in German legal philosophical discussion as "no guilt without moral guilt" [152]. Under that concept, it may appear that offenses which are not moral offenses would be eliminated. In fact, however, very often the offense remains and instead receives a spurious or specious "moral" reinforcement. Thus the person who rides a streetcar without paying may be guilty not simply of an infraction of regulations of public order, but also of the questionable "moral" crime of "accepting a service without compensation". The philosophical dilemma this may entail by extension is not necessarily apparent until, for example, the logical consequences of the newly attributed "moral purposiveness" of the state arises. Violations of public order, then, or perhaps of merely an administrative regulation, can be magnified out of proportion to its former significance into a "moral offense".

More significant consequences for our current American situation would occur when, for example, an inductee refuses to serve in the

[151] See n. 132 above.

armed forces in a war he considers politically intolerable or even morally objectionable. He may be tried and found guilty of a deliberate violation of the Selective Service Act. But the further condemnation of this particular individual as guilty of an immoral act because he has not met his moral obligation to the United States can be extremely unfortunate for what that notion of a fixed moral purpose can later entail for a host of morally indifferent acts. Ultimately to maintain that what the law—or the administration—says is what is moral can undermine all moral considerations by individuals and not only inconvenient ones.

There is an important *moral* question as to whether those who in effect interpret patriotism as assent to the policies of any particular administration, can also impose a "moral obligation" to join in responsibility for the "immoral" consequences of official policies. Surely under the law a man may be guilty of refusing induction. He acts, furthermore, with intent and purpose, thus with *mens rea,* the element of criminality which it is morally incumbent upon us to find in order to convict him, not of a moral crime, but of a violation of a legal enactment. The law itself remains—for the Anglo-American legal tradition—morally indifferent. The moral decision of the violator is, however, that it is morally more defensible to act contrary to the law than to participate in what is to him a morally unjustifiable conflict.

The issue of the moral element in guilt under law is then what it is morally incumbent upon us, in legal justice, to find in order to convict. But the guilt for which the accused is liable under the law is legal guilt. For moral guilt man must answer for himself, to mankind, or his Maker.

They call *a free country* one in which the constraints of law are supposed to be the act of the greatest number. The strictness of such constraints does not feature in this definition. However hard they may be, so long as they emanate from the majority, or so long as the majority believes they emanate from itself, that is enough: that country is *a free country*.

...For centuries, almost the whole of organized society consisted of two categories of individuals whose status was not the same; the first were slaves and others were called "free". In Rome, freemen who were born of free parents were called *ingenui;* but if they had been set free, they were called "libertines". Much later they called "libertines" those who were deemed to have freed their thoughts; not long after, that fine title was reserved for those who knew no trammels in the order of morals.[152]

(Paul Valéry)

[152] From Paul Valéry: "Fluctuations on Liberty," in *Reflections on the World Today,* transl. by Francis Scarfe, Pantheon, New York, 1948, pp. 56f., 53f.

CRIMINAL LAW AND REFORM IN THE UNITED STATES

CHAPTER II

HISTORICAL AND THEORETICAL PROBLEMS

Criminal law reform is not simply an issue between those who favor liberalization of the existing systems (because they themselves are too weak to face the appropriate measures to eliminate crime or to uphold traditional standards or values) and those who are strong enough to take a stand against crime and the deterioration of standards which they associate with crime. Certainly, all decent people oppose crime and its increase. But still misleading theoretical over-simplifications are resorted to by those who want to settle the problem of crime by more laws but will not face the more difficult sociological question: "What are the reasons for crime?" and "How can we combat crime effectively?" Fear of crime and distress over social conditions has been used by hard line advocates of retributive justice and liberal reformers alike to popularize viewpoints and programs. We are well aware of the tactics of scare speeches and headlines about the rising crime rate. But, to avoid the pitfalls of misrepresentation, it is not enough only to recognize the social and personal impact of crime or only the disheartening quality of its social origins. One must himself retain the personal moral judgment to distinguish willful and destructive crime and violence from circumvention of subjectively or historically established regulations and social controls which may no longer retain the respect of many people who look for a modern rational basis for the laws they follow. A person who is a champion of law and order must either recognize what the law guarantees or the order he is talking about is not justice under law. At the same time we must consider the purpose and again the history of the laws in question, or the controversy over the justice of one law becomes challenge to law in general. That is in fact the attitude—no objective—of some radical groups, precisely the challenge to law as such—at least the law of present authorities. But that is in another way also the attitude of many who claim to advocate law and order, but mean the enforcement of prohibitions they favor while forgetting the guarantees of due process of law. The latter undermine the law by selective enforcement of it. The former want the power of the latter to abuse the law in the same way.

To uphold the law, one must have respect for all it promises: guarantees, and procedures, as well as sanctions. Reform of the law properly requires attention to the purpose the particular law is to serve. Purposes of these laws must be suitable purposes for a society of law. And the pursuit of social purposes under law can only proceed in harmony with the expectations of society, its tradition of guarantees, and respect for due process.

A.   WHAT IS A CRIME?

There are basic theoretical assumptions underlying any criminal law system which, once they are established, provide a point of departure for the elaboration of the structure of that system. These center on the problems of what constitutes a crime; what acts ought to be considered criminal, and why; and how and under what circumstances can and ought these acts be prohibited under law? These questions have to do both with the social context in which the act occurs, and the practical legal outlook which determines that such acts are to be prohibited by law. These questions also concern the internal aspects of the act itself which tell us the degree of responsibility with which the act was committed.

(1) *The Social Context of an Offense and the Extent of Criminalization.*

Our attitudes toward crime and the criminal have changed markedly in the last half century, and crime has come to be approached much more as an understandable and soluble problem, rather than as a mysterious and enduring affliction subject to only minor correction through strong retribution.[1] In recent years it has been considered that with a proper balance of law, law enforcement, and correction and punishment, crime could be greatly reduced and criminals rehabilitated. Along with changing social attitudes and conditions, there has also been

---

[1] Hermann Mannheim surveyed approaches to the sociology of crime in: *Comparative Criminology*, Vol. II, Routledge and Kegan Paul, London, 1965, pp. 419-443.

a tendency to relax or eliminate old prohibitions which have seemed no longer to reflect the public morality or social sense of the modern day.[2]

But changes in social attitudes and conditions do not always come uniformly or easily, nor would this necessarily be desirable in a pluralistic society, although the protagonists of partisan ideas continue to urge us to believe that they should be. At the present time, there are a variety of strong movements to reform or liberalize important areas of the criminal law, which are considered to be applying legal sanctions where no threat to our social or moral well-being is involved, and where the idea that there were a danger appears to be outdated.

At the same time, there are strong counter-movements acting to extend the coverage of the criminal laws to broader areas,[3] and to enforce provisions often long neglected or no longer viewed with the same eyes as when they were first enunciated.[4] The same person may

---

[2] Several examples of this kind come to mind: the new abortion statutes in New York, Hawaii and Alaska (see p. 139 below). Other changes have occured in the direction of greater leniency for homosexual offenders (p. 162f. below) and drug offenders (p. 150 below).

Furthermore, if the attitudes of police and prosecutors develop the same degree of tacit acceptance as those of the rest of society, there can be little question that patterns and emphases in enforcement of existing laws may change dramatically over a period of years; see e.g. Dunning: "Discretion in Prosecution," 1 *Police Journal* 39 (1928), at p. 47.

[3] See e.g. the debate over preventive detention between Ramsey Clark, former U.S. Attorney General, and Richard G. Kleindienst, then Assistant Attorney General, in the *Congressional Quarterly*, May 29, 1970, p. 1441f. Clark accused the government of: "responding to fear with morally unconcerned postures.... [they] propose inherently immoral and violent practices such as wiretapping, entering premises without knocking, and now jailing persons we say we presume innocent before trial...." Clark went on to urge reforms in other areas. Kleindienst answered: "Society has the inherent right to protect its members for limited periods through due process procedures from persons who pose a serious threat...." Both of these spokesmen advocated specific changes in criminal procedure and law enforcement which they maintained would improve social conditions.

[4] Concerning the entire D.C. crime program, then Attorney General John M. Mitchell stated: "This model anticrime program will point the way for the entire nation at a time when crime and fear of crime are forcing us, a free people, to alter the pattern of our lives." ("Nixon Crime Control Proposals Stalled in Controversy," *Congressional Quarterly*, June 5, 1970, pp. 1496-1497, at p. 1497). Mitchell's view poses the paradox that if police are given greater powers over the rights of individuals the entire society may become freer. In all fairness, however, although the fear of crime is an area of major public concern, in a free society protection from fear of real injuries cannot be extended to protection from all

have one attitude on one issue, and a seemingly conflicting one on another. One attractive yet frustrating aspect of trends in American criminal law is that they are generally not based upon fixed doctrine. This allows a desirable flexibility, yet makes a systematic analysis complex and difficult.[5]

But groups which are particularly incensed by appearances frequently blame relaxation of enforcement of criminal morals laws for what they view as the apparent degeneration of moral standards leading to an increase in violence, crime, and moral corruption.[6] Whether or not this claim is justified, it demonstrates that many people are very much concerned with appearances and political, social, or moral nonconformity which they often tend to identify with crime. But there always seem to be other people equally dedicated to shocking the former groups and outraged when they are attacked themselves.[7] Regardless of where one sides on any one issue, it is easy when looking at things from a distance to see the futility of the employment of the law and

associations that may inspire fear in the citizen suddenly exposed to all the world of legitimate private idiosyncracies. See also J. Edgar Hoover, "The Increase of Crime," in R.D. Knudsen (ed.): *Criminological Controversies*, Appleton-Century-Crofts, New York, 1968, pp. 6-13, esp. p. 12.

[5] G.O.W. Mueller (*History of American Criminal Law Scholarship* Walter E. Meyer Research Inst. of Law, Inc., New York, 1962, pp. 1-21; 227) shows us how American jurisprudential and criminological theories have not followed consistent overall patterns. In part, Mueller attributes this to the common law's being the "law of the craftsman" or practitioner in the criminal law field, while the civil law has been the "law of the scholar" in the sense that European jurists are more concerned with doctrinal purity and logical consistency.

[6] See e.g. "First Lady's Press Secretary Lauds Daley, Scores Yippiness," *The New York Times*, Aug. 30, 1970, p. 15; and J. Edgar Hoover: "The Increase of Crime," *loc. cit.*

[7] These remarks are not intended to over-simplify or dismiss the problems of legitimate representatives of unpopular opinions making themselves heard when both the government and the public choose not to listen. Confrontations on the scale of those at the 1968 Democratic National Convention in Chicago are brought about by provocations on both sides. But far more people than provoke get hurt. For the power groups, that is interpreted as a warning to those who challenge their power and legitimacy. For the doctrinaire, if enough innocent by-standers and liberals get hurt it will "radicalize" them. See especially: *Rights in Conflict*, The Violent Confrontation of Demonstrators and Police in the Parks and Streets of Chicago During the Week of The Democratic National Convention of 1968, A Report Submitted by Daniel Walker, Director of the Chicago Study Team, to the National Commission on The Causes and Prevention of Violence, Introd. by Max Frankel of *The New York Times*, Bantam Books, New York, 1968.

police on peripheral irritations, while the rate of violent and dangerous crime increases unabated.[8]

In 1967, the President's Commission on Law Enforcement and the Administration of Justice pointed out that between 1960 and 1965 reported crimes against the person had increased from 148.3 per 100,000 of population to 184.7, or 24.5%. During the same period, crimes against property had increased from 916.1 per 100,000 of population to 1,249.6, or 36.4%.[9] These dramatic and well-publicized statistics have contributed to a demand for a more effective criminal law system, not only from those who favor more stringent controls but also from those favoring varying degrees of liberalization.

(2) *Actus Reus* and *Mens Rea*: *The Criminal Act and The Measure of Guilt*

Before embarking on the further discussion of the social context of the law, it is necessary to return to a fuller consideration of the theoretical analysis of the internal aspects of the criminal act itself. Regardless of proposals for the increase or reduction of sanctions, or the questions of liberalization versus extended criminalization of various kinds of behavior, there are important principles of legal analysis to consider which determine the degree of criminal liability, or the exclusion of guilt altogether for any act prohibited by law. For it is the question of intent or awareness of wrongdoing which decides an individual's criminal liability in a particular action.

A classic statement of the common law doctrine on this point is enunciated by Salmond:

The general conditions of penal law liability are indicated with sufficient accuracy in the legal maxim, *Actus non facit reum, nisi mens sit rea*—the act alone does not amount to guilt; it must be accompanied by a guilty mind. That is to say there are two conditions to be fulfilled before penal responsibility can rightly be imposed....The material condition is the doing of some act by the person to be held liable....The formal condition, on the other hand, is the *mens rea* or guilty mind with which the act is done.[10]

---

[8] Cf. U.S., President's Commission on Law Enforcement and Administration of Justice: *The Challenge of Crime in a Free Society: A Report by the ...*, U.S. Gov't. Printing Office, Washington, D.C., 1967, p. 22f.

[9] *Ibid.*, p. 24. These statistics represent reported crimes.

[10] Sir John Salmond: *Salmond on Jurisprudence*, 11th ed., Glanville Williams (ed.), Sweet and Maxwell, London, 1957, p. 398. This basic concept is described elsewhere, for instance in Rudolf von Ihering: *Law as a Means to an End*, translated by Isaac Husik, MacMillan, New York, 1924, pp. 8f, cited in Jerome

The development of the concept of a "guilty mind", or guilt arising from intent, as a necessary constituent element of a crime is one of the most intriguing and complex chapters in the history of the common law tradition. In addition to requiring the positive descriptive elements of a crime to establish criminal liability, it allows for the defenses of insanity, involuntary action, and mistake of fact and mistake of law.

It is indicative of the importance of the individual responsibility with which the average person is normally considered to act that every individual is assumed to be able to exercise his discretion at least within the guidelines existing in the criminal law, unless it is proved otherwise. This is to assume that everyone is normally capable of making conscious, rational decisions as to whether or not he will act within the law. Here is the heart of the dilemma that trial judges have faced in enforcing the doctrine of *mens rea*. Was an act done with intent? Was an act done with knowledge? With recklessness, or what in the German frame of reference is called "conscious or unconscious negligence"? [11] Or was the act done purely by accident? A vast amount of consideration and formulation has gone into decisions, commentaries, and other writings in often futile attempts to give adequate expression to these elusive distinctions. A modern and cogent elucidation of the levels of *mens rea* believed to be present in human activity as it relates to the criminal law has been provided for in the American Law Institute's *Model Penal Code*, § 2.02:

Hall (ed.): *Readings in Jurisprudence,* Bobbs-Merrill, Indianapolis, 1938, p. 186. As Ihering sees it: "…in every act, it is never the act we want…we want only the purpose." This contention arose very early in the history of law. It appears in one of the laws of Aethelred (ca. 1000): "And if it happens that a man commits a misdeed involuntarily, the case is different from that of one who offends of his own free will voluntarily and intentionally," (VI *Aethelred,* 521) (translated by A.J. Robertson cited in Theodore F. T. Plucknett: *A Concise History of the Common Law,* Little, Brown and Company, Boston, 1956, p. 464). Black provides the following definition of *mens rea:* "A guilty mind; a guilty or wrongful purpose; a criminal intent;" and secondarily: "Guilty knowledge and wilfulness" (*Black's Law Dictionary,* 4th ed., West Publishing Company, Minneapolis, 1951, p. 1137). See also, James Marshall: *Intention—in Law and Society,* Funk & Wagnalls, New York, 1968, pp. 4-11. Marshall provides a very extensive discussion of the concept of *mens rea.*

[11] H. Schroeder: "German Criminal Law and its Reform." 4 *Duquesne Univ. Law Rev. 97* (1965), p. 105, note 24.

[12] American Law Institute (ALI): *Model Penal Code,* Proposed Official Draft, 1962, § 2.02. The *Model Penal Code* is an ongoing effort by various scholars

GENERAL REQUIREMENTS OF CULPABILITY

1. Minimum Requirements of Culpability.

Except as provided in Section 2.05, a person is not guilty of an offense unless he acted purposely, knowingly, recklessly, or negligently, as the law may require, with respect to each material element of the offense.

2. Kinds of Culpability Defined.

(a.) Purposely.

A person acts purposely with respect to a material element of an offense when:

(1.) if the element involves the nature of his conduct or a result thereof, it is his conscious object to engage in conduct of that nature or to cause such a result; and

(2.) if the element involves the attendant circumstances, he is aware of the existence of such circumstances or believes or hopes that they exist.

(b.) Knowingly.

A person acts knowingly with respect to a material element of an offense when:

(1.) if the element involves the nature of his conduct or the attendant circumstances, he is aware that his conduct is of that nature or that such circumstances exist; and

(2.) if the element involves a result of his conduct, he is aware that it is practically certain that his conduct will cause such a result.

(c.) Recklessly.

A person acts recklessly with respect to a material element of an offense when he consciously disregards a substantial and unjustifiable risk that the material element exists or will result from his conduct. The risk must be of such a nature and degree that, considering the nature and purpose of the actor's conduct and the circumstances known to him, a law-abiding person would observe.

(d.) Negligently.

A person acts negligently with respect to a material element of an offense when he should be aware of a substantial and unjustifiable risk that the material element exists or will result from his conduct. The risk must be of such a nature and degree that the actor's failure to perceive it, considering the nature and purpose of his conduct and the circumstances known to him, involves a gross deviation from the standard of care that would be exercised by a reasonable man in his situation.

3. Culpability Required Unless Otherwise Provided.

When the culpability sufficient to establish a material element of an offense is not prescribed by law, such an element is established if a person acts purposely, knowingly, or recklessly with respect thereto.

4. Prescribed Culpability Requirement Applies to All Material Forms.

When the law defining an offense prescribes the kind of culpability that is sufficient for the commission of an offense, without distinguishing among the material elements therof, such provision shall apply to all the material elements of the offense, unless a contrary purpose plainly appears....[12]

working under the auspices of the American Law Institute to provide the most adequate expression of the criminal law they can develop.

These definitions, which noticeably avoid the actual use of the word "intent", no doubt because of its varying implications, bring up several questions. Glanville Williams divides the issues between those who would limit the *mens rea* to intentional acts, and those who would expand it.[13] By limitation to intent he means recognizing only acts committed "purposely" or "knowingly", as described in the *Model Penal Code* (§ 2.02 cited). Those for an expanded *mens rea* would, he says, extend the notion of intent—and consequently the degree of criminal liability—to include the category of recklessness. For the purposes of the limited definition of intent, however, Williams is not so sure that simply sticking with the more general word "intent" itself would not be better, merely ascribing to "intent" those acts done with purpose, and those done with knowledge.[14]

The *Model Penal Code* indicates a belief in the need for recognition of the separate category of purpose when considering the *mens rea* of the crimes of treason, attempt, and conspiracy.[15] But Williams sees no practical necessity in maintaining this distinction. He reasons that acts done with full knowledge of their almost certain consequences are really little different from acts performed intentionally. He illustrates this contention with the example of two men walking along the edge of a cliff, who see a watch lying on the ground. They both run to get it, and one of the men attempts to push the other off the cliff to keep him from reaching the watch first. Williams says that the intent of the man who made the attempt to push the other off the cliff was to obtain the watch, but his act was done with full knowledge of the likely result of giving his companion a shove, and, therefore, he should be held as accountable as he would have been had his act had as its primary goal the death of the other individual. Since he would be held equally accountable under the definition provided by the *Model Penal Code,* Williams sees no real need for the distinction between "purposely" and "knowingly".[16]

---

[13] Cf. Glanville Williams: *The Mental Element in Crime,* The Magnes Press of the Hebrew University, Jerusalem, 1965, pp. 21-51, esp. pp. 21; 25. Marshall, *op. cit.,* p. 6, also discusses including reckless acts within the category of intention.

[14] Cf. Williams, *op. cit.,* p. 24f.

[15] A.L.I.: *Model Penal Code,* Tentative Draft No. 4, 1955, Comments for § 2.02, pp. 123-29.

[16] Williams, *op. cit.,* p. 24. R. Cross reviews Williams' ideas in 83 *Law Quarterly Rev.* 215 (1967). He questions the wisdom of eliminating the distinction between "purpose" and "knowledge".

The authors of the *Model Penal Code,* however, argue in defense of their carefully drawn distinction between purpose and knowledge:

> In defining the kinds of culpability, a narrow distinction is drawn between acting purposely and knowingly, one of the elements of ambiguity in the legal usage of "intent"....Knowledge that the requisite external circumstances exist is a common element in both conceptions. But action is not purposive with respect to the naure or the result of the actor's conduct unless it was his conscious object to perform an action of that nature or cause such a result. The distinction is no doubt inconsequential for most purposes of liability; acting knowingly is ordinarily sufficient. But there are areas where the discrimination is required and is made under existing law, using the awkward concept of "specific intent". This is true in treason, for example, in so far as purpose to aid the enemy is an ingredient of the offense....[17]

The question remains, however, whether it is necessary to separate the various aspects of intent so that they describe the elements of three specific offenses. These subdivisions appear to be little more than slight variations of one another.

Williams criticizes equally the idea of expanding the doctrine of intent. This would extend culpability attributed to intentional acts to those done recklessly as well. Williams rejects this solution as confusing ostensibly foreseeable consequences with intended results.[18] It is also difficult to imagine how under these circumstance an attempt would look: a "reckless attempt" seems like an implausible construction.

There are a variety of potential problems which would also be expected from such a broad definition. The expanded doctrine of intent would distinguish a *mens rea* as grave as that ascribed to acts done with full intent or knowledge from acts committed with only slightly more than a reasonable foreseeability of resulting harm. And the conclusion that the individual should have foreseen the result of his action may be arrived at according to how unorthodox or careless the accused's acts appear afterwards at the time of trial. The imputation of foreseeable results may not be an accurate determination according to the circumstances at the time of the event, but more important, this would judge the offender's acts to have been intentional when they were merely ill-considered or reckless. Williams considers such an extension as based upon faulty logic, and, therefore, ultimately prejudicial to any notion of true determination of the facts during the trial. This is, however, a recourse which

---

[17] A.L.I.: *Model Penal Code,* Tentative Draft No. 4, 1955, pp. 123-24.
[18] Cf. Williams, *op. cit.,* p. 38.

some have adopted, expanding the concept of intent in order to gain convictions in certain instances.[19]

Closely related to such an expansion upon the role of intent is the logic of those who seem to advocate abandonment of *mens rea*. Not surprisingly, after one has blown up a definition to so great a generalization that it includes almost all possible cases, one may come to question whether it has any definitional meaning at all, and then be persuaded rather to turn to the simple criminalization of specific acts in themselves, regardless of the degree of intent of the accused, for whom the question of intent becomes only one of extenuating circumstances. But a kind of presumption of legal guilt would attach itself to the simple identification of someone committing a prohibited act, if one disregards the mental state of the accused. In the end this would have the same questionable effect as would occur in the blanket identification of recklessness with intent. An abandonment of the *mens rea* concept might also mean punishing those persons who acted merely negligently, the same as those who acted recklessly. Individual acts may or may not be negligent or reckless according to the standards the law acknowledges and courts attempt to establish. But, if one were to abandon the concept of *mens rea,* the results of acts done recklessly, negligently, or otherwise unintentionally could be equally liable with those done deliberately—unless punishment were specifically excluded under certain circumstances.

A well known example of a major offense which may occur without specific *mens rea* is described in *United States v. Dotterweich.*[20] In this case, Dotterweich, the President of the Buffalo Pharmaceutical Company was found absolutely liable for the mislabeling of a certain drug in violation of the *Federal Food, Drug, and Cosmetic Act,* when he had no personal contact with the drug in question. The point first made by the United States Supreme Court in *United States v. Balint.*[21] is rephrased and clarified in *Dotterweich:*

The prosecution to which Dotterweich was subjected is based on a now familiar type of legislation whereby penalties serve as effective means of regulation. Such legislation dispenses with the conventional requirement for criminal conduct— awareness of some wrong-doing. In the interest of the larger good, it puts the

---

[19] *Ibid.,* p. 38.
[20] 320 U.S. 277 (1943). Compare A. L. Goodhart: *English Law and Moral Law,* Stevens and Sons, Ltd. London, 1953, p. 86. Goodhart explains the "legal" as opposed to "moral" reasons for such vicarious liability.
[21] 285 U.S. 250 (1921).

burden of acting at hazard upon a person otherwise innocent, but standing responsible in relation to a public danger.[22]

The Court construed the public danger to constitute grounds to enforce absolute liability on the offender in the absence of any specific statuatory limitation to personal liability. They did this, as is indicated, to reduce the social costs of impure or mislabeled substances of this type, assuming that this had been the intent of Congress in the Act. The abandonment of the need for *mens rea* in this situation might have been simply a notable exception in the case of offenses under regulatory legislation; in both the United States and England, however, this malleable doctrine has been applied in other areas. In *Morrisette v. United States,* for example, a junk dealer gathered up and sold old shell casing on a United States Air Force bombing range. He was convicted of "knowingly converting" government property, although he reasonably believed the property abandoned since it had lain neglected for a long time. The conviction in this instance was reversed by the Supreme Court on appeal, the Court insisting that the required *mens rea* for what was really a theft offense was not present.[23] But as Kadish and Paulsen point out in their innovative text on the criminal law, in most states absolute liability is extended in principle to cases of bigamy and sex offenses concerning minors.[24]

However, controversy surrounding required mental states for proof of culpability does not completely explain the elements of a crime. For there to be criminal guilt, there must also be some act. Individuals are not punished for their thoughts, no matter how reprehensible they may be. The act may be relatively inconsequential—such as some small assistance to a thief—or once removed from what is commonly recognized as criminal action—such as participation in a conspiracy—but some action is required.[25]

---

[22] 320 U.S. 280f.

[23] *Morrisette v. United States,* 342 U.S. 246 (1952).

[24] Sanford Kadish and Monrad Paulsen: *Criminal Law and its Processes,* Little, Brown and Company, Boston, 2nd ed., 1969, pp. 247-49.

[25] See, among others, Immanuel Kant: *The Philosophy of Law,* translation by W. Hastie, T&T Clark, Edinburgh, 1887, pp. 24-25: "...no external legislation can cause any one to adopt a particular intention, or to propose to himself a certain purpose; for this depends upon an internal condition or act of the mind itself. However, external actions conducive to such mental condition may be commanded, without its being implied that the individual will of necessity make them an end to himself." See also, Glanville Williams: *Criminal Law: the General*

It is often difficult to consider the act without discussing *mens rea*. There are instances in which an omission to act, alone, will satisfy the requirements of culpability. Most offenses, however, require a certain *mens rea* as well. Nonetheless, the question of criminal guilt or liability can be approached from the standpoint of the act rather than that of the mental state.

Salmond does this by categorizing acts which result in criminal liability as, "...any event which is subject to the control of the human will".[26] Others speak of "voluntary acts" as opposed to "involuntary acts".[27] The problem arises from ascribing to acts qualities which are really a function of various kinds of mental control, or its absence. This can be confusing, since there is nothing outwardly "voluntary" or "involuntary" about many acts. Some occurrences may seem involuntary —an individual's car leaves the road on a tight curve. Others may seem voluntary—one man severely beats another in a fight in a bar. Yet without some investigation into the surrounding circumstances and the thoughts of those involved, one can only speculate that the first event actually was involuntary, and the second voluntary. The driver of the car may have decided to commit suicide, while the man who gave the other a beating may have been acting in an autistic state. Thus an act is only the external side of a fact and with the few exceptions of absolute liability cited, it must be coupled with the requisite *mens rea*

Part, 2nd ed., Stevens & Sons, Ltd. London 1961, pp. 16-21, for further discussion. As Kant implied, short of mind reading, proof of particular thoughts is simply not possible, let alone coercing the thinking of particular thoughts, or punishing for the thinking of particular thoughts.

[26] *Salmond on Jurisprudence,* p. 399.

[27] See e.g., H. L. A. Hart: *Causation in the Law,* O.U.P., Oxford, 1959, p. 38: "In common speech, and in much legal usage, a human action is said not to be voluntary or not fully voluntary if some one or more of a quite varied range of circumstances are present: if it is done 'unintentionally' (i.e., by mistake or by accident) or involuntarily (i.e., where normal muscular control is absent), unconsciously; or under various types of pressure exerted by other human beings (coercion or duress); or even under the pressure of legal or moral obligation, or as a choice of the lesser of two evils which is often expressed by saying that the agent 'had no choice' or no 'real choice'." See also Sim: "Involuntary Actus Reus," 25 *Modern Law Rev.* 741 (1962): "The coupling of an abstract quality of the mind with substantive acts is usually attempted when the mental quality was simply absent. Apparently the requirement of *mens rea* is thought to be so imperative that one must make some reference to it when it does not exist. Why not rather than involuntary acts, acts without the presence of the mental element?"

if the individual involved is to be held criminally liable. However, since physical facts are easier to describe and establish in the courtroom, it remains tempting to develop formulas which allow conviction for these particular acts alone.

(3.) *The Defense of Insanity and the Problems of Limited Responsibility*

The basic assumption of the law—and hence the basis for the presumption of criminal responsibility—is the conviction that, except under special or extraordinary circumstances, a person is free to act or not to act.[28] The logic of the defense of legal insanity derives, paradoxically perhaps, from this same proposition. For, in order to defend the consistency of the theory of personal responsibility, the theories of limited responsibility had to be developed to explain known exceptions.

An unwarranted retreat from the basic proposition of personal responsibility to widen the scope of the exceptions might produce an escape route through which many who are presumably guilty under the present doctrine might pass, thereby possibly undermining the general deterrent of the system of criminal law.[29] Yet a natural limitation for any over-extension of the exceptions in a full-scale resort to a general theory of only limited personal responsibility, or only relative personal responsibility, might be that it could also mean an end to the usefulness of the exceptional defenses altogether. For, if we are only relatively responsible anyway, the degree of diminished responsibility (unless it were total and permanent mental incapacity) would become meaningless, so far as escaping punishment completely is concerned, and would serve only to provide a measure for compensatory penal social re-education.

The basic test for insanity originated with the famous *M'Naghten Case.* The decision in *M'Naghten* indicated that innocence due to insanity may be allowed only in instances where the accused was either unable to appreciate the nature and quality of his act, or was unable to distinguish

---

[28] 45 *ALR* 2d 1447: "The law is based upon, and probably irretrievably committed to the theory that, in the absence of special conditions, individuals are free to exercise choice between possible courses of conduct, and, hence, morally responsible." Cf. also David Acheson: *"McDonald v. United States:* The Durham Rule Redefined," 51 *Georgetown Law Journal*, 580 (1963), p. 580.

[29] Acheson, *loc. cit.,* p. 589: Cf. also testimony before the Subcommittee on Constitutional Rights of the Senate Judiciary Committee, March 11, 1958, as cited by James Clayton in "Six Years After Durham," 44 *Journal of the American Judicature Society* 18, (1960), p. 19.

whether his act was right or wrong.[30] In some jurisdictions a supple-
mentary test was added to determine whether the action was the result
of an irresistable impulse regardless of the accused's ability to distinguish
right from wrong at the time of his act.[31]

For the past twenty years a controversy has existed over the modifi-
cation of the *M'Naghten* rule in the form of the *Durham* rule in the
District of Columbia by the Federal District Court of Appeals for that
jurisdiction. This formulation allows the jury to acquit on grounds of
insanity if the criminal act was "...a product of a mental disease or
defect." [32] An attempt to establish the New Hampshire rule which has
existed since 1870,[33] *Durham* has not been adopted in any other Federal
District or in any of the states. Two basic criticisms are made of this
more recent rule. First, that it leaves to the psychiatric profession the
key definition of the phrase "mental disease or defect". In one instance
the definition at St. Elizabeth's Hospital in Washington, D.C. was
changed between a Friday and a Monday so that, where formerly,
sociopathic individuals had not been considered to be suffering from
a mental disease, suddenly they were included in that category with
others traditionally so regarded.[34] In that case, an appeal was successful,

---

[30] *M'Naghten's Case*, House of Lords, 10 *Cl. & F.* 200 (1843), 719.

[31] *Smith v. United States*, 36 *F.2d* 548 (1929): The degree of insanity which will
relieve the accused of the consequences of a criminal act must be such as to create
in his mind an uncontrollable impulse to commit the offense charged. This impulse
must be such as to override the reason and judgment and obliterate the sense
of right and wrong to the extent that the accused is deprived of the power
to choose between right and wrong...his reasoning powers were so far dethroned
by his diseased mental condition as to deprive him of the will power to resist
the insane impulse to perpetrate the deed, though knowing it to be wrong." See
also 22 *CJS* 208 61: There is a conflict of authorities as to whether or not one
knowing the nature and quality of his act and also knowing that it is wrong,
but who is unable to control his conduct, may properly be considered criminally
responsible. See also the A.L.I.: *Model Penal Code*, Tentative Draft No. 4 (1955)
§ 4.01, «Mental Disease or Defect Excluding Responsibility». The draft presents
a formulation which incorporates the "mental disease or defect" phrase from
Durham (see below) but is similar in effect to *M'Naghten* in that it requires the
determination of whether or not the accused could appreciate the criminality
of his act. It adds a restatement of *Smith* in the alternative, exculpating those
who cannot make their conduct conform to the requirements of the law because
of mental incapacity.

[32] *Durham v. United States*, 214 *F.2d* 862 (1954), 874-875.

[33] *State v. Pike*, 49 *N.H.* 399 (1870), as cited in 214 *F.2d* 874.

[34] *Blocker v. United States*, 288 *F.2d* 853 (1961), 859-862.

when the "sociopathic" defendant was suddenly determined to be suffering from a mental disease, and, therefore, coming under the provisions of the *Durham* formulation. The second major criticism is that the word "product" is vague, and raises the fundamental problem of causality.[35] As was quickly pointed out, once a defendant is found to be suffering from a mental disease or defect, very little else is needed to establish a causal link between his condition and his act.[36] Very often a directed verdict has been quickly forthcoming, since once the mental disease or defect was established, that was all that was needed to raise reasonable doubts about the accused's guilt.[37]

However, a subsequent case has reduced the confusion surrounding the application of the *Durham* rule. In *McDonald v. United States* the same Federal Court of Appeals ruled that the jury was bound not only to find that a mental disease or defect exists, but also that it "...substantially affects mental or emotional processes and substantially impairs behavior controls." [38] This was a great step toward reducing the over use of the words "mental disease or defect" as a slogan which encompassed the accused's condition, and was often established by expert witnesses to a degree which barred any real discussion by the jury. Under *McDonald*, juries are free to determine in light of expert and other testimony whether they consider that the defendant was suffering from a mental disease or defect, and then is bound to determine the effect this condition had on the behavior which led to the defendant's act.

Ironically, in the *Blocker* case and in *McDonald*, the role of the *M'Naghten* test was raised, and reinstated, at least as a relevant consideration in determining insanity. In a concurring opinion to *Blocker,* Judge

---

[35] H. Fingarette: "The Concept of Mental Disease in Criminal Law Sanity Tests," 33 *Univ. of Chicago Law Rev.* 229 (1966) 229f: for the author's conceptual analysis of the term "mental disease", see pp. 235-248; see also, *Carter v. United States,* 252 *F.2d* 608 (1957), 617: "Mental disease means mental illness. Mental illnesses are of many sorts, and have many characteristics. They, like physical illness, are the subject matter of medical science." This definition appears to leave determination of the condition to medical experts. The Court indicates as well that the relationship of a mental disease to the act is a critical one, and that causality must be established to some degree, although how certain the jury must be is left unclear.

[36] See Acheson: *loc. cit.,* p. 583: "A second major difficulty with the 'product' rule has been a virtually automatic presumption, once mental disease is shown, that the act was a product of the disease."

[37] *Ibid.*

[38] *McDonald v. United States,* 312 *F.2d* 847 (1962), 851.

Burger (now Chief Justice Burger of the United States Supreme Court) stated:

The defendant is not to be found guilty as charged unless it is established beyond a reasonable doubt that when he committed the act, first, that he understood and appreciated the act was a violation of the law, and, second, that he had the capacity to exercise his will and choose not to do it.[39]

This, formulation, which Judge Burger proposed, is a restatement of the *M'Naghten* rule, with the "irresistable impulse" test added.

Although Burger's suggestion has not been adopted in that jurisdiction, the Court stated in *McDonald* the rule now in use:

We think the jury may be instructed, provided there is testimony on the point, that capacity, or lack thereof, to distinguish right from wrong and ability to refrain from doing a wrong or unlawful act may be considered in determining whether there is a relationship between the mental disease and the act charged. It should be remembered, however, that these considerations are not to be regarded as independently controlling or alternative tests of mental responsibility, in this circuit. They are factors which a jury may take into account in deciding whether the act charged was a product of mental disease or defect.[40]

Consequently, even in the District of Columbia, which supposedly had changed the rule, the *M'Naghten* test is allowed, although only as one criterion. Before *McDonald,* the number of acquittals by reason of insanity had risen, and it was thought that the fears of the critics of the *Durham* rule would be realized.[41] *McDonald* can be seen as an attempt to clarify *Durham,* and also to restrict its application to fewer cases.

There are other instances in which individuals may not be liable for their acts, although these have not produced as great a concern that large numbers of individuals would unjustifiably escape criminal responsibility as did alteration of rules governing the defense of insanity. Generally persons who act without conscious awareness of their actions are exonerated. This may be true whether or not the lack of awareness is permanent or intermittent, such as in the case of an epileptic.[42] Intoxicated

[39] 288 *F.2d* 871.

[40] 312 *F.2d* 851.

[41] Cf. Acheson: *loc. cit.,* chart on page 589.

[42] When driving a car, or performing other potentially dangerous acts, an epileptic or other person who is aware that he is subject to temporary autistic behavior may be liable for injuries caused while in an autistic state (an *actio libera in causa*). In *Regina v. Charlson,* 39 *Cr.App.R.* 37, (1955), however, a father's apparently unforeseeable and unconscious bludgeoning of his son was considered an action without any intent or knowledge, and the father was acquitted; see also

persons are generally liable for their acts since they chose to become intoxicated in the first place, and since courts have generally not recognized that reduction of inhibitions through intoxication releases from criminal responsibility.[43] However, mental incapacity or insanity which results from drunkeness may mean an individual will not be liable for a crime requiring specific intent or knowledge. The logic is similar to that employed in establishing a defense by reasonable mistake of fact: a person cannot intentionally perform an act if he has no awareness of the nature of his act.[44] However, this defense has been used successfully in only a few instances.

(4) *The Defense of Mistake of Fact and of Mistake of Law*

There are two other instances of limited liability: the defenses of mistake of fact and of mistake or ignorance of law. These are the results of lack of information on the part of the accused, either of the circumstances attending his act or of the law.

For a mistake of fact to be recognized as a defense, the lack of information must be a reasonable one. A burglar entering a second story window may claim that he thought that the building was open to such intrusion, but it is unlikely that this would be considered a reasonable error. Furthermore, reasonable error must also preclude the possibility of the *mens rea* required for the offense.[45] For instance, an individual is in a candy store. On the counter is a basket containing English Toffee. The basket has a sign on it which reads, "Try our

S. J. Fox, "Physical Disorder and Criminal Liability," 63 *Columbia Law Rev.* 644 (1963), especially at p. 646 for a list of kinds of conditions producing impaired or aberrant conduct. Cf. also generally, Weihofen and Overholser: "Mental Disorder Affecting the Degree of Crime," 56 *Yale Law Journal* 959 (1947).

[43] Cf. 8 *A.L.R.* 30, 1236, 1240, 3: See also Jerome Hall: *General Principles of Criminal Law*, Bobbs Merrill, Indianapolis, 1960, p. 533. One might have imagined that the exculpatory rule would have completely undermined the rigorous traditional liability, since *mens rea* is the requirement of fundamental principle. But major limitations persist. The situation where the agent has acted freely to put himself into a state where he might no longer be able to form the *mens rea* of a foreseeably resulting action is referred to as *actio libera in causa*.

[44] Cf. 8 *A.L.R. 3d* 1236, 1246, 4, especially 1240 and 1251; cf. also Moore: "Legal Responsibility and Chronic Alcoholism" 122 *American Journal of Psychology* 748 (1965) and Beck and Parker: "The Intoxicated Offender—A Problem of Responsibility," 44 *Canadian Bar Review* 563 (1966).

[45] Cf. e.g. Jerome Hall: *General Principles of Criminal Law*, 2nd ed., Bobbs-Merrill, Indianapolis, 1960, pp. 365-366: "...mistake of fact is a defense if

English Toffee". Thinking the basket contains free samples for customers, the person takes one of the candies and walks out of the store. The clerk, seeing this, stops him on the street and has him arrested for shoplifting. As it turns out, many similiar stores in the area offer free samples. The accused made what is ruled a reasonable mistake of fact. He thought the candies were to be taken as free samples when they were actually intended for sale only. Because of his error, the accused performed an illegal act, but the intent to steal was lacking. Because the offense of theft requires intent, in this instance, where the reasonableness of the error can be established, the required *mens rea* may be precluded, and the accused cannot be found guilty of the charge.

The defense of ignorance or mistake of law has been used successfully in only very few instances, however. One often hears the statement. "Ignorance of the law is no excuse", and generally it is not accepted as one.[46] Recently, however, a few exceptions to this rule have been recognized by the Supreme Court. In *Lambert v. California* [47] the appellant failed to register under a Los Angeles Municipal Code Section requiring that all convicted felons register with the police.[48] Although a convicted

---

because of the mistake, *mens rea* is lacking.... Anglo-American criminal law restricts the scope of *ignorantia facti*...the mistake must be a reasonable one...[and] certain sexual offenses, bigamy and other types of strict liability [are excepted]." See also 22 *Corpus Juris Secundum* 182, American Law Book Company, New York, 1961, 47: "Since ignorance or mistake of fact, not due to negligence, in the commission of an otherwise criminal act results in the absence of a requisite element of malice or criminal intent, it is generally a defense."

[46] For two classic statements, see: John Austin: *Lectures on Jurisprudence,* 3rd ed., rev., ed. by Robert Campbell, John Murray, London, 1869, pp. 497f. Austin exposed a fallacy of the doctrine that ignorance is no excuse because supposedly, all men are bound to know the law. The law may, as he points out, be unknowable to jurist and layman alike: "The solution of this difficulty is to be found in the principles of judicial evidence. The admission of ignorance of the law as a specific ground of exemption would lead to interminable investigations of insoluble questions of fact, and would, in effect, nullify the law by hindering the administration of justice" (p. 489). See also Hans Kelsen: *General Theory of Law and State,* transl. by Anders Wedburg, Russell & Russell, New York, 1961: "The juristic statement that an individual is legally obligated to certain conduct holds even if the individual is wholly ignorant of the fact that he is obligated. That ignorance of the law does not exempt from obligation is a principle which prevails in all legal orders, and must prevail, since otherwise it would be almost impossible to apply the legal order" (p. 72).

[47] 355 *U.S.* 225 (1957).

[48] *Los Angeles Municipal Code,* §§ 52.38; 52.39.

felon, she had no knowledge of her obligation under the city ordinance. The court indicated that there was no "proof of probability of such knowledge" and added that her actions were of a passive nature and no different from those of an average member of the community.[49] The ordinance punished an omission to act. For that reason, and because the accused's action was both reasonable and passive, the conviction was overturned as a contravention of the due process of law guaranteed under the United States Constitution. Consequently, an omission to comply with the requirements of a statute which the accused cannot reasonably be expected to know, may be excused when no wrongful intent can be established.[50]

Whether such a rationale might extend to laws prohibiting affirmative acts is questionable. In *Long v. State*,[51] a case involving what the

---

[49] 355 *U.S.* 229 (1957).

[50] In a similar German decision rendered in 1952, the highest federal court declared that "awareness of unlawfulness" is an essential element of the complete description of a criminal act. (Cf. *Entscheidungen des Bundesgerichtshof in Strafsachen*—BGHSt 2, 194-212). This is, however, not acceptance of the defense of "ignorance of law" pure and simple (see further discussion of this point in Chapter IV: A., n. 7 below), but a definite requirement of *mens rea* in establishing guilt.

There are no unquestioned guarantees under American law against legal culpability on the part of someone who, without wrongful intent, violates a law he did not or could not know about. Yet, even here the theory of absolute culpability is not undisputed. G.O.W. Mueller has described the role of *mens rea* in the common law: "On Common Law *Mens Rea*," 42 *Minn. Law Rev.* 1043, (1958) and discusses recent Supreme Court decisions where a defense built on ignorance of the law or error in regard to it was successful cf. *Lambert v. Calif.*, 355 U.S. 225 (1957); *Smith v. Calif.*, 361 U.S. 147 (1959). He concludes hopefully:

Once it is recognized that the common law regards *mens rea* as a universal requirement, technical and jurisprudential difficulties are at an end. In terms of due process this recognition simply means: that judges no longer confound intent and *mens rea;* that judges apply the common law rule according to which *mens rea* is a universal requirement whether or not the statutory definition contains words indicative of *mens rea,* such as "intentionally"; that act-and-intent statutes are codifications of the common law requisite of *mens rea* and should be treated as such; and that statutes attempting to abolish a universal *mens rea* requirement—and these are rare—are unconstitutional, as are judicial utterances, in the nature of judicial legislation, to that effect. (p. 1103f.)

(See also: American Law Institute (A.L.I.): *Model Penal Code*, Tentative Draft No. 4, Philadelphia, 1955, § 2.04 (1) a-b; and G.O.W. Mueller: "Mens Rea and the Penal Law Without It: A Study of the German Penal Law in Comparison to the Anglo-American Penal Law," Thesis, Columbia Univ. Law Sch., 1955, MS.).

[51] *Del.* 262 (1949).

defendant reasonably believed to be a valid divorce decree, a re-
marriage, and a subsequent charge of bigamy, the court stated:

A mistake of law, where not a defense, may nevertheless negative a general
criminal intent as effectively as would an exculpatory mistake of fact.[52]

The decision goes on to say that this paradox is the result of the
desire that knowledge of the law should be encouraged, and the availability of the defense of ignorance of law would tend to discourage
gaining such knowledge by those who wished to save such an argument
for future use.[53] In this instance, however, the accused had sought
the advice of counsel. The Court indicated that in such cases when
bona fide efforts to ascertain the law were made, the concern that others
might calculatedly maintain their ignorance, and then use it as a
defense was not justified. For ignorance to qualify as reasonable. "...an
affirmative showing of effort to abide by the law, tested by objective
standards rather than the defendant's subjective state of mind...."[54]
would be required. This provides a narrow range for the use of the
defense of mistake of law. It has not been accepted within all jurisdictions in the United States, however. And because of resistance to the
idea that consulting an attorney would be an objective standard, it is
unlikely that the defense will be recognized except in a few cases
where equity weighs strongly for acquittal.

Although maintaining interest in learning the content of the law is
of some importance, more significant is the fact that most people are
aware that something is considered wrong even if they do not know of
the exact law they are violating. In a television interview a member
of the Hell's Angel's motorcycle gang in California once announced
in reply to questions concerning a report that several members of his
gang had had sexual relations with two underage girls, that the girls had
not been raped, because, "whatever happened to those girls, they were
willing." Of course, the men who had participated in this escapade

---

[52] *Ibid.,* p. 497. Cf. also Bulgar: "The Present Function of the Maxim *Ignorantia
Juris Neminem Excusat—A* Comparative Study," 52 *Iowa Law Rev.* 626 (1967),
p. 633: "This excuse points again to the evidential value of the *ignorantia iurus*
rule and to the possibility inherent in the judicial process of evaluating also the
subjective motives of the parties. This process would lead in time to equating
ignorantia iurus with *ignorantia facti.*"

[53] 44 *Del.* 277.

[54] *Ibid.,* at 272.

were still guilty of relations with underage girls or statutory rape. Their spokesman was apparently ignorant of the law in this area, but because of the widely known social prohibition against this kind of activity, it is hardly conceivable that ignorance of law could negate the required intent in this case. It must be recognized, however, that in a society with unsettled standards of conduct, a case could arise where ignorance of the law and ignorance that certain conduct was generally unacceptable could reasonably coincide. In such an instance, it could no longer be argued that there was any high probability that members of the society at large would not act in much the same way, and a public policy doctrine that one should have a sense of the prohibition from his society even if he is not aware of the specific prohibition could be maintained only as an accepted legal fiction.

B.   INDIVIDUAL RIGHTS DURING ENFORCEMENT OF THE LAW

A distinguishing characteristic of the theory of criminal justice in the United States has been an overriding concern for procedural safeguards for individual rights, particularly as they are guaranteed in the first ten amendments to the Constitution and secured and elucidated in numerous civil rights decisions. Under the constitutional provision for the separation of powers, the final test of effectiveness of "rule of law" in constitutional democracy may rest with the courts' ability to protect what theorists refer to as "security of law", not simply by guaranteeing a fair trial to those accused of crimes, but, equally important, by insuring against the danger of the abuse of civil rights during law enforcement. Obviously, the difficulty for the courts to attempt to uphold these rights lies in the fact that the courts have only judicial power. Adherence to the rulings of the courts, not so much as seen by the example of the conduct of particular individuals, who may be within the law or outside it, but by the general compliance of the other branches of government and the acceptance of this as law by society as a whole, demonstrates the standing of the law in that society, and the dedication of the government, and the people, to government under law.

It is the irony of the call for "law and order" that many of those who call loudest are often those least concerned with law in the sense described above. In times of mounting social problems and a rising crime rate, it is plain that effective measures are necessary to guarantee the rights and safety of those endangered. But unless the same standards of justice apply then, as in situations where there is less apparent direct challenge, the institutional structure is no longer in a position to maintain the general high regard for the law and the confidence in the basic impartiality and justice of the judicial system, both of which seem to be, in fact, necessary conditions of functioning legal democracy. The courts can interpret the law laid down in the Constitution, the statutes, and the basic decisions; declare what the law is; and direct compliance with the law. But they are dependent on the powers of other branches, and upon the acceptance of the public for carrying out the decisions of the courts. Prudent recognition of what the limits are on what the law can do is probably just as instrumental as tacit acceptance in maintaining a general climate of confidence in the law and in our present system of legal justice.

The decisive test for maintaining the reputation and authority of the law comes both in the manner in which the law enforcement agencies carry out their obligations and the manner in which the courts respond to a challenge to constitutional rights and protections. Any discussion of current questions of hope of liberalization of the law, and of more effective means of law enforcement, has, therefore, to consider carefully not only the matter of over-criminalization and the frequent problems of the enforcement of morals legislation in a pluralistic society, it must also consider the challenge to individual rights during enforcement of the law and the response of the courts to any infringement of individual rights. For, it is, in the final analysis, this system of legal rights and legal guarantees, which distinguishes the libertarian democratic system of law from many a more "efficient" system. And it is in fact in the Supreme Court, at least, that the greatest attention to individual rights has been observed. For, in declaring where and how specific constitutional guarantees should be applied, wider recognition of individual rights has been obtained and greater understanding of what these rights must entail, to be secure, has been achieved, at least for those who could afford the appeals, who benefit from others' rulings, or who are held in some jurisdiction where anonymity or public ignorance or attitude does not cost them their civil rights .

(1) *Search and Seizure*

A key provision concerning any initial investigation of a crime, and the first measure both of effectiveness in law enforcement and in safeguarding the rights of individuals, is the guarantee against unreasonable searches and seizures outlined in the Fourth Amendment:

The right of the people to be secure in their persons, houses, papers, and effects, against unreasonable searches and seizures shall not be violated, and no warrants shall issue, but upon probable cause, supported by oath or affirmation, and particularly describing the place to be searched and the persons or things to be seized.

A search and seizure may be unreasonable, then if it is not based on probable cause which allows issuance of a warrant, from the appropriate magistrate, and particularly describing the place to be searched and whoever or whatever is to be seized.

Because the power of the Supreme Court is only judicial it has been most decisive and illuminating that the Court could uphold this provision by excluding from use as evidence anything seized in a manner not consistent with these constitutional limitations. It was not until fairly recently that the rule was developed, however, in order to deal with illegal searches and seizures. Helpless to obstruct illegal searches or seizures in any other way, the Court refused to accept evidence obtained by illegal means.

In *Weeks v. United States*,[55] in 1914, the Supreme Court ruled that an illegal seizure of papers in an attempt by a federal marshall to gain evidence of a violation of a lottery statute not only violated the defendant's rights under the Fourth Amendment, but that the papers illegally seized could not be introduced as evidence at a trial.[56] That decision resulted in the now famous "exclusionary rule" which continues in effect.

In *Mapp v. Ohio,* in 1961, the Supreme Court determined that this interpretation and safeguard of Fourth Amendment rights, applicable previously only to federal officers, would be applicable to state officers as well.[57] The Court recognized that since the vast majority of criminal prosecutions occur at the state level in this country, the most effective standard available must be applied to the states in order to prevent abuse by the states of the individual rights outlined in the Fourth

---

[55] 232 *U.S.* 383 (1914).

[56] *Ibid.,* at. p. 398; for description and analysis of developments since *Weeks* see Jacob W. Landynsky: *Search, Seizure and the Supreme Court,* The Johns Hopkins Univ. Press, Baltimore, 1966; see also F. A. Allen, "Exclusionary Rule in the American Law of Search and Seizure," 52 *Journal of Criminal Law, Criminology, and Police Science* 245 (1961); The German procedural rule generally does not provide for exclusion of evidence illegally obtained. In this regard, see Walter Clemens: "The Exclusionary Rule Under Foreign Law, Germany," 52 *Journal of Criminal Law, Criminology, and Police Science,"* 277 (1961).

[57] 367 *U.S.* 643 (1961); see also Roger Traynor, "*Mapp. v. Ohio* at Large in the Fifty States," *Duke Law Journal* 319 (1962).

Amendment.[58] This was, from the practical standpoint of sheer numbers of cases, a major step, and meant that the federal doctrine concerning search and seizure was now applicable in every jurisdiction in the United States.

Since the time the exclusionary rule itself was promulgated attempts have been made both to limit and to extend the application of both the Fourth Amendment warrant requirements and the exclusionary rule. There are, first of all, certain instances in which no warrant must be obtained in order to conduct a legal search. For instance, searches and seizures without a warrant but pursuant to a valid arrest are permissable. Here two questions arise: First, was the arrest itself based on probable cause, and, therefore, valid. In *Johnson v. United States,* in 1947, federal officers acting on a tip, identified themselves and were admitted to a room in a boarding house (although not with express permission), then on the basis of an odor of opium in the room, they arrested the occupant and searched the room, seizing some narcotics.[59] In this instance, the arrest was not considered a basis for the search. The odor of opium could, however, have provided probable cause for the issuance of a search warrant, which then would have led to a valid arrest based on the evidence discovered. The key rule is that the neutral magistrate must be allowed to declare whether there is probable cause for a search warrant.[60] Evidence obtained from a search subsequent to an arrest cannot be used to substantiate the validity of the arrest. Second, the question remains whether the scope of the search was reasonable. This becomes a matter of degree once it is determined that the arrest is valid. Could the arresting officers search just the person of the defendant, for instance? Could the search extend to the room in which he was arrested? Or could the search be extended to his entire house, perhaps. If the arrest occurred on the street, or on other premises, could the officers then proceed to the defendant's house and search it? The courts have been lenient in allowing officers discretion in this area once the validity of the initial arrest was established. In *Agnello v. United States,*[61] in 1925, the Court stated:

The right without a search warrant contemporaneously to search a person lawfully arrested while committing a crime, and to search the place where the arrest is

---

[58] *Ibid.* 657.
[59] 333 *U.S.* 10 (1947), 17.
[60] *Ibid.* 14; Cf. *United States v. Harris,* 403 *U.S.* 573 (1971).
[61] 269 *U.S.* 20 (1925).

made in order to find and seize things connected with the crime, as the fruits, or as the means by which it was committed, as well as weapons and other things to effect an escape from custody is not to be doubted.[62]

The case involved the illegal sale of cocaine at one defendant's house to government informers. The Court did limit the search, however, to areas under the physical control of the defendants at the time of the arrest, and did not allow admission of evidence seized at Agnello's house which was some distance from the defendant's home where the arrest had occurred.[63]

The questions above point out the rather fine practical distinctions which must be developed in order to force adherence to the general provisions of the Bill of Rights.

A further instance in which warrants have not been required are those in which the evidence or persons sought have a high degree of mobility— such as when they are in an automobile—or when the evidence sought is in imminent danger of destruction. Again, the Court has responded to the practical demands of such situations, and allowed searches, without warrants, if officers had probable cause to proceed on the assumption that such conditions existed.

In *Carroll v. United States,* decided in 1925, a case involving violations of the prohibition amendment, the Court indicated,

...the warrant requirements of the Fourth Amendment might be dispensed with where considerations of time prevented the issuance of a warrant as in the case of an automobile which can be quickly moved....[64]

Recently, however, in *Coolidge v. New Hampshire,* the Supreme Court refused to allow admission of evidence found in a defendant's car which had been seized without a warrant and towed to the police station where it was searched, also without a warrant.[65] The reasoning of the Court was that there was no probable cause to suspect flight or removal of the evidence. It was also indicated that the notion that the car could be searched as incident to a valid arrest was incorrect.

There is a second group of exceptions to the exclusionary rule which allow evidence to be admitted even though it was obtained during an illegal search. First, evidence which is uncovered in an illegal search of premises which were not under the control of the person against whom

[62] *Ibid.* 30.
[63] *Ibid.* 32f.
[64] 267 *U.S.* 132 (1925), 153.
[65] 403 *U.S.* 433 (1971).

the evidence is to be used may be introduced in court. If this is done, the accused person has no standing to object, since he had no direct connection with the premises searched illegally. The key to this exception is how broadly the concept of control of premises is construed. In *Jones v. United States,* in 1960, the Supreme Court indicated its intention to construe control of premises fairly widely, even to the point of considering a person to be in control of premises which a friend is allowing him to use only temporarily.[66]

A second exception which allows the admission of illegally seized evidence occurs when the defendant seeking to suppress the evidence in question is unable to prove that the government would not have recovered the evidence in some other legal fashion. In *Wayne v. United States,* in 1963, police entered an apartment illegally on a tip that an abortion was in progress. They discovered the defendant, his attorney, and the body of the dead patient. The Supreme Court upheld admission of the corpse as evidence on the reasoning that the police would have discovered it from the County coroner anyway [67] (see also *Harlow v. United States* [1962]).[68]

A third, and little known exception to the exclusionary rule, is when a private individual illegally seizes evidence and turns it over to law enforcement authorities. In *Burdeau v. McDowell* (1921) [69] such evidence was permitted despite its origins. This is an exception parallel to what was once called "the silver platter doctrine", which allowed evidence seized in an illegal search by state officers to be turned over to federal officers as if on a "silver platter". That doctrine, described in *Lustig v. United States* in 1949, stipulated that evidence from an illegal state search might be introduced at a federal trial if there were no violations by federal officers during the search, and no federal officers or agencies were involved.[70] The question of application of the exclusionary rule to state proceedings had been resolved temporarily in the same year as *Lustig,* states being required to adhere to the requirements of the Fourth Amendment under the due process clause of the Fourteenth Amendment, but left free to choose any reasonable method to achieve this (see *Wolf v.*

---

[66] 362 *U.S.* 267 (1960).
[67] 318 *F.2d* 205 (D.C. Circ. 1963), cert. denied 375 *U.S.* 860 (1963).
[68] 301 *F.2d* 361 (5th Circ. 1962), cert. denied 371 *U.S.* 814 (1962).
[69] 256 *U.S.* 465 (1921).
[70] 338 *U.S.* 74 (1949) 78f.

Colorado [1949]).[71] That exception was eliminated in 1960 in *Elkins v. United States,* a case involving a search by Oregon police which was directed at finding obscene movies, but turned up evidence of illegal wiretapping by the defendent.[72] In that instance, the Supreme Court rejected the silver platter doctrine in a decision which was followed closely by *Mapp v. Ohio* [73] which applied federal search and seizure standards, including the exclusionary rule, to the states.

It must be pointed out that the exclusionary rule has been expanded as well as circumscribed. If law officers learn of additional evidence during an illegal search, they are not allowed to use knowledge arising from the illegal search as evidence of probable cause to obtain a warrant in order to conduct a legal search to obtain the other materials. In *Silverthorn Lumber Co. v. United States,* decided in 1920, knowledge of illegally seized records which had been ordered returned by the court could not be used as probable cause for their subpoena and eventual admission in evidence.[74] In a second case, *Nardone v. United States* (1937), an instance in which the Supreme Court ordered that the prosecution must reveal the use to which they put evidence obtained from wiretapping, Justice Frankfurter made the following statement:

The burden is, of course on the accused in the first instance, to prove to the trial court's satisfaction that wiretapping was unlawfully employed. Once that is established—as was plainly done here—the trial judge must give opportunity, however, closely confined to the accused, to prove that a substantial portion of the case against him was a fruit of a poisonous tree.[75]

This now well known doctrine was reaffirmed in *Wong Sun v. United States* in which the Supreme Court ruled knowledge from an inadmissable confession could not be used to obtain additional evidence, and that any such evidence would be excluded.[76]

If one examines the basic reasons for the exclusionary rule, and the exceptions to its application in the event of illegal searches, it is clear that the courts have not been consistent in applying this rule to safeguard individual rights. The rationale for the rule is that hopefully it will deter law officers from searches which violate the provisions of the

---

[71] 338 *U.S.* 25 (1949).

[72] 364 *U.S.* 206 (1960).

[73] See note 57 above.

[74] 251 *U.S.* 385 (1920).

[75] 308 *U.S.* 338 (1937); see also "Fruit from the Poisonous Tree—A Plea for Relevant Criteria," 115 *Univ. of Pennsylvania Law Rev.* 1136 (1967).

[76] 371 *U.S.* 471 (1963) 378-388.

Fourth Amendment, and will insure the integrity of the judicial process by refusing to allow the prosecution to build its case using methods in violation of the Constitution. If deterence and ethical consistency are goals, it would seem to be logical to disallow the introduction of evidence from any illegal search, regardless of the accused's standing to object, the likelihood that the evidence would have been uncovered by other means or channels, or who conducted the illegal search.[77] In fact, considering the question of standing, alone, it would seem equally desirable to provide for the protection of the Fourth Amendment to someone not under investigation for any crime as it is for the defendant himself.[78]

Very recently, in *Bivens v. Six Unknown Agents,* the Supreme Court allowed recovery of a money judgment against the state for an illegal search.[79] This may be a new and added deterrent to illegal search and seizure, and if the exclusionary rule is discarded at some point, a new way to halt unconstitutional practices. Another potential benefit of such a ruling may be its application to illegal searches of persons not a party to the case.

One challenge to search and seizure guarantees which is unique not only from the standpoint of the rule developed initially to cope with it, but also because of the nature of the "search" conducted, is that of electronic eavesdropping and wiretapping. Undoubtedly because of the science fiction quality of the devices employed, and the fact that physical penetration of the defendant's premises was not necessary, there was reluctance to include such practices within the protections of the Fourth Amendment. There had been concern regarding the use of such devices as wire taps soon after the introduction of the telegraph and telephone. In 1874, Illinois passed a statute which prohibited interception and disclosure of telegraph news dispatches,[80] in 1905, California prohibited all telephone wire taps.[81] In 1918, Congress passed a similar law.[82]

But in the first decision concerning wiretapping, *Olmstead v. United States,* decided in 1928, the Supreme Court interpreted the Fourth Amendment quite literally, and determined that because the wire tap involved no physical penetration of the defendant's premises, no search

---

[77] See esp. Landynski: *Op. cit.,* pp. 76f.
[78] 403 *U.S.* 388 (1971).
[79] *Ibid.*
[80] *Ill. Stat.* Ch. 134, § 7 (1874).
[81] *Calif. Penal Code,* § 620 (1905).
[82] 40 *U.S. Stat.* 1017-1018.

was involved.[83] It is not surprising that literal interpretation had this result, since such devices were hardly contemplated by the framers of the Bill of Rights.

As the sophistication of eavesdropping and wiretapping devices developed and the use of such devices became increasingly widespread, it grew apparent that some restriction beyond the physical penetration rule would be necessary. *Olmstead* itself was not received well by the public, and in 1932 no less than eight bills were introduced in Congress to end the use of wiretapping devices by federal officers. Although all of these failed at that time, their supporters were successful in having a rider attached to an appropriations bill forbidding use of federal funds for wire taps to enforce the prohibition amendment. [84]

In 1934 the *Enabling Act of the Federal Communications Commission* was passed. It included the following prohibition in Section 605 pertaining to wiretapping and electronic eavesdropping:

...no person not being authorized by the sender shall intercept any communications and divulge or publish the existence, contents, substance, purport, effect or meaning of such intercepted communication to any person.[85]

The Supreme Court, more or less on its own,[86] extended this to cover interception of telephone messages in the first case of *Nardone v. United States* in 1937 when evidence was ruled to have been obtained in a wire tap violating Section 605 of the *Enabling Act of the FCC*, and was thus excluded.[87]

In *Goldstein v. United States* in 1942 the Supreme Court held that since Goldstein was not a party to the telephone conversations in question, he did not come within the protection of Section 605.[88] This was the equivalent doctrine to that of lack of standing in conventional search and seizure cases.[89] In *Goldman v. United States*, delivered in 1942 at the same time as *Goldstein*, an electronic eavesdropping device was held to be no violation of the defendant's Fourth Amendment Rights since it

---

[83] 277 *U.S.* 438 (1928); on wiretapping generally, see Landynski: *Op. cit.*, pp. 198-244; also K.I. Solomon, "Short But Happy Life of *Berger v. New York*," 45 *Chicago-Kent Law Rev.* 123 (1968-69).

[84] 47 *Stat.* 1387.

[85] 48 *Stat.* 1103, 47 *U.S.C.* 605; for penalties see 47 *U.S.C.* 501.

[86] Cf. Landynski: *Op. cit.*, p. 206.

[87] 302 *U.S.* 383 (1937).

[88] 316 *U.S.* 114 (1942).

[89] *Ibid.* 129.

was merely held against the wall of the room adjoining the defendant's and constituted no physical penetration.[90] The Court had relied on *Olmstead,* and refused to extend Section 605 to such devices.[91]

In *Schwartz v. Texas,* a decade later, the court refused to apply the standard drawn from Section 605 to a state proceeding.[92] Two thieves had quarrelled, and state officials had persuaded one to telephone the other while they listened in by means of a wire tap. Such evidence, although illegally obtained, was not excluded. The restraint shown in *Wolf v. Colorado* was applied here as well.

In 1957 a further development occurred. In *Benanti v. United States,* the Supreme Court refused to allow use of evidence, in federal court, which had been obtained through a wire tap by New York state officials although that was illegal under that state's laws.[93] Section 605 was used in this instance as a device to overturn the "silver platter doctrine".[94]

In *Berger v. New York,* decided in 1967, the Court faced the question of eavesdropping devices and Fourth Amendment guarantees.[95] The "silver platter doctrine" had by this time been discarded for other search and seizure matters in *Elkins.* The Court finally applied the Fourth Amendment in this case to eavesdropping, ruling that a New York state statute allowing eavesdropping and wiretapping, did not require sufficient particularity.[96] That is, it did not require that a warrant specify the offense believed committed or the particular evidence sought. Indeed, the comprehensive nature of either of these practices—comprehensive in the sense that the entire intellectual exchange is recorded—made them vulnerable to a "vacuum cleaner effect" which almost by its nature violates the principle of particularity.

In *Berger* the court also deplored the fact that the statute allowed for an indefinite wire tap,[97] and gave the defendant no notice of the incursion.[98]

In *Katz v. United States* the court is more specific in overruling *Olmstead and Goldmann,* and rejecting the proposition that wiretapping and

[90] *Ibid.*
[91] *Ibid.*
[92] 344 *U.S.* 199 (1952), 212f.
[93] 355 *U.S.* 96 (1957).
[94] *Ibid.* 102.
[95] 388 *U.S.* 41 (1967).
[96] *Ibid.*
[97] *Ibid.* 59f.
[98] *Ibid.* 60.

eavesdropping are not subject to protections provided by the Fourth Amendment because they involve no physical penetration of the premises.[99] Because the Court is now concerned with protecting what the defendant sought to protect himself—in this instance by entering a telephone booth—the exchange of words, not the physical area is what is important.[100] As the Court stated:

The Government's activities in electronically listening to and recording the petitioner's words violated the privacy upon which he justifiably relied while using the telephone booth and thus constituted a "search and seizure" within the meaning of the Fourth Amendment. The fact that the electronic device employed to achieve that end did not happen to penetrate the wall of the booth can have no constitutional significance.[101]

The Court thus reversed the conviction in this instance, because federal officers had not sought a warrant before a neutral magistrate, a fundamental requirement in all searches and seizures with the few exceptions described above.[102]

Recent attempts have been made to codify a balanced position as regards wiretapping and electronic eavesdropping. One such attempt is found in the *Omnibus Crime and Safe Streets Act of 1968,* Title III, "Wiretapping and Electronic Surveillance".[103] This title provides that federal officers who have obtained prior approval from the Attorney General may apply to the appropriate federal judge for permission to employ eavesdropping devices. An order for "Authorizing or approving the interception of wire or oral communications" can be obtained. The Act goes on to specify offenses for which such application can be made. An important exemption from its requirements is made for matters involving national security (this was specified in *Katz* as well).[104] The Act requires probable cause that such an offense has been committed, satisfying the requirement in the Fourth Amendment against unreasonable searches; but this Act, unlike the Supreme Court's interpretation of the Fourth Amendment, applies only to federal officers (and only in the District of Columbia).

[99] 389 *U.S.* 347 (1967).
[100] *Ibid.* 353.
[101] *Ibid.* 353.
[102] *Ibid.* 357f.
[103] 18 *U.S.C.* 119.
[104] 389 *U.S.* 347. 364.

Most recently in *United States v. White,* the Supreme Court upheld the admission of testimony of an agent hiding in a closet who related statements which he had overheard from the defendant.[105] The defendant was speaking to an individual he trusted, but who had arranged for the conversations to occur within earshot of the police agent. This followed the precedent established in *On Lee v. United States* which allowed introduction of testimony by an agent who had listened to the conversation of the defendant with an informer who had concealed a microphone and transmitter on his person.[106]

As a consequence of recent decisions, however, wiretapping and electronic eavesdropping have been brought generally under the requirements and safeguards of the Fourth Amendment. Obviously, the lack of physical intrusion into private quarters is no longer a significant distinction. But by acknowledging that the guarantee against unreasonable search and seizure was intended to cover private communication and activity in the home, as well as goods, effects and papers, the privacy of oral communications has been recognized, by extention, as one of the rights protected by the Fourth Amendment, although there is no explicit statement to that effect in the language of the Amendment. Clearly searches and seizures have been subject to considerable scrutiny by the Supreme Court during the past several decades. Certain basic safeguards outlined in the Fourth Amendment have been emphasized, and insured, partly through the exclusionary rule. As has been pointed out, inconsistencies do exist in this rule's application. There is the further issue which must now be resolved since the passage of the present Administration's *District of Columbia Omnibus Crime Bill,* which includes among other matters the controversial "no knock" provision.[107] This will allow Washington, D.C. law officers, in certain

---

[105] 401 *U.S.* 745 (1971).

[106] 343 *U.S.* 747 (1952).

[107] See "Congress Clears Controversial D. C. Crime Control Bill," *Congressional Quarterly Weekly Report,* July 24, 1970, Vol. XXVIII, no. 23, p. 1887, "description of HR 12806 and S 2601. New York has a similar provision, *N.Y. Code Crim. Proc.* 799, which allows entry without knocking if the magistrate agrees that "...the property sought might be easily and quickly destroyed or disposed of, or that danger to the life and limb of the officer or another may result if such notice were given." See also, William Siegal: "The New York 'Frisk' and 'No Knock' Statutes: Are They Constitutional?" 30 *Brooklyn Law Rev.* 274 (1964), p. 278: the author concludes that the "no knock" provision will most likely be permitted, since in *Kerr v. California,* 374 *U.S.* 23 (1963), a search pursuant to a valid

instances after they have obtained a warrant, to be authorized to enter a dwelling without knocking or, presumably, without presenting the occupants with a warrant. The hope is to prevent destruction of evidence (such as narcotics), flight, or danger to the police themselves while they are waiting for a response to their knock. This draws attention to the entire issue of conduct of officers who have obtained a warrant. Similar to other search and seizure issues, this one is eventually reduced to the practical level of just what police may or may not do concerning a person or his residence when they have a warrant. Since contacts between police and those they seek to investigate or arrest present inevitable conflict, this and similar issues will be debated for some time to come.

Criticism of the exclusionary rule and the complexity of the interpretation of the Fourth Amendment guarantee is not limited to those who realize a political benefit from the cry for law and order. Dissatisfaction extends to those whose efforts are oriented toward more effective and professional police work. As the notes to the text in this section indicate, this group includes a number of distinguished legal thinkers. They deplore the fact that relevant evidence which would prove that particular acts occurred, or in some way bear on the case at hand, is denied consideration in order to prevent violation of basic Fourth Amendment rights. The anomaly of the disregard of relevent evidence is so far inadequately defended by even the most ardent civil libertarian, and may prove the undoing of the use of the exclusionary rule, particularly in light of the *Bivens* case, and the availability of a civil action against unlawful police practices as an arguably more effective deterrent.

In the final analysis the public is entitled to protection of person and property and redress of grievances, where justified. It is the duty of the police to investigate crime and gather evidence. But the role of the courts is equally clear, to provide guidelines to insure that lawful investigation shall not become a means of contravening the rights of individuals and the public which the law and its enforcers serve.

(2) Rights of the Arrested Party

If a valid search is conducted, evidence may be uncovered which will lead to the issuance of an arrest warrant. As has been pointed out,

---

arrest conducted without knocking or other notice was permitted. The warrant would, of course, provide greater safeguards than were available in that instance.

an arrest may also occur spontancously if the officer observes a crime being committed, is told of a crime which was or is being committed,[108] or has some other substantive reason to believe an offense has been or is being committed or will occur. This brings us to the critical area of rights of arrested parties. A basic right, and one which is a safeguard for other rights, is that of right to counsel for individuals accused of certain offenses.[109]

In *Gideon v. Wainright*, decided in 1963, states were required in such cases to provide counsel for all defendants, who were unable to obtain their own.[110] And this may still be necessary even if a defendant waives this right, but does not do so, as was stated by the Court in *Minor v. United States* in 1967, with,

...an apprehension of charges, the statutory offenses included within them, the range of allowable punishment thereunder, possible defenses of the charges, circumstances in mitigation thereof, and all other facts essential to a broad understanding of the whole matter.[111]

In *Massiah v. United States,* 1963, the time when right to counsel begins was held to be after arrest and indictment, and during interrogation by police.[112] In that instance, Massiah had been indicted for illegal importation and possession of narcotics, released on bail with a co-defendant, and then tricked by the government in collusion with the co-defendant into making incriminating statements which were heard by government agents using an electronic eavesdropping device.[113] It was held that at any interrogations counsel was to be present. In this instance, the subterfuge used was considered to be a form of interrogation and investigation. The court avoided the Fourth Amendment eavesdropping issue.[114]

---

[108] The issue is complicated if officers are acting on a tip. The Supreme Court has ruled that this is permissable if the tip is from a source known by the officers to be reliable, see *Draper v. United States,* 358 *U.S.* 307 (1959).

[109] Ostensibly counsel will keep the defendant from prejudicing his case by providing information or doing things he has the right to refrain from; as indicated in *Hamilton v. Alabama,* 368 *U.S.* 52 (1961), 54: "...since rights 'may be irretrievably lost,' if not then and there asserted, as when an accused represented by counsel waives a right for strategic purposes." On the right to counsel generally, see Walter V. Schaefer: *The Suspect and Society,* Northwestern Univ. Press, Evanston, Ill., 1967.

[110] 372 *U.S.* 335 (1963) 344-45.

[111] 375 *F2d* 170 (1967).

[112] 377 *U.S.* 201 (1963).

[113] *Ibid.* at 202-03.

[114] *Ibid.* at 206-207.

In *Escobedo v. Illinois* [115] in 1963, right to counsel was insured after arrest, but prior to indictment. The court reasoned that the investigation was no longer a general inquiry into an unsolved crime.[116] Since it had focused on the defendant, he was now entitled to counsel, since, as in *Massiah,* the case had reached a "critical stage".[117] This critical stage test was expanded to include post-indictment police line-ups in *United States v. Wade.*[118] It also extends to juvenile delinquency hearings as ruled in *In re Gault.*[119]

In order to insure an awareness of rights to counsel, as well as the right to refrain from giving incriminating statements, *Miranda v. Arizona* provided that police officers read the now famous *Miranda* warning, or its equivalent, a statement of the rights of the arrested party.[120]

Many critics have labelled this treatment of "supposed criminals" overly lenient. Many people feel that police should have a freer hand in interrogation to enable them to obtain evidence needed for convictions. The assumption seems to be that only "bad" or "guilty" people are arrested, and so the legal system should be as heavy handed as necessary to bring such individuals to justice quickly. This ignores the fact that everybody is supposed to be protected from misuse of state power, besides the obvious fact that innocent defendants would receive equally short shrift with such tactics.

The Supreme Court modified the *Miranda* rule itself during the 1971 Court term by limiting its application in the well known ruling in *Harris v. New York.*[121] Here the Court said that if the trial judge is convinced that a confession obtained without first giving the *Miranda* warning was obtained without coercion, it can be admitted during the prosecution's cross-examination of the defendant in order to contradict or impeach his statements made on the witness stand. This will make defendants even more unlikely to testify in their own defense in such cases. When they do, it is hard to conceive of juries actually disregarding the factual import of their alledged confessions, considering them only as they tend to undermine the witness's credibility.

---

[115] 378 *U.S.* 478 (1963).
[116] *Ibid.* at 485.
[117] *Ibid.* at 486.
[118] 388 *U.S.* 218 (1967).
[119] 387 *U.S.* 1 (1967).
[120] 384 *U.S.* 436 (1966).
[121] 401 *U.S.* 222 (1971).

(3) Bail and Pre-trial Detention

The basic presumption that the accused is innocent until tried and convicted, and should not be confined or punished until then is the basis for the procedure of granting bail. In addition to right to counsel, to trial by jury in certain instances, to due process of law, and the intricate procedures and safeguards which that phrase implies, individuals are also protected against excessive bail by the Eighth Amendment. This guarantee lies at the heart of a current issue because of the recent passage of the *District of Columbia Omnibus Crime Control Act* which allows for preventive detention in certain instances, from the time of arrest and indictment, and continuing for sixty days.[122] The question arises whether for non-capital crimes, the Eighth Amendment implies that bail must be set.

The history of the bail system in America tells a sorry story. The fact that the well-to-do go free while the poor and indigent are held for lack of even the amount necessary to meet the ten percent of the bail set, required by the bail bondsman, is far from just. Considering that the system is designed with the intended goal of preventing flight before trial, it affords an even less justifiable form of descrimination if one acknowledges that the economic risk of the financially well off person who may be inclined to flee is further reduced if he is in fact posting only a percentage of the bond; on the other hand pursuit by bonding companies has become more of a threat to reckon with.[123]

---

[122] HR 12806 and S 2600 as reported in "Nixon Crime Control Proposals Stalled in Controversy" *Congressional Quarterly Weekly Report,* June 5, 1970, Vol. XXVIII, No. 23 p. P1496. The report gives the following qualifications for utilizing preventive detention: 1. A dangerous crime (robbery, or attempted robbery; burglary or attempted burglary; arson or attempted arson; rape; unlawful sale or distribution of drugs, if the offense is punishable by more than one year's sentence). 2. A violent crime (murder, rape, mayhem, kidnapping, robbery, burglary, voluntary manslaughter, extortion or blackmail with threats of violence, arson, assault with intent to commit any of those offenses, assault with a dangerous weapon, or conspiracy to commit any of those offenses, if punishable by more than one year's sentence) committed by a person free on bail, probation or parole, or a person convicted of a violent crime within the previous ten years. In Germany, as well as elsewhere in Europe, preventive detention, or pre-trial detention, exists where a court determines that there is a strong suspicion present that a criminal act has been committed; see "Note; Preventive Detention: A Comparison of European and United States Measures" 4 *N.Y.U. Journal of Int'l Law and Politics* 29, 294 (1971).

[123] Cf. e.g. Caleb Foote: "Coming Constitutional Crisis in Bail," 113 *Univ. of Pennsylvania Law Rev.* 959 (1965).

Under the 1966 Federal Bail Reform Act, every effort was made to avoid discrimination against indigents by providing criteria besides the posting of bail to give indication that an accused person would appear for trial.[124] Preventive detention would depart from this idea, that only those who do not seem likely to appear for trial may be held, when accused on non-capital offenses.

There are various arguments both for and against the new Act. Attorney General John Mitchell maintained in its support:

I believe that pre-trial release of potentially dangerous defendants constitutes one of the most serious factors in the present crime wave.... danger to the community must be made a significant consideration in the ultimate decision to release a suspect.[125]

The validity of such fears is questioned by a study, commissioned by Mitchell's own department, to be used in the defense of that position. The report indicated that during a four week period in 1968 only 11 % of those accused of crimes in the District of Columbia, and, who were released pending trial, were re-arrested for the same crime for which they had originally been charged. Two of every three re-arrested were charged with minor offenses. As Senator Samuel D. Ervin (Democrat, North Carolina), a major opponent of the scheme, pointed out, twenty individuals would have to be detained to restrain one potential recidivist.[126] An additional argument advanced by Senator Ervin was that the detention would occur at the wrong time, since the majority of such recidivism occurs after two months from the date of release. Opponents also argue that assurance of a speedy trial would eliminate most crimes in this category.[127]

These arguments were countered by the Administration which argued that 50 % of the crime in the District of Columbia is not reported, and since only 20 % of these reported crimes result in an arrest, fully 90 %

---

[124] 18 *U.S.C.* 3146 (a). See generally, B.D. Beaudin: "Bail in the District, What it Was and What it Will Be," 20 *American Univ. Law. Rev.* 432 (1970-71). Projects similar to that under the 1968 Bail Reform Act have been successful in several states, most notably in Illinois and California; see Note: "Tinkering With the California Bail System," 56 *Calif. Law Rev.* 1134 (1968).

[125] Cf. *Congressional Quarterly Weekly Report,* June 5, 1970, *loc. cit.,* p. 1496. See also J.N. Mitchell: "Bail Reform and the Constitutionality of Pre-trial Detention." 55 *Virginia Law Rev.* 1233 (1969); J.P. Hickey: "Preventive Detention and the Crime of Being Dangerous," 58 *Georgetown Law Journal* 287 (1969).

[126] *Ibid.* 1497.

[127] *Ibid.*

of the crimes committed by repeat offenders are not revealed by the statistics above.[128] What this means in terms of detaining those who are arrested is dubious.

The issue is complicated by the fact that judges are currently able to set relatively high bail which many defendants are unable to post. Such practices vary widely, and result in many cases in longer pre-trial detention than sixty days because of crowded court calendars. The 1966 *Bail Reform Act* was an attempt to alleviate this problem through release on one's own recognizance when a reasonable basis is provided for the expectation that a defendant will appear without having posted bail. Some indigent defendants, however, cannot provide either such reasons or the amount of bail. Yet, the new law might provide some unhoped for benefit to such individuals affected if it could guarantee a sixty days maximum detention. As it is, however, crowded court calendars make the imprisonment for those who cannot post bail much longer, as a function of an administrative problem rather than of any aspect of their case. However, practical limitations on the expected results of the *Act,* plus its inconsistency with established interpretation of the Constitution and the historic purpose of bail procedures, continues to raise difficult questions.

As has been mentioned, the fact that an individual could be held without bail, although not accused of a capital offense, raises the issue of the implication of the Eighth Amendment. In *United States v. Melville,* in 1969,[129] confinement of defendents in non-capital cases prior to trial, on the basis that they are likely to commit a crime, was not allowed under existing federal legislation. The same decision indicated that: "...the task of setting conditions for release consists exclusively of ascertaining the least onerous conditions," which will reasonably assure the appearance of the person arraigned for trial.[130] Whether the new preventive detention system is constitutional also remains unresolved.

To some extent existing vagrancy laws already allow a kind of preventive detention, however. Vagrancy laws are often vague enough that they can be used to hold a suspect on otherwise insufficient evidence.[131]

---

[128] Cf. Jack Landau; "Preventive Detention: Public Safeguard," *Trial,* Dec.-Jan. 1969-70 (pp. 23-25) p. 23.

[129] 306 *F.Supp.* 124 (1969).

[130] Cf. 18 *U.S.C.* § 3146 (a).

[131] In a recent challenge to the loose construction of such laws, the Supreme Court struck down a loitering ordinance which had been applied to keep young

Generally, such laws prohibit public idleness or loitering without visible purpose or at unusual hours. In *State v. Grenz,* for instance, a burglary suspect was held on a vagrancy charge.[132] The Supreme Court of the State of Washington sustained this practice, saying:

The obvious intent of the legislature in enacting subdivision 8 of the vagrancy statute was to enable law enforcement officers to keep the streets clear, at late and unusual hours of the night, of those persons who by reason of being bent upon serious mischief, theft, or burglary, have no visible or lawful mission in the locality.[133]

The logical, and yet worrisome aspect of such laws is that they allow the detention of persons for something less than probable cause for a specific violation. The unfortunate possibility is that when one of those caught in such a net is not guilty of any specific offense, he may still be guilty of the crime of being no more than suspicious. How does one prove he was not being suspicious when the time and place of one's arrest are *prima facie* evidence of his guilt?

C.   APPROACHES TO CRIMINAL LAW REFORM

(1) *The Theory and The Form of Correction*

There are four basic theories for what the punishment provided for in the penal law is supposed to accomplish. [These are: deterrence (divided into general deterrence and special or individual deterrence); restraint of dangerous persons in order to protect society; resocialization or rehabilitation; and retribution.][134] The last two of these require qualification:

people from gathering at a fountain in downtown Cincinnati [*Coates et al. v. City of Cincinnati,* 402 *U.S.* 611 (1971)]. The ordinance made it a criminal offense for "three or more persons to assemble...on any of the sidewalks...and there conduct themselves in a manner annoying to persons passing by...". The Court held that on its face it violates "the due process standard of vagueness and the constitutional right of free assembly and association". While loitering is not vagrancy as such, considering the numbers, the means, and the publicity advantage of young people and their defenders today, and the fact that they often have nothing to do which is more pressing, they might be the best advance guard for testing the constitutionality of such laws. All too often the vagueness of present laws is interpreted by policemen as license to move along citizens who happen to be out at late hours, rather than protecting them from being accosted on the streets.

[132] 26 *Wash. 2d* 764, 175 P.2d 633 (1946).

[133] *Ibid.*

[134] Cf. e.g. Gardiner: "The purposes of Criminal Punishment," 21 *Modern Law Rev.* 117 (1958), pp. 117-23; Gardiner adds the category of "expiation and atone-

resocialization or rehabilitation is considered by some to be something
other than punishment, and if it alone were the goal of commitment
to a correctional institution, no doubt the notion of punishment could
be discarded altogether.[135] An exclusively retributive policy is generally
rejected today as a primitive reaction which reflects as much on those
who exact it, as on those being punished.[136] If one rejects the retribution
theory as a basis for punishment, the controversy becomes one between

ment". This rests on the moralistic notion that society also has a duty to punish
sin. Retribution, he feels, is simple revenge, which is somewhat difficult to justify
since a balance must be achieved between the crime and the punishment. Crimes
defy quantification in terms of years in prison or fines. Gardiner questions the
possibility of general deterrence, and completely rejects individual deterrent
effects—a prison sentence is a "passport to the underworld". Gardiner favors
rehabilitation as a single goal. Johannes Andenaes: "General Preventive Effects of
Punishment," 114 *Univ. of Pennsylvania Law Rev.* 949 (1966), pp. 949-960, says
that although general deterrence clearly does not work for hardened criminals, it
may work for others. He says, in any case, that deterrent effect cannot be altogether
disregarded; that deterrent theories do not urge logically harsher penalties for widespread and hard to detect crimes since crime is not to be deterred at all costs (one
criticism of this theory is that if it were followed logically, extremely harsh penalties
would have greater effect than more moderate ones); and that "even the simplest
kind of common sense indicates that the degree of risk of detection and conviction
is of paramount importance to preventive effects of penal law" (at 960). See also
his: "The Moral or Educative Influence of Criminal Law", 27 *Journal of Social
Issues* 17 (1971).

[135] Cf. e.g. A. C. Ewing: "A Study of Punishment II: Punishment as viewed
by the Philosopher," 21 *Canadian Bar Rev.* 102 (1943): Ewing questions whether
rehabilitation can be called punishment. He regards resocialization measures
as another category from those designed to punish individuals (p. 111). Punishment
is simply a way to point out and impress as to the "wrongness" of certain acts,
and has little deterrent effect according to Ewing. See also F.A. Allen: "Criminal
Justice, Legal Values, and the Rehabilitative Ideal," 50 *Journal of Criminal Law,
Criminology and Police Science* 266 (1959), p. 230. Allen indicates that since
any isolation of the individual from society "presents to any community the most
extreme issues of the proper relation of the individual citizen to state power,"
such measures are punishment whether penal theorists choose to call them that or not.

[136] Cf. e.g. Gardiner: *loc cit.,* pp. 118-119: "...the theory of expiation rests
upon the premise that it is man's duty to punish sin—a legacy from the times of
taboo breaking." And at p. 120: "...to allow feelings of hatred and revenge to
enter into the consideration of what is a just punishment is to substitute passion
for reason;" see also Ewing: *loc. cit.* p. 105: "Few philosophers would, therefore,
defend a thoroughgoing retributive view today, but there has been a considerable
reaction, how extensive is difficult to judge, in favor of a theory which would
still be partly retributive." Ewing does not reject retribution altogether; it is, for
him, a logical end to the moral-legal force which he feels justifies any prohibition.

those who accept deterrent effects and stress the protection of society through restraint of dangerous individuals, and those who would prefer a system directed exclusively towards resocialization. However, even those who stress deterrents and restraint would encourage some effort toward rehabilitation secondarily, and many of those emphasizing rehabilitation do not deny the existence of some deterrent effect as well as the efficacy of restraint in certain instances.[137]

Considering the state of prisons throughout America today, none of the goals is fully achieved, and even restraint is effective only for the society outside the prison; the inmates themselves are relatively unprotected from each other, and depending on the prison, from attack by the guards. Certainly where crowding, homosexual attack, brutality and intimidation are usual occurrences, the typical prisoner is far more concerned about his psychological and physical survival than about any of the goals which are reputedly reasons for his detention. As Teeters describes the situation:

Brutality, regimentation, despair (experienced by inmates and staff), lack of funds, political interference (commissioners picked through politics rather than through experience and continued in office despite pedestrian performance), poor physical conditions, wholesale homosexuality, exposed not long ago in a Philadelphia prison —not unique, but actually, the usual—and many other unwholesome conditions exist almost everywhere. Indeed, the prison presents an abysmal graveyard of blighted expectations which shows little promise of improvement.[138]

---

[137] Andenaes: *loc. cit.,* p. 951, also note 1. Andenaes makes a qualified reference to instances in which general deterrence operates. He deplores the lack of research in this area (p. 952), and the belief that no supporting data exists on the subject (p. 973). One point overlooked by those urging pure rehabilitation, and one which Andenaes makes, is the possibility of deterrence as a by-product of such measures (p. 971). Andenaes feels, however, that such programs are based on imprecise methods, and should be used only on certain categories of offenders. He goes on to describe research which might be done in this area (p. 473). See also F. A. Allen: *loc. cit.,* p. 229: Allen makes his way through the jargon of rehabilitation, and recognizes essential issues and factors existing in this area: "...the language of therapy has frequently provided a formidable obstacle to a realistic analysis of the conditions that confront us." For a rehabilitative view which rejects deterrent effect, see Barnes and Teeters: *Criminology,* p. 338; see also Gardiner: *loc. cit.,* pp. 121-126. Gardiner presents a body of evidence which he feels indicates the futility of individual and general deterrence. He feels deterrence, when it operates, is more a result of social disapprobation.

[138] N. K. Teeters: "State of Prisons in the United States," 33 *Federal Probation* 18 (1969), p. 19. Teeters is a harsh critic of prison systems, and a strong advocate of a rehabilitative system.

Unfortunately, creative efforts to change this situation,[139] based on one or another theory of correction, have been on such a small scale that the prison systems within the United States remain largely unreformed. With conditions as they are, whether one chooses deterrence and restraint or rehabilitation, it makes little practical difference.

Perhaps one beneficial result of the current social turmoil in the United States may be to lead eventually to penal reform, once the sons and daughters of the comfortable and respectable "Middle Americans" (and maybe one or two of them—as the reports of curious bystanders being swept up in police sweeps increases) begin returning home from unexpected "busts" or civil disobedience prestige arrests in the jails long kept respectably far from their awareness. Once those who count have seen and come back from the degrading and debilitating conditions of our "houses of correction", perhaps there will be a chance for reform in this side of American life too. The problems of penal reform, we will surely find is much more serious and demanding than the problems of reform of the criminal law itself. But that is another story.

(2) Sentencing and Grading of Punishment

There are three basic sentencing systems in the United States. Many feel that none of these has proven satisfactory.[140] One system provides that the judge first determine whether or not there shall be commitment to prison in a particular instance, and a board appointed by the state then actually determines its duration within the guidelines provided by statute. In most such states only a maximum term is prescribed. This has been sharply criticized as granting too much authority to a non-

---

[139] Cf. Barnes and Teeters: *op. cit.*, part IV, "The Resocialization of the Offender in the Community," pp. 543-584, and particularly, "Substitutes for Imprisonment," p. 592; most innovations up to 1959 are discussed here; for an analysis of the phenomenon of the halfway house, see Hobbs and Osman: "From the Prison to the Community: A Case Study," 13 *Crime and Delinquency* 317, (1967) pp. 321-322.

[140] For an analysis of each of these systems see: Sol Rubin: "Allocation of Authority in Sentencing-Correctional Decisions," 45 *Texas Law Rev.* 455, 1967, esp. pp. 455-463. Mr. Rubin is a strong advocate of the judge set maximum term, and cites in detail the reasons provided in the text supporting its adoption. See also "Statutory Structures for Sentencing Felons to Prison," 60 *Columbia Law Rev.* 1134 (1960). This presents very extensive analysis of sentencing structures and systems as they existed in 1960. Particularly useful is a chart indicating the system employed in each of the states (between pp. 1144-45).

judicial body—the sentencing or parole board—in an area supposedly protected by the Eighth Amendment to the Constitution. In addition, the offender often has the feeling that little attention is paid to the question of sentencing, a question which may well be more crucial to him than his actual conviction. Such boards, at least in California and Washington, may also alter sentences and determine eligibility for parole.

A second system allows the jury to set the sentence within a minimum and a maximum length fixed by statute. This method has defects as well. Juries either do not have vital pre-sentencing information, or, because of their size, are less effective in integrating and using such information. Judges should have had more experience in such matters, and be better able to make the sentence fit the offense and the offender. Judges, as professional men, ought also to be less swayed by emotion than the average jury. Some argue, further, that, because they deal with a large number of similar cases, judges can reduce the disparities between sentences; however, experience in jurisdictions in which judges set sentences has not necessarily borne this out.[141]

Arguments favoring jury sentencing center on the possibility, at least in rural counties, that the jurors will have personal knowledge of the defendants, and that twelve men will be fairer than a single judge.[142] Considering the accuracy of information available to typical members of such communities, the first of these points is hard to accept. And whether twelve heads are better than one is also debatable.

In most states, a judge sets a maximum sentence under the maximum allowed by statute. The parole board then has the power to shorten this term at their discretion. There are many who consider this the most satisfactory system, for the following reasons: First, it allows parole when the board feels the individual is capable of returning to society. When a minimum sentence is set, this is not possible until that minimum has been served.[143] Second, under the maximum sentence

---

[141] See "Appellate Review of Primary Sentencing Decisions: A Connecticut Case Study," 69 *Yale Law Journal* 1453 (1960). This study reveals disparities among sentences appealed in Connecticut, and the reluctance of the appellate body to change more than a small fraction of these. See also Sol Rubin: "Disparity and Equality of Sentences—A Constitutional Challenge," 40 *Federal Rules Decisions* 55 (1967), especially pp. 56-58. See also Wechsler: "Sentencing, Correction and the Model Penal Code," 109 *Univ. of Pennsylvania Law Rev.* 465 (1960-61).

[142] Cf. Sol Rubin: *loc. cit.,* pp. 459-460.

[143] For a discussion of this point, see Sol Rubin: *Ibid.,* pp. 463-464. See also Will C. Turnbladh: "A Critique of the *Model Penal Code* Sentencing Proposals," 23

system, the convict knows the maximum time he might serve, and realizes that earlier parole is possible for good behavior [144] and is, therefore, hopefully motivated to try for parole. Third, so far as the sentencing procedure is concerned, the judge has access to the pre-sentencing report, and the possibility of weighing it within the context of his experience.

Unfortunately, this system has not proved wholly satisfactory either, despite its favorable aspects. In most cases there is no way for the convict to discover the contents of the pre-sentencing report, although pressure for a partial reform in this area is building.[145] Judges are not required to provide a rationale for a particular sentencing decision. And, finally, only eleven states allow any appeal from the sentencing decision as long as the sentence is within the limits set by statute.[146] As a consequence, despite the judicial nature of the process, convicted persons have no way to learn how sentences in their cases were determined. This can be particularly distressing to the individual and counterproductive to the system if the convict hears about others in prison who are serving a shorter term for the same offense.

All of this brings us to the essential issue that with fifty-one separate state jurisdictions and hundreds of judicial districts and levels with thousands of judges, there is no way to enforce a semblance of uniform sentencing. As one critic points out:

Law and Contemporary Problems 544 (1958) at 548: One of the truly destructive elements in present day sentencing practice is the imposition of minimum terms, especially those which, at the discretion of the sentencing judge may (in some states) be inordinately high. It must be recognized that a high minimum term limits parole flexibility and handicaps the entire correctional process. See in addition: "Statutory Structures for Sentencing Felons to Prison," 60 *Columbia Law Rev.* 1140 (1960).

[144] See Turnbladh: *op. cit.,* p. 548; see also Rubin: *loc. cit.,* p. 462.

[145] Frank J. Remington: "Pre-sentencing Reports: Should Secrecy be Removed?" 3 *Trial* 16 (1966), p. 16. Remington points out the concern expressed by judges that the sources used to obtain the individuals pre-sentencing report should not be disclosed. The fear is that those individuals giving unfavorable but necessary information concerning the defendant could either suffer reprisals or be intimidated into silence. See also the *Proposal of the Advisory Committee on Federal Rules of Criminal Procedure,* Rule 32 (c), which as Remington points out, guards against this by keeping sources of information confidential. This safeguard was also incorporated into the A.L.I. *Model Penal Code,* Proposed Official Draft, 1967, § 7.07 (5), which recommends disclosure of "factual contents" only.

[146] Cf. 69 *Yale Law Journal, loc. cit.,* p. 1453.

It is not surprising that such discretion should give rise to great abuse. It was intended that disparity of sentence for the same offense would result from the wide range of dispositions made possible, for individualization required in treatment, but the disparity has been so great, so apparently illogical, and so prejudicial to the rehabilitation of offenders that demands for reform have been widespread.[147]

Thus the creditable ambition of a system capable of individualization of treatment has also led to arbitrary and unacceptable disparities. The situation is further complicated, Wechsler protests, because state legislatures have "...run wild, both from the standpoint of the size and number of sentencing regulations they have imposed." [148] So while the judge set maximum sentence is only the least undesireable system, none of the three alternative schemes used in this country for determining the length of prison terms has provided a satisfactory solution to the problems of sentencing.

One suggested reform is the *Model Sentencing Act*.[149] Under that proposal, a judge would have discretion as to the maximum sentence he imposes for a dangerous convict. This might include up to a statutory maximum of thirty years, considerably less than the statutory maximums allowable in many jurisdictions at the present time. A person who is not dangerous could be sentenced to no more than five years. Again, this is under the minimum that is allowed in most jurisdictions now. "Dangerous" and "non-dangerous" are defined according to criteria provided by the act. However, the judge would have to justify his classifying a person as dangerous, and disclose why a particular sentence was imposed. One might hope that the requirement for more careful specification would oblige more judicious consideration.

The *Model Sentencing Act* would also provide judges with the option of deferring conviction and imposing probation. If the defendant successfully fulfilled the terms of that probation, he would have no conviction on his record.

The A.L.I. *Model Penal Code* (Proposed Official Draft, 1962) also includes a proposal for sentencing process and structure.[150] Minimum

---

[147] "Due Process and Legislative Standards in Sentencing," 101 *Univ. of Pennsylvania Law Rev.*, 258 (1952-53).

[148] Wechsler: *loc. cit.* 473.

[149] Advisory Council of Judges of the National Council on Crime and Delinquency: *Model Sentencing Act*.

[150] A.L.I.: *Model Penal Code*, Proposed Official Draft (1962) §§ 6.06, Alt. 6.06, 6.07; for parole requirements see § 6.10: These are also controversial because they provide for a separate parole term which, it is believed, will lengthen the period of

as well as maximum sentences would be fixed. In section 6.06 sentences for felonies of the first degree are prescribed for a minimum sentence of between one and ten years, the maximum would be life imprisonment. For felonies of the second degree, the minimum would be set at between one and three years, and the maximum at ten years. For felonies of the third degree, the minimum would be between one and two years and the maximum five years. Obviously, a person serving a sentence for a felony of the first degree might serve less time than someone convicted of a felony of the third degree, supposedly a lesser offense. The degree of a felony is determined by the *mens rea* of each defendant as well as the gravity of his act.

An alternative section retains the minimum described above, but narrows the maximum allowed to either life imprisonment, or twenty years, or less. Anyone sentenced to anything less than life imprisonment would come under this twenty year maximum.

The *Model Penal Code* sections have been strongly criticized. Some feel that the terms are simply too harsh.[151] As suggested above, others

imprisonment and parole since boards may be reluctant to exercise their authority and impose an entirely new parole sentence, and when they do, will impose an unusually long one. The authority and procedure of the court and board is outlined in Article 7, of the same draft of the *Model Penal Code:* Concerning the separate parole sentence see 60 *Columbia Law Rev., loc. cit.,* 1143. The opposing view presented here, suggests that a separate sentence without a maximum provided by the original prison term will allow a parole period to be terminated when the board considers the parolee ready, rather than at a time set by the trial judge in his post-conviction sentence.

[151] Cf. e.g. Hermann Mannheim: "Comparative Sentencing Practice," 23 *Law and Contemporary Problems* 557 (1958), Mannheim provides a broad study of trends in sentencing in Western European countries over the past half century. He also provides reasons for leniency or severity which could be applied to the situation in the United States: (1) the state of criminal law—the variety which it offers in the choice of sanctions and the scope it leaves to judicial discretion by providing minimum and maximum penalties (2) Other forms of legislative guidance regarding choice of sanctions; (3) sources of information made available to the courts on the background of the offender by mandatory or discretionary pre-sentence inquiries; (4) the views of judges and magistrates on the value of available sanctions and their philosophy of punishment; (5) guidance by courts of appeal or cassation and the influence of ministerial circulars or public prosecutors and counsel for the defense; (6) the state of crime and economic conditions at a given time in a certain area; (7) the state of public opinion concerning crime and punishment, and the influence of the press; and (8) the teachings of criminology and penology and research in these fields. See also Turnbladh: *op. cit.,* p. 545. Turnbladh cites Weihofen in *The Urge to Punish:* as stating "...it is time we

oppose the minimum proposed as an added restraint in cases when a felon might be eligible for earlier parole.[152] The criticism can also be made that no provision is included for either written findings or appeal,[153] although this could responsibly be left to change through procedural reform. Although the *Model Penal Code* sections are a disappointment to many reformers, they strike a balance somewhere in the middle of practices contained in the various state codes today. For this reason they are probably more likely to be adopted in an era when many call for minimum sentences and more restrictive parole requirements. Although not satisfactory to the reform-minded, the sections present a coherent formulation free of the plethora of restrictions and disparities found in most state codes.

There are additional problems concerning sentencing in the United States. At times, sentences are compounded when each aspect of a single criminal act is tried as a separate criminal offense.[154] For instance, the sale of a marijuana cigarette may also bring charges of illegal possession of narcotics, or an act causing death may violate a number of homocide statutes. There is also the questionable practice of punish-

Americans realized that we have probably the most ferocious penal policy in the whole civilized world" (p. 148). Weihofen cites the retention of capital punishment as evidence. Further indication is the fact that in most Western European Countries there has been an absolute drop in the prison population (see Mannheim: *op. cit.*, pp. 562-582). In the United States the prison population has been increasing faster than the general population has, indicating according to Turnbladh (*op. cit.* p. 545) not only an increase in crime, but also a severe sentence structure. Cf. also Paul W. Tappan: "Sentencing Under the *Model Penal Code*," 23 *Law and Contemporary Problems* 528 (1958), p. 536, with sentences imposed in Western European countries as indicated by *Mannheim: loc. cit.*, pp. 562-582.

[152] Cf. notes 140 and 143 above.

[153] Cf. e.g. D.A. Thomas: "Sentencing—the Case for Reasoned Decisions," *Criminal Law Rev.* 243 (1963), p. 243; also 69 *Yale Law Journal, op. cit.*, p. 1453. The first of these two articles presents many of the arguments for written findings and second indicates the status of appeals systems in the United States today.

[154] For a discussion of the matter of multiplication of statutory penalties see: "Consecutive Sentences in Single Prosecutions: Judicial Multiplication of Statutory Penalties," 67 *Yale Law Journal* 916 (1958); see also, Remington and Joseph: "Charging, Convicting and Sentencing the Multiple Offender," *Wisconsin Law Rev.* 528 (1961); this provides a detailed description of the situation in Wisconsin. Finally, *Model Penal Code*, Proposed Official Draft, 1964: § 7.06. (1) "Sentences for more than one crime when multiple sentences of imprisonment are imposed on a defendant for more than one crime...such multiple sentences shall run concurrently or consecutively as the court determines." The section restricts consecutive sentences to those totaling one year or less.

ing the recidivist more harshly than the first offender.[155] And the entire area of sentencing youthful offenders uncovers the surprising fact that for many acts, young persons are liable for longer terms than adults would be if convicted of the same offense.[156] These difficulties, together with those already considered, demonstrate that sentencing structures and procedural matters are as clearly in need of reform as many of the titles themselves. Because of many politicians' fears of appearing too soft on crime and because it is often assumed that most people are probably strict adherents of retributive justice, there is little hope at present of a successful movement toward a realistic reassessment of gradings of punishment, major strides or comprehensive changes in this area are exceedingly difficult. Yet, because of the large number of defendants who plead guilty, the primary issue—particularly as far as the defendant himself is concerned—is as often the sentence as the conviction.

(3) Full-scale Reform vs. Piecemeal Revision: American Attempts at Recodification

The controversy between those who believe that law should essentially follow, not lead, and that it should do so slowly, in response to clearly formulated social sentiment, and those who believe that the law should be a determined agent in the creation of new norms is one of the recurrent themes in the history of legal thought.[157]

---

[155] Turnbladh: op. cit., pp. 546-547. For an explanation of the Model Penal Code, Proposed Official Draft, 1964, § 7.06, on this point, see Wechsler: op. cit. pp. 480-81.

[156] These are not only youthful offenders (those under 16 or 18 years of age in most states) but also young adult offenders. They are out of the juvenile court's jurisdiction, but still as Wechsler points out "within the formative years of character and personality development" (ibid. p. 489).

Under the A.L.I. Model Youth Correction Act, 1940, a design for a separate court system was provided for, and has been adopted in ten states. Turnbladh questions the effectiveness of this (op. cit., pp. 552-53). He cites the superfluous nature of such a system, and the fact that it almost invariably suffers from a lack of financial support; also that within a few modifications, regular criminal courts could perform these same duties. The problem of disparity of sentencing for young offenders may result in anomalies like those reported in California or Minnesota where maximums imposed may be longer than those allowed for adults. Indeterminate reformatory sentences may have the same result (see Rubin: loc. cit. p. 466).

[157] W.G. Friedmann: Law in a Changing Society, Univ. of California Press, Berkeley, Calif., 1959, p. 3.

Since the time of Savigny, these schools have been identified with what was supposed to be the gradual responsive legislation and case law tradition on the one hand, and the systematic codification of the law on the other. And if one accepts this dichotomy, then American criminal law is commonly regarded to have emerged through the more gradual process. As one commentator indicates:

Continental Europe has followed the Roman tradition and has consistently favored codification; but the Anglo-American world, in spite of such scholars as Bentham, Livingston, Macaulay, Field, and Stephan, has consistently opposed it.[158]

Historically there have been significant efforts at codification both in the United States and Great Britain. The literature of Anglo-American legal history makes this aspect of American legal development clear. And the partisans of systematic codification have not been wanting. In the view of some commentators, theirs is even the dominant tendency:

The dominant view of legal specialists has been that the legislature should assume the major responsibility for making basic policy decisions in the field of criminal law.[159]

In Europe there is a long tradition of codification and systematic legal science, and from a European point of view, the overwhelming impression of Anglo-American law is one of case law. In a relatively recent commentary on American criminal law for Europeans, Honig applied a generalization, Wieacker had once made for Roman law, to American legal experience:

...it is essentially the law of judges, and the spirit visible is not of legal science, but jurisprudence.[160]

Legal science in this sense is used as a synonym for the German *Rechtswissenschaft,* which Wieacker, and Honig, apparently consider to be a more systematic, or "scientific", method in contrast to the development of case law jurisprudence, or the reasoning of judges,

---

[158] Frederick Cohen: "Criminal Law, Legislation and Legal Scholarship," 16 *Journal of Legal Education* 253 (1964), p. 253.

[159] Frank Remington and Victor Rosenblum: "The Criminal Law and the Legislative Process," 1960 *Univ. of Ill. Law Forum* 451, (1960), p. 451.

[160] Richard M. Honig: "Das Amerikanische Strafrecht," in *Das Ausländische Strafrecht der Gegenwart,* Duncker und Humblot, Berlin, 1962, Vol. (pp. 15-262), p. 15.

as the word is used in this instance. This impression of what the law
is like in the common law countries can, however, lead to a basic
misapprehension of the role of *stare decisis,* which ostensibly provides
a continuing guideline, or precedent, for the situation before the judge.
This impression is often weak on representing the ability of such a
"case law" system to allow for basic departures from doctrines laid
down by precedent particularly in this present era which is often
characterized as one of judicial activism. In certain recent developments
in American law—such as the Supreme Court's determination of the
demands of due process in protecting the rights of arrested parties
and in clarifying First Amendment liberties—it is possible to see a more
"systematic" result brought about by judges than might have been
readily possible by legislation. This is a development which probably
would not have been thought foreseeable by European scholars without
a systematic *"Rechtswissenschaft".*

The incredible diversity in the American situation is also nettlesome
to those who are accustomed to a more systematic, universally applicable
law. With fifty-one separate state jurisdictions, this diversity is reflected
both in the criminal codes and in the case law. Viewed from traditional
American perspective, however, many consider this diversity to be
beneficial evolution of legal norms in terms of local values and needs.[161]

As already indicated, there have been attempts at recodification of
state codes within the United States. One such document which has
been regarded as a brilliant work of legal scholarship, but was rejected
by the state for which it was intended was Livingston's Code of 1824
for Louisiana. Another example the Field Code of 1865, was adopted
in New York state, and had a decided effect on the drafting of codes
in other states. Louisiana eventually did adopt a new code draft in
1942; Wisconsin adopted one in 1956; Illinois followed in 1961; and
Minnesota in 1964.[162] These were patterned substantially after the
American Law Institute's (A.L.I.) *Model Penal Code.* New York completed it's first comprehensive revision of the Field Code in 1965.[163]
California, Connecticut, Delaware, Georgia, Kentucky, Maryland, New

---

[161] Cf. e.g. Herbert Wechsler: "The Challenge of the Model Penal Code," 65
Harvard Law Rev. 1097 (1952) pp. 1131-32.

[162] *Louisiana Rev. Stat.* (West's) 14:1-14:201; *Wisconsin Criminal Code,* Laws
of 1955 ch. 696, effective July 1, 1956 *Illinois Ann. Stat.* ch. 38 (Smith-Hurd,
1961); *Minn. Stat. Ann.* 609.01-618.21 (1964).

[163] *New York Sess. Laws* 1965 Chs. 1030-1031.

Mexico, and Texas are at present in the process of developing comprehensive penal code revisions.[164]

Although such individual state efforts are naturally undertaken separately, there are a number of unifying factors which not only shape the content of the reforms along similar lines, but bring some considerable uniformity to criminal law throughout the United States. Supreme Court decisions play an important role in this process. As Ernst Freund pointed out fifty years ago:

> The great opportunity of the courts lies in construction. Construction is essentially supplementary legislation, and it was the recognition of this fact that has made codifiers jealous of the judicial power to interpret, which they sought to supercede by prescribing a recourse to the source of legislative authority in cases of ambiguity and doubt. Statutory construction is, however, inseparable from adjudication, and ultimately the courts are sure to regain and retain it.[165]

Freund was proven right since the courts have lived through an extremely active interpretative period since that was written. But there is not only the direct effect of such high court decisions in ordering various lower courts or law officers to adhere to their decisions for us to consider. One must also realize that those drafting the new codes review what the courts have decided in certain areas, and then include appropriate applications, or codifications, of these decisions in their new codes.[166]

Decisions of state judges also have an effect, and the decisions of judges in certain key states are invoked throughout the country on occasions when similar problems arise. This interaction of the judicial pronouncements of various states provides for a national judicial dialogue on particular problems, and from such comparisons and emphases comes greater uniformity in case law.[167]

---

[164] See concerning various revisions, Bowman: "The Illinois Criminal Code of 1961," 50 *Ill. Bar Journal* 34 (1961); "Drafting a New Penal Law for New York," 18 *Buffalo Law Rev.* 251 (1968-1969); Pirsig: "Proposed Minnesota Revised Criminal Code," 47 *Minn. Law Rev.* 417 (1963). A. H. Sherry: "Penal Code Revision Project-Progress Report," 43 *State Bar Journal* 900 (1965).

[165] Ernst Freund: *Standards of American Legislation,* 2nd ed., University of Chicago Press, Chicago, 1965, p. 275.

[166] Cf. Schwartz: "Criminal Law Revision Through a Legislative Commission—The New York Experience," 18 *Buffalo Law Rev.* 215, Interview with Richard Bartlett, Chairman of the Temporary Commission on Revision of the Penal Law and Criminal Code.

[167] Cf. B. J. George „A Comparative Analysis of the new Penal Laws of New York and Michigan," 18 *Buffalo Law Rev.* 233 (1968-69) p. 249.

One must also consider the predominantly national outlook of leading scholars in criminal law. Even when focusing on a particular state's problems, they generally review developments which parallel it in other states. American legal scholars do not, of course, have the direct influence on judicial decisions and legislation which their European counterparts have had. In Europe legal scholars are commonly cited in interpretation and development of legal doctrine.[168] John Kaplan points to an important difference between the European and American situation:

> In contrast with the Continent, England and the United States have very few professors of criminal law. Radzinowicz indicates that in Italy, France, Germany, and Austria,—with a multiplicity of courts and sources of law, and without the doctrine of *stare decisis*—the legal scholars could move in and claim a degree of importance never attained in England and the United States.[169]

Some change in this situation has occurred with the naming of prominent law professors to various state criminal code revision commissions. But the recent example of California has shown that if their proposals seem too novel or arouse moralistic sensibilities they may be fired by the legislators. It is questionable how much influence legal scholars may have on commissions unless they have constituencies of their own, special patronage, or exceptional persuasive ability. In the case of the recent New York state revision only one law professor was included on the commission and the chairman was a former state legislator. Few controversial changes were suggested, however necessary they may or may not have been. But, passage was better assured through this strategy. In New York, the approach was far more to provide a new structure for the code, and to eliminate contradictions and duplications, leaving controversial, substantive areas to the legislature itself.[170] Considering the social and political implications of matters such as abortion and homosexuality, it may be that politically sensitive state legislators will themselves be better able to revise the law in terms of what is acceptable to a majority of the population in these critical areas.

---

[168] Cf. Cohen: *loc. cit.*, p. 262. For an informative discussion of "the wholesome influence" of continental scholars on American criminal law, see G.O.W. Mueller; *Crime Law and the Scholar*, London, Heinemann Educational Books Ltd., 1969, pp. 133-37.

[169] John Kaplan: *Marijuana—The New Prohibition*, World Publishing Company, Cleveland, 1970, pp. 370-72.

[170] Cf. Schwartz: *loc. cit.*, p. 214.

Legal scholars do have another kind of influence, however, insofar as they provide comparisons and evaluations in terms of developments in other countries. In the United States, developments in England enjoy particular attention. One need only consider the influence of the discussions surrounding the *Wolfenden Report* and the legalization of abortion, to realize that evaluation of such foreign developments can be even more effective than original, but only theoretical, contributions.

Finally, there are purely political or public media influences to be considered in the climate of legal development. Nationally circulated magazines, national television news programs, and radio broadcasts have a general impact which not only produces a response to matters of national interest, but keeps that interest alive, circulates the most widely accepted views on such matters, and at times creates the interest and legitimizes certain viewpoints almost single-handedly. National pressure groups have a similar impact: Both the Catholic Church and conservative Protestant ones have, for example, played a dramatic role in the formulation of abortion laws in all of the states, although their influence in this area seems to be waning; and the National Rifle Association goes so far as to mount political and defamatory campaigns against the proponents of gun control legislation.

There is a further example of collective scholarship which must be mentioned separately because of its considerable but specialized influence. The American Law Institute's *Model Penal Code*, begun shortly after the end of World War II, is considered at one time or another by all who are involved in redrafting a state code. As has been pointed out, the *Model Penal Code* is not expected to be adopted in its entirely,[171] it is a model which legislators and revision commission members can turn to in their discussion of various provisions. As was indicated in a study of the development of the recent New York state revision, the code was used for certain sections, but rejected for others.[172] Its importance may be more that it raises the central issues involved in each section, rather than in any perfection it has achieved in the sections it includes. It also has been a significant force adding to general support for recodification throughout the United States.

---

[171] Cf. e.g. Wechsler: *loc. cit.*, p. 1130.
[172] Cf. Richard H. Kuh: "A Prosecutor Considers the *Model Penal Code*," 63 *Columbia Law Rev.* 608 (1968-69), p. 630.

The code has been attacked by some who feel that it proposes sections which few legislatures can seriously consider.[173] Although full-scale adoption is unlikely anywhere that is not a fatal defect. It is hard to imagine that a purely non-political document would have much chance of full-scale acceptance by a political body. Yet, the model serves as a systematic outline of the consensus of modern criminal law opinion. As George Desson and Harold Lasswell point out:

> The legal counselor may be working with an assembly or a committee in which many diverging views must be dealt with—differing conceptions of the common good, and differing degrees of selfless devotion to that good.... There is no drug capable of imbuing a trance state in the seasoned politician (or the unseasoned for that matter) by which he becomes a dispassionate spokesman for the common good.[174]

Kaplan and his colleagues fired by the California state legislature after their consultant body recommended legalizing marijuana (see Chapter III: B, page 149f. below) found this out through bitter experience. And since politicians and state legislators have far greater access to, and experience with, the media which shape public opinion, it is unlikely that the voice of the legal scholar, however reasoned, will soon dominate the public discussions in this area.

But systematic and logical attempts at recodification remain necessary and will continue to. For in the words of Roscoe Pound:

> It is futile to expect that the preliminary work of searching for, organizing, and making available data required for law-making, judicial law finding, and administrative enforcement will do itself. Nor may it be done by the old machinery of legislative committees working under pressure at the crisis of law-making, of courts deciding controversies on local fragments of national questions, under limitations of jurisdiction, venue, parties, and of administrative tribunals treating every case as unique. Even more, it is futile to expect sound results from research done to order for some special interest, or done in a commercial or partisan spirit.[175]

As Pound's statement reveals, there are a great number of influences on the lawmaking process in the United States. Some of these are

---

[173] Cf. Schwartz: *loc. cit.*

[174] George Desson and Harold Lasswell: "Public Order Under the Law: The Role of Advisor Draftsman in the Formulation of Codes or Constitutions," 65 *Yale Law Journal* 174 (1965), p. 175.

[175] Roscoe Pound: *The Formative Era of American Law*, Little, Brown and Company, Boston, 1938, p. 71.

brought to bear on redrafting criminal codes from time to time. And the success met by these actions is just as variable as the circumstances from which they arise.[176]

The substance of the law can be changed drastically by such efforts, or this task may be left to state legislatures. Such recodification at whatever level it occurs, may or may not have an effect on crime. It may, however, improve the law, or imbue it with further moralistic provisions which will be imposed on those with differing conceptions of what is acceptable behavior. If the work is done well, however, it will result in a streamlining of the code in question. Part of being free is believing oneself able to be free. But part of being free to make laws is the feeling that one ought to make laws for all occasions—some of which are not necessarily governable by law. So if all men are to be able to believe themselves to be free, some may have to give up making some laws which often have no effect but to sooth the consciences of the lawmakers, for having made them. Basic guarantees can make men free. But basic morals laws do not often succeed to make men moral. In a society whose constitution is libertarian, whose stated political principles are characterized by tolerance, and whose citizens represent such wide diversity, individual freedom becomes necessary lattitude for maintaining the social fabric without constant conflict between the individual and the authority of the state.

---

[176] Walter O. Weyrauch discusses one of the most pervasive if unintended sources of distortion, introduced through the use of commentaries and citations drawn upon to support arguments and conclusions both in lawyers' briefs and judicial decisions. Dependence upon unverified citations makes the West Publishing Co. into a quasi-codifier of American case law, as a result of the influence of their standard reference works:

It is not unlikely that a real examination of the precedents occurs only rarely. This system can continue to function relatively without difficulty, despite the steadily increasing inflation of precedents. Basicly it is a matter of a kind of private codification, which still refers to the precedents although they slowly lose their importance. As a result it is not much a question of exactitude any more, nor when the precedent was set, nor in which state.

(*Zum Gesellschaftsbild des Juristen: eine vergleichende Studie über die subjektiven Faktoren im Recht*, Luchterhand, Neuwied; Berlin, 1970, p. 212f., n. 10. See also F. Schmidt: "The Ratio Decidendi: A Comparative Study of a French, a German, and an American Supreme Court Decision, 6 *Acta Instituti Upsaliensis Iurisprudentiae Comparativae* (1965) 12, 17f.; and A. Ehrenzweig: "Das Common Law," 1 *Zeitschrift für Rechtsvergleichung* (1960), 145, 149).

CHAPTER III

CURRENT ISSUES AND SELECTED SUBSTANTIVE REFORMS

There are some areas of the criminal law which have been the subject of greater concern than others; some offenses seem somehow to be more at the forefront of public consciousness although they are not necessarily typical offenses when considered from the statistical standpoint of numbers of arrests made—except in case of marijuana and drug abuse arrests. Yet when public concern about law and order grows, certain morals issues seem inevitably to be identified with that concern.

The issues considered in this section—abortion, homosexuality, drug and narcotics abuses, and obscenity—have all been subject to shifting value judgments but still seem almost certain to arouse moral sensibilities. Yet, in these same areas where emotional, moral concern is greatest, there has also been the greatest effort at reform. In the case of the first issue, abortion, abortion statutes have actually been reformed in three states, and considerable political, moral and religious concern has been and still is focused on these reform efforts. Laws concerning homosexuality have remained the same, for the most part, although enforcement patterns show some fluctuations. In the third area, drug and narcotics abuse, the incidence of the offense itself has increased so dramatically, that the public and its representatives have been forced to re-examine the law in this area because it has so clearly not met the needs of the situation. Yet, whatever the emotional, moral response to the idea of issues named so far, their actual occurance can often be lost sight of, or never come to the notice of the average person, since they generally do not arouse public notice. When it comes to obscenity, however, by definition it has to be a public occurance, but it may depend very much on where one lives, where one goes, or how much one is steeled against it, how much one encounters this offense, too.

There has definitely been some considerable change of public and private attitudes so far as the issues chosen for analysis here are concerned. In some cases there has been corresponding success in changing the law regarding these matters, or at least some changes have occurred in the judicial interpretation of the law. In other cases, however, although some change of attitude has occurred, no general shift in the criminal law has followed. It is probably in the area of abortion that the change in public attitude has been most noticeable, so that in some few states there has been a sudden and dramatic change by direct legislation.

It is obviously impossible to treat here all the substantive changes which have occurred in these areas of the American criminal law in recent times. But we hope some idea of the nature of these changes can be gained from our discussion of the background of these particular emotional issues. We hope in this way to do a little not only to illuminate the social, political process, which can bring about law reform, but also to explore the often mysterious historical by-ways where the social, moral attitudes are formed, which either demand sanction or reject the role of temporal law, for the preservation of accepted social, moral values.

A.   ABORTION: WHEN DOES HUMAN LIFE BEGIN? *

The resort to abortion has been characterized in many different ways in the history of Western social and legal thought. The Greeks and Romans seem not to have objected to the practice as one means of population control.[1] Aristotle suggested various other methods but then allowed:

When couples have children in excess, and there is an aversion to exposure of offspring, let abortion be procured before life and sense have begun.[2]

The Aristotelian measure of when "life and sense have begun" seems to have been adopted by the early Church Fathers and remained influential in various criminal codes until fairly recent times. Aristotle

---

* See page 263 for "A Note on the U.S. Supreme Court's Decision on Abortion."

[1] Cf. e.g. Bernard M. Dickens: *Abortion and the Law*, MacGibbon & Kee, Bristol, 1966, p. 15; and George Devereux: *A Study of Abortion in Primitive Societies*, Julian Pr., New York, 1955.

[2] *Aristotle's Politics*, transl. by Benj. Jowett, Clarendon Pr., O.U.P., Oxford, 1905, p. 295, VII. 16 § 15.

believed that during pregnancy three "souls" succeeded one another at different stages. The first, the "vegetable soul" existed from conception. It was succeeded by the "animal soul" after forty days for the male child, and after eighty or ninety days for the female child. For Aristotle the "animal soul" was perceptible from the time of quickening but abortion was acceptable until this time.[3]

Among the Church Fathers the distinction was made between the inanimate and animate unborn child. Noonan quotes St. Augustine, for example, as expressing the opinion on abortion before quickening that "If the embryo is still unformed, but yet in some way ensouled while unformed... the law does not provide that the act pertains to homicide, because still there cannot be said to be a live soul in a body that lacks sensation...." [4] The early Church was not unanimous in allowing abortion in the early stages of pregnancy, however. And Tertullian, for one, argues that the embryo has a soul from the time of conception, although it may not be considered man (*homo*) until it has attained final form.[5] Therefore, Tertullian maintains, "it does not matter whether one snatches away a soul after birth or disturbs one as it is being born." [6] The Augustinian view seems to have prevailed, however, and thus, until the 19th Century, abortion before animation, or "quickening", seems to have been allowed by the Church of Rome.

The dialogue continued within the Church, however, with those who adhered to the strict construction of the idea that God had constituted matrimony not to satisfy lust, but that couples might have children, condemning even methods of contraception as homicide. For much of this time, however, the official position even on abortion was more liberal. What was important from a practical standpoint, so far as abortion was concerned, was the question of quickening. If a woman was not yet quick with child, then abortion could still be performed. The strict construction doctrine won out for a time under Pope Sixtus V (1585-90), and the church departed from this liberal doctrine on abortion briefly, before its rejection of all abortion some centuries later. According to the bull *Effraenatam* of Pope Sixtus V (issued in 1588) "All abortion

---

[3] Aristotle: *History of Animals*, 7.3, cited by John T. Noonan, Jr in: *Contraception: A History of Its Treatment by the Catholic Theologians and Canonists*, Belknap Pr., H.U.P., Cambridge, Mass., 1966, p. 90.

[4] "On Exodus 21.80," from *Corpus Scriptorum Ecclesiasticorum Latinorum* (CSEL), Vienna, 1866, 28²:147, quoted by Noonan: *Ibid.*, p. 90.

[5] "The Soul," 25.2, 37.2, cited by Noonan: *Ibid.*, p. 90.

[6] "Apology," 9.8, *CSEL*, 69:24, quoted by Noonan: *Ibid.*, p. 91.

and all contraception by potion or poison were to be treated as murder." [7] Noonan attributes this short-lived official puritanism "almost wholly" to "the personality of Sixtus V". His successor, Gregory XIV (1590-91) ended this interlude, returning to the traditional formula in 1590 with the bull *Sedis Apostolicae*. It was not until 1869, at a time perhaps not so troubled by Renaissance morals and social conditions that Pope Pius IX ended this rather liberal policy and reverted to the position of *Effraenatam* on abortion.[8] It is possible that this was, to some extent, in response to the discovery of the manner of human fertilization by Ferdinand Keber in 1853, since the beginning of life was now said to occur at the point of fertilization rather than at quickening. But for whatever reason the new definition of the onset of human life was decided upon, Church doctrine has remained unchanged since that time.[9]

The English common law had historically utilized the Aristotelian rule as well. Blackstone, whose authoritative *Commentaries* revived English jurisprudence in the 18th Century, wrote: " . . . life begins in contemplation of law as soon as the infant stirs in the mother's womb." [10] But, similar to the Roman Church, in the 19th Century, the common law countries, too, began to move away from this doctrine, although the shift was not abrupt. In 1803, the Ellenborough Act was passed.[11] It outlawed the use of poison or "medical substances" to induce abortion after quickening, and was designed primarily to protect women from growing dangers from the use of such substances. It is important to note that surgical abortions, and use of medicines before quickening were not prohibited. Lord Landsdowne's Act of 1828 replaced the earlier prohibition, but retained the provision concerning poisons and "medical substances" and added surgical abortions after quickening.[12] It was not until 1837 that all abortions were prohibited in England.[13] This was altered slightly in 1861 to include the mother as a principle in any abortion proceeding.[14]

---

[7] Noonan: *Ibid.*, p. 362.
[8] See discussion in Noonan: *Ibid.*, p. 404f.
[9] Cf. also Lawrence Lader: *Abortion*, Bobbs-Merrill, New York, 1966, p. 81.
[10] I *Blackstone* Ch. 1. § 175. Blackstone bases his rule in turn on Coke.
[11] 43 *George III*, c. 58.
[12] *Offenses Against the Person Act*, 9 *George IV*, c. 31.
[13] 7 *William & 1 Victoria*, c. 85.
[14] 24 & 25 *Victoria*, c. 100.

Similar development occurred in the United States at about the same time. In 1821, Connecticut passed the first abortion statute which prohibited those performed after quickening.[15]

A recent article indicates:

Of nine states whose courts ruled on quickening, seven held that abortion before quickening was not an offense of any kind at common law . . . .[16]

And as late as 1869, a Kentucky court ruled that it:

never was a punishable offense at common law to produce, with the consent of the mother, an abortion prior to the time when the mother became quick with child [17]

Arkansas did not punish abortion before quickening until 1947,[18] and Mississippi not until 1956.[19] Rhode Island had no abortion section in its criminal code until 1896.[20] Returning to earlier formulations, the New York statute of 1828 included the exception of allowing abortion when it proved necessary to preserve the life of the mother.[21] Ohio adopted this rule in 1834,[22] and Indiana and Missouri followed in 1835.[23] Of the fifty jurisdictions which eventually prohibited abortion, forty-two included this exception.[24] The other eight included it, and allowed abortion in instances which would serve to preserve the woman's health as well.[25] These statutes have continued in effect until the recent reform efforts.

The scope of the illegal abortion problem in the United States has been immense, however. It had been estimated that there were a million or more illegal abortions in the United States every year,[26] before the liberalization of abortion laws in New York, Hawaii, and Alaska. It

---

[15] *Conn. Stat.*, Title 22, §§ 14, 16 at 152, 153 (1821).

[16] Loren G. Stern: "Abortion Reform and the Law," 60 *Journal of Criminal Law, Criminology, and Police Science* 3 (1969). See pp. 85-87 for a complete review of American statutes in this area, i.e. as of 1969.

[17] In *Mitchell v. Commissioner*, 78 Ken. 204, 210 (1869).

[18] Cf. Lader: *op. cit.*, p. 86.

[19] *Ibid.*

[20] *Ibid.*

[21] *New York Rev. Stat.*, pt. IV, Ch 1, Title II, §§ 8 and 9 at 550 (1828).

[22] *Ohio, S & C Stat.* 440 (1834).

[23] *Indiana, 2 G & H* 469 Sec. 36. *Mo. Rev. Stat.* (1835) 168-70, Art. 2, §§ 10; 36.

[24] Cf. Stern: *loc cit.*, p. 86.

[25] *Ibid.*

[26] Approximately one million illegal abortions per year is as accurate an estimate as exists. See e.g. A. L. Ziff; "Recent Abortion Law Reforms," 60 *Journal of Criminal Law, Criminology, and Police Science* 3, (1969), p. 5.

has been pointed out that because of the advances in medicine there are very few instances in which the life of the woman might be endangered by the birth of her child.[27] Consequently, the exception which exists in most jurisdictions resulted in very few legal abortions. The woman seeking an abortion had, therefore, been driven to resorting to an illegal practitioner. The poor, in particular, have been at the mercy of quacks and unskilled abortionists, the social critics maintain. But because of the secrecy which used to surround the whole affair, the rich were often no better off, although a well-to-do family which knew about the operation could conceivably manage to have it done within the confines of a private clinic or hospital whenever one might be induced to carry out the operation for a price.[28]

In response to this situation, a number of proposals have been made. In three states, Alaska, Hawaii, and New York, virtually all restrictions were recently eliminated.[29] These reforms make abortion a matter between the woman and her physician. In each instance, only licensed physicians are permitted to perform the operation.[30] Hawaii and Alaska have residency requirements of three months and one month respectively. No doubt these were designed to prevent the states from becoming Meccas for women seeking abortions. New York did not include such a provision.

In New York, the operation must occur within the first 24 weeks of pregnancy. This clause may have little effect on the practice under the new law since early abortion is normally recommended. But it was included mainly as a concession to religious and humane attitudes.[31]

---

[27] Cf. Stern: *loc. cit.*, p. 87.

[28] Cf. Edwin M. Schur: *Crimes Without Victims*, Prentice Hall, Englewood Cliffs, N.J., 1965, p. 21.

[29] 103 *Laws of Alaska* 11.15.060 and 08.64.105: *Hawaii Rev. Stat.* 453-16; *McKinney's Session Law News of New York*, May 10, 1970, § 125.05.

In March, 1972, the Federal Commission on Population Growth and the American Future, appointed by President Nixon the year before, made its second report including the recommendation that the states be encouraged to follow these examples: "... women should be free to determine their own fertility ... the matter of abortion should be left to the conscience of the individual concerned, in consultation with her physician, and ... states should be encouraged to enact affirmative statutes creating a clear and positive framework for the practice of abortion on request" (*New York Times*, 17 Mar., 1972, p. 180; 1:3-7).

[30] *Ibid.*

[31] Cf. "Final Approval of Abortion Bill Voted in Albany"; *New York Times*, April 11, 1970, p. 1:1.

Eleven states have passed a partial reform patterned after the American Law Institute's (A.L.I.) *Model Penal Code* provision.[32] Also called the *Therapeutic Abortion Act,* it broadens the number of exceptions to the complete prohibition of abortion except when the mother's life is endangered. Under this act, pregnancy resulting from rape or incest or other felonious union may be terminated, as well as those which will result in the birth of a deformed child. Most important, pregnancies which would "gravely impair the physical or mental health of the mother" may be terminated. However, as many critics have pointed out, this reform is a very limited one, affecting only a relatively small number of cases each year.[33]

It would appear in light of these recent developments, however, that a general reform in this area may follow. Many states now have one or the other of these proposals before their legislatures, and in Maryland and Arizona, the complete reform only narrowly failed in the 1969-70 legislative session.[34] Although such measures are hardly assured of success, as political leaders around the nation learn from their colleagues in Alaska, Hawaii and New York, that the political consequences, public uproar, and political defeats do not occur in a magnitude first imagined, the movement may grow.

It is significant for any reform in this area that the Catholic Church remains opposed to any lessening of restrictions or narrowing of definitions for this offense,[35] and after the state legislature in New York passed the bill removing existing restrictions, the Archbishop on behalf of all the bishops in New York requested that Governor Rockefeller veto the new act.[36] Some within the Church have been quite outspoken in rejecting or criticizing the Church's official position. The significance

---

[32] American Law Institute (ALI): *Model Penal Code* (Proposed Official Draft, 1962) § 230.3.

[33] See A. L. Ziff: *Loc. cit.,* p. 14: "The reforms simply substitute one 'dead letter' law for another...."

[34] Cf. "Governor Mandel Explains Abortion Law Veto," *New York Times,* May 27, 1970, p. 43:2; "Arizona House Passes End to Abortion Law Curbs," *New York Times,* Feb. 27, 1970, p. 72:1.

[35] See page 243 at n. 103, below for a discussion of the encyclical *Humanae Vitae,* the most recent papal doctrinal statement in this area.

[36] "Final Approval of Abortion Bill Voted in Albany," *loc. cit.* (n. 31, above). Amidst considerable controversy a repeal bill did manage to pass both houses of the legislature in 1972 (cf. *New York Times,* 10 May, 1972, p. 1:1-2; 11 May, 1972, p. 1:1). President Nixon who had just rejected the recommendations for liberalized abortion laws made by his Commission on Population Growth (see n. 29),

of this internal resistance to doctrine may have greater effect in blunting general Catholic opposition to abortion, than in bringing about any pervasive reversal in Church policy. But there is also substantial opposition to any change from prominent non-Catholic segments of the population. The traditional moral attitude still espoused by many is that abortion involves the taking of human life, and hence murder. Governor Ronald Reagan of California has taken this position, suggesting no difference between abortion, selective infanticide, and perhaps euthanasia: "If we allow people to decide to abort an unborn foetus, soon we will be allowing people to perform abortions a year after birth."[37]

The contrary view is defended by those who believe that the parents, or the mother, possibly within certain guidelines, should decide whether they want to, or she wants to, continue the pregnancy. One of the most telling arguments of ordinary reason (if not supported by theology) is the feeling that a foetus early in the pregnancy does not yet enjoy the quality of a separate individual human life. This argument cannot obviate the fact that, in any case, by procuring an abortion a human-life-to-be is denied a theoretical "right to live", or to be born. And an unborn child does enjoy certain uncontested rights and protections under the law.

Critics of these reservations point to the fact that an average woman is capable of bearing many other children. Just as undeniably, however, the particular foetus aborted will not develop into a particular child, regardless of what other children that woman might bear. It is argued that contraception produces a similar result, but inhibiting conception (again in contemporary ordinary reason) is not the same order of act as taking a life.[38] Consequently, a woman's rights in most American jurisdictions extend to preventing conception, but not to an abortion at her own discretion.[39] Obviously the crucial question that underlies the debate on any change in the law protecting the unborn child is, "When does human life begin?"

---

associated himself personally with the cause for repeal in a letter to Cardinal Cooke of New York (cf. *New York Times,* 8 May, 1972, p. 1:1; 9 May, 1972, p. 1:1-2; 11 May, 1972, p. 1:2-3).

[37] Statement covered on the San Francisco NBC Affiliate KRON-T.V.'s 6:00 p.m. *Newswatch,* February 19, 1970.

[38] One may note that the Encyclical, *Humanae Vitae,* is no less firm on the prohibition of contraception than of abortion, however. See page 243,n. 103 below.

[39] Cf. e.g. *Griswold v. Connecticut* 381 *U.S.* 479 (1965) 498.

Until recently (i.e. until legalization of abortion in New York, Hawaii, and Alaska) it was estimated that over a million women underwent abortions illegally every year. Lawmakers and the public must, therefore, realize that regardless of how far along we are at answering any ultimate questions on the beginnings of human life, the liberalized abortion laws have probably had as much effect as public health measures, as possibly in changing the number of abortions performed. No doubt the movement for eliminating restrictions on abortion will grow, perhaps not so much as the result of the practical considerations on the side of leniency, as of the difficulty of either disestablishing or restricting the growth of an institution for which there is considerable public demand, and as information on the availability of abortion clinics in a few states is publicized.

A new physiological test of the presence of human life has been applied to determine legal death for the purpose of organ transplants. When a so-called "flat" electroencephalogram indicates that there is no measurable brain wave activity, a vital organ may be transplanted from that body.[40] By application of this measurement at the other end of life, a foetus which does not yet exhibit brain wave activity might be said to be not yet able to be classified as exhibiting the most vital characteristic of human life.[41] This test has the advantage of ease of application of a verifiable measurement, but that does not escape the obvious fact that the foetus is in the process of developing human life and is, therefore, not strictly speaking comparable to a body which has stopped functioning and no longer has the potential to recover. This development in the discussion of the beginning of the existence of life is no doubt a refinement. However, in practice it does not take us much beyond the old theory of quickening. We would merely be able to employ a mechanical measurement to determine when that moment had arrived.

One final aspect of the abortion problem should be emphasized. Abortion is not as obvious a problem—or an offense—as the other issues considered here since where legal prohibitions have applied all parties have endeavored to conduct the matter secretly. The nature of the prohibition was a protection of the public conscience. And while a

---

[40] See Still: "Objective Diagnosis of Human Death," 59 *Journal of the Washington Academy of Science* 46, 48 (1969) in review of Daniel Callahan: *Abortion: Law Choice and Morality, 58 California Law Rev.* 1257, 1261 (1970).

[41] *Ibid.*: see also generally, Daniel Callahan, *Abortion: Law, Choice and Morality*, MacMillan: New York (1970).

social problem existed, that need not imply public realization of its dimensions. Formerly every case was hushed up. No doubt many people were aware that an abortion could be procured, and they may even have known of a channel available for this purpose. But the actual consequences of any changes in this situation, legal or otherwise, or even the maintenance of the *status quo,* may have only personal reality for the vast majority of people. For this reason, perhaps, once a system of legal abortion clinics is established and if the furtive and illicit associations disappear it may be less difficult for the remaining states to ease further legal restrictions concerning abortion, without long enduring recriminations or accusations of moral permissiveness.

B.   DRUG ABUSE AND MARIJUANA:
MORAL RESPONSIBILITY VS. CONTROL OF MORALS

The use of drugs, although an ancient practice, only fairly recently became a legal offense in the United States. Prior to 1914, there had been only sporadic attempts to regulate the use of drugs. In 1874, for instance, Connecticut passed a law providing for civil commitment to institutions for drug addicts.[42] In 1877, Nevada passed a more general provision outlawing the use of particular narcotic substances.[43] It was not until the signing of the *Hague Convention* of 1912, however, that any systematic attempt was made to regulate drug use.[44]

Until that time, various detrimental practices had been growing in significance. Medical misuse was widespread.[45] Morphine addiction was called the "soldier's disease", since many Civil War veterans who had been administered the drug in military hospitals became addicted to it.[46] Doctors were indiscriminate in their prescription of such drugs,[47] and

---

[42] *Conn. Laws,* 1874, p. 256.

[43] *Nevada Stat.,* 1877, p. 69.

[44] *Suppression of the Abuse of Opium and Other Drugs, Convention and Final Protocol Between the United States and Other Powers,* Jan. 23, 1912; July 9, 1913, 38 *Stat.* 1912, T. S. No. 612.

[45] Cf. William B. Eldridge: *Narcotics and the Law,* American Bar Foundation, New York, 1962, pp. 4-9. The author gives detailed description of the growth of the drug problem in the United States. A dialogue between Yale professors D. Musto and A. Trachtenberg: "As American As Apple Pie," *Yale Alumni Magazine,* Jan. 1972, pp. 16-21, discusses the prominent role of drug use in American social history. Musto's book: *Narcotics and America* is to appear in 1972.

[46] *Ibid.*

[47] *Ibid.*

medical texts urged little caution in their use.[48] Use of opium in various patent medicines became a national problem.[49] Often even stronger opium compounds were urged on the unwary as they experienced the pain of withdrawal from the original potion.[50] The large Chinese community's use of opium in San Francisco became the object of national curiosity.[51] Considering these separate problems together, a significant proportion of the population seems to have been suffering from drug addiction long before the time the *Hague Convention* was signed.

It is important before proceeding further with the historical development of drug and narcotics laws to consider what the various substances involved are. They fall into six general categories: (1) opiates and opium derivatives, principally heroin and morphine; (2) derivatives of the coca plant, including cocaine; (3) strong hallucinogens, including peyote, mescalin, psilocybin, psilocin, LSD and DMT; (4) weak hallucinogens, including marijuana; (5) stimulants or amphetamines; and (6) barbiturates—either penobarbital sodium or secobarbital sodium.[52] Of these, the first two, plus the strong hallucinogens, peyote and mescalin and the weak hallucinogen marijuana, were more or less freely available in the United States in 1912. The others on the list were developed or derived later through the miracles of modern science.

In 1914, the *Harrison Act* was passed. It was the first attempt to deal comprehensively with the narcotics and dangerous drugs known at that time.[53] It was essentially a tax measure, or more aptly, a series of prohibitive taxes. Use was restricted to medical purposes and research by licensed individuals and facilities.[54] The structure of the act made it probable that in most instances of one violation, multiple violations of its provisions would be committed. [55]

---

[48] *Ibid.*

[49] *Ibid.*

[50] *Ibid.*

[51] *Ibid.*

[52] U.S. President's Commission on Law Enforcement and the Administration of Justice, Task Force Report: *Narcotics and Drug Abuse,* U.S.G.P.O., Washington, D.C. 1967, pp. 1-6. See also "Hallucinogens," 68 *Columbia Law Rev.* 521 (1968), pp. 524-39.

[53] The present edition of the *Harrison Act,* which really comprised three separate enactments can be found as *Int. Rev. Code,* 1954, §§ 4701-36.

[54] *Ibid.*

[55] In other words, possession in substantial quantities is also *prima facie* evidence of intent to sell and possibly of illegal importation.

The *Harrison Act* was followed in 1932 by the *Uniform Narcotic Drug Act,* designed for the states,[56] which, to date, has been accepted by all states except California, New Hampshire and Pennsylvania, and has also been accepted by Puerto Rico, the Virgin Islands and the District of Columbia.[57] A pre-psychedelics measure, it includes strong prohibitions concerning the use, possession and sale of opiates, marijuana and coca derivatives. In § 2 it provides:

It shall be unlawful for any person to manufacture, possess, have under his control, sell, prescribe, administer, dispense, or compound, any narcotic drug except as authorized in this act.

In addition, many states made it a crime to be addicted to a particular narcotic, regardless of whether one had the drug in his possession. In *Robinson v. California,* decided in 1962, the United States Supreme Court ruled such statutes unconstitutional, reasoning that since narcotic addiction was an illness, punishment of an illness was a "cruel and unusual punishment" and therefore a violation of the Eighth and Fourteenth Amendments to the Constitution.[58]

Returning to the development of federal and state laws, the federal government added a provision concerning marijuana to the *Harrison Act* sections passed in 1914.[59] This placed a tax of one dollar per ounce on sales to a person or organization registered for a medical research project allowed to use such substances, and one hundred dollars per ounce on sales to those who were not registered.[60]

World War II brought some changes in the drug and narcotics trade. With markets in the Middle East and Far East suddenly inaccessible, Mexico became an important source for marijuana and low grade opiates.[61] Since the war, the Middle East and particularly Turkey, as well as the Far East has, reassumed an important position in the drug

---

[56] National Conference of Commissioners on Uniform State Laws, *Uniform Narcotic Drug Act,* 1932.

[57] Cf. Eldridge: *op. cit.* p. 45. The author points out that California, Pennsylvania, and New Hampshire adopted similar laws.

[58] 370 *U.S.* 660 (1962).

[59] *Marijuana Tax Act* of 1937, 50 *Stat.* 551, as amended, *Int. Rev. Code,* 1954, §§ 4741-76.

[60] *Ibid.,* § 4741 (1) & (2).

[61] Cf. John B. Williams: *Narcotics and Dangerous Drugs,* California Peace Officers Training, Bureau of Vocational and Technical Education, The California Community Colleges, 1969, p. 9.

trade, while Mexico has remained an additional source of supply, especially convenient to the market on the West Coast.[62]

Drug use of all kinds grew steadily in the 1950's.[63] In response to this fact, the *Federal Narcotic Control Act* of 1956 raised penalties for possession of narcotics or dangerous drugs to a minimum of five years in prison for the first offense. A second offense could bring a minimum sentence of ten years, while sale to a minor was punishable by death.[64]

With the blossoming of the psychedelic revolution, the *Drug Abuse Control Amendments* of 1965 were passed by Congress.[65] They allowed the Department of Health, Education and Welfare to designate certain substances as dangerous drugs so that they would come under the control of previous legislation. In 1967, the United States also signed the *Single Convention on Narcotic Drugs,* an attempt to gain international cooperation to stem the tide of what was becoming a flood of narcotics and drugs of various kinds into the United States.[66]

In the past ten years, the scope of what was a nagging, but relatively minor law enforcement problem, confined, at least in the popular and official minds to the poor, and particularly to the minority group poor, has burgeoned into a full-scale social revolution which continues to shake the foundations of most communities in the United States. Drug use did not simply rise sharply, it sky rocketed during the decade of the 1960's. A glance at the statistics of arrests made in California alone —frankly the nexus of the "drug scene"—shows the tremendous increase of all kinds of drug and narcotics use. The use of marijuana and dangerous drugs—strong hallucinogens, stimulants and barbiturates—rose at a fantastic rate, especially among young people, although as the accompanying chart indicates, the increase in the use of opiates cannot be ignored either. When one considers that the arrests represent only a fraction of the rise in incidence of use, the size of the problem is staggering.

---

[62] Cf. *Narcotics and Drug Abuse, op. cit.,* p. 6.

[63] Cf. Williams: *op. cit.* p. 10.

[64] 70 *Stat.* 567 (1956). For a complete description of penalties for drug offenses in each state as of October, 1961, see Eldridge, *op. cit.,* "Appendix C", pp. 149-87. For comment on American penalties for drug offenses, see F. A. Allen, "American Narcotics Legislation," in Wilner and Kassenbaum: *Narcotics,* McGraw-Hill, New York, 1965, pp. 23-24.

[65] 21 *U.S.C.* §§ 321, 331, 352, 360, 360a, 372 (Supp. I, 1965).

[66] *Single Convention on Narcotic Drugs,* July 12, 1967, *TIAS* No. 6298.

TABLE 1 — ADULT DRUG ARRESTS REPORTED BY CALIFORNIA LAW ENFORCEMENT AGENCIES, 1960 THROUGH 1969*

Offense by Year of Arrest

Offense	1960	1961	1962	1963	1964	1965	1966	1967	1968[a]	1969[a]	Percent change	
											1969 over 1968	1969 over 1960
Total	17,649	16,917	16,277	16,787	19,707	21,685	28,267	47,032	69,413	94,745	36.5	436.8
Marijuana . . .	4,245	3,386	3,433	4,883	6,323	8,383	14,209	26,527	34,323	38,670	12.7	811.0
Opiates	9,135	8,171	5,939	5,972	7,597	6,104	6,364	8,197	8,497	9,990	17.6	9.4
Dangerous drugs .	3,533	4,530	5,865	4,768	4,577	5,930	6,064	9,558	22,150	41,230	86.1	1,067.0
Other offenses . .	736	830	1,040	1,164	1,210	1,268	1,630	2,750	4,443	4,855	9.3	559.6

[a] Expanded from sample data.

TABLE 2 — DRUG ARRESTS OF JUVENILES (UNDER 18 YEARS) REPORTED BY CALIFORNIA LAW ENFORCEMENT AGENCIES, 1960 THROUGH 1969*

Offense by Year of Arrest

Offense	1960	1961	1962	1963	1964	1965	1966	1967	1968[a]	1969[a]	Percent change	
											1969 over 1968	1969 over 1960
Total	1,616	1,271	1,336	1,439	2,022	2,689	5,355	14,760	32,620	35,970	10.3	2,125.9
Marijuana . . .	910	408	310	635	1,237	1,619	4,034	10,987	18,991	16,180	−14.8	1,678.0
Opiates	160	136	83	92	104	60	118	272	540	755	39.8	371.9
Dangerous drugs .	515	709	906	675	639	951	1,007	2,809	11,076	17,595	58.9	3,316.5
Other offenses . .	31	18	37	37	42	59	196	692	2,013	1,440	−28.5	

Note : Percentages not computed on bases smaller than 50.

[a] Expanded from sample data.

* From : State of California, Department of Justice, Bureau of Criminal Statistics : *Crime and Delinquency in California, Drug Arrests and Dispositions in California : Reference Tables, 1969*, Sacramento, 1969, p. 1.

Although some continue to claim that law enforcement officials have reduced addiction through enforcing existing laws, most admit that enforcement efforts have largely failed. Schur recalls that:

The former U.S. Commissioner of Narcotics himself has been quoted as saying that the combined efforts of the Army, the Navy, the Narcotics Bureau and the F.B.I. could not eliminate drug smuggling.[67]

He would probably agree that the same group could have little effect on possession and sale within the United States as well.

An interesting and well-publicized failure to increase the effectiveness of anti-smuggling efforts was Operation Intercept, heralded by the Nixon Administration as a new and effective means to stem the flow of drugs and narcotics crossing the border from Mexico.[68] The program foundered amidst protests from the Mexican Government that border searches were inhibiting commerce and tourism.[69] Yet, one self-described marijuana smuggler took pains to point out:

One of the reasons Operation Intercept was such a joke to professional marijuanos is the silly conception behind it. The idea that officials could stop the marijuana traffic by searching every car crossing the border is absurd. The only effects Operation Intercept had were to hassle the tourists, disrupt the economy of Mexico and the U.S. and help the professional marijuana smuggler.
One of the things most people don't realize is that any really big operation is going to have reasonably high-placed officials working for it on both sides of the border.... The increasingly heavy bust statistics reflected along the border are a result of most amateur operations.[70]

The present authors are in no position to give such inside dope on the marijuana smuggling trade. However, there does seem to be an enormous number of people from the youth class involved—who can hardly be considered agents of organized crime—especially in the marijuana trade. In a front page report the *New York Times* draws on the authority of drug dealers and law enforcement officials to characterize the nature of the trade in marijuana and hashish, a concentrated form of

---

[67] Schur: *op. cit.,* p. 134: see also Williams, *op. cit.,* p. 9.

[68] Cf. "Marijuana Farm Seized in Mexico," *New York Times,* Oct. 13, 1969, p. 20:1.

[69] *Ibid.*: "The adverse effects on regular commerce and tourism resulting from the rigid inspection procedures at the Mexican border points produced official Mexican protests."

[70] Roger Tichborne: "Tales of Mexico and Marijuana," *Scanlon's,* Vol. 1, No. 6, August, 1970, pp. 6-20, p. 9.

marijuana extracted from the resins of the cannabis plant. There are primarily three groups involved, it says:

The established Mexican and Mexican-American Organizations operating on both sides of the border: These deal in large shipments and are said to account for a major portion of the Mexican marijuana smuggled into the United States.

The new American groups that have sprung up in the last 18 months to two years: These are said to involve mostly young Americans in their 20's. The groups range from two or three friends who carry out a "one-shot" expedition—to bring back anywhere from a few "kilos"... to perhaps a hundred pounds or more of marijuana—to large, well-financed organizations that operate elaborate smuggling ventures utilizing airplanes, pleasure craft, lobster boats, skin-diving equipment and other exotic paraphernalia.

Young American amateurs: Largely tourists and vacationers, this group probably accounts for most of the border arrest statistics. Given to such devices as stuffing marijuana into automobile doors and spare tires, they usually bring back no more than a few kilos, often for their own use and usually only once.[71]

It reports customs men conceding that they "stop probably no more than 10 per cent" of this smuggling. "By that estimate," it calculates, "over 1.3 million pounds of marijuana and 34,000 pounds of hashish found its way into the counrty last year [1970]." Over a 10 month period, King finds this equally revealing breakdown of those arrested:

91 per cent of the hashish smugglers and 85 per cent of the marijuana smugglers were under 30 years of age. Nearly three-quarters in both categories were under 25. Over a fifth of those caught bringing marijuana into the country were teen-agers, as were 14 per cent of those trying to smuggle hashish.[72]

It might seem with the bleak enforcement picture, officials would develop creative reforms for the law and law enforcement to deal with what has become a situation so out of proportion with existing legislation and enforcement techniques that they are almost becoming irrelevant. For the most part, this has not been the case.

One suggestion advanced in California recently to legalize and control the use of marijuana—noted for its mild effect, non-addictive quality, and widespread use—resulted in the firing of the entire consultant body which had made this suggestion to the California State Legislature.[73] This group, made up of distinguished members of the Law School faculties in the University of California system and from the School of

[71] Wayne King: "A Rising Demand for Marijuana Lures the Young into Smuggling," *New York Times,* Tues. 16 Feb., 1971 (p. 1 : 5-6), p. 23.

[72] *Ibid.,* p. 23.

[73] Cf. "If Pot Were Legal," *Time,* July 20, 1970, p. 41.

Law of Stanford University, had pointed out that marijuana law enforcement attempts were exceedingly expensive and nonetheless ineffective, so that law enforcement efforts might better be directed towards truly dangerous addictive drugs, such as heroin.[74] Many legislators seemed scandalized by this, protesting that they would maintain the blanket prohibition of all drugs and narcotics proscribed by law at the present time, no matter how difficult this made the focus of enforcment efforts.

About the only reform which has occurred in this area is the reduction of federal and state penalties for first offenders convicted of possession of either marijuana or a narcotic or a dangerous drug. The United States Senate recently passed a measure which reduced the minimum sentence for possession of narcotics or dangerous drugs from five years to one year, and provided for a maximum five thousand dollar fine.[75] Twenty-three states have reduced penalties for possession of marijuana as well.[76] This is in fact perhaps the most important area for law reform —and may hopefully also lead to penal reform as well. For the most numerous offenders, and statutory criminals, under the drug abuse laws are the youthful, or *cavalier* offenders. Conservative and upstanding members of society, who have been led to believe, from earlier years that drug offenders were un-social elements who wanted to make victims of their children, must now come to realize that it is the children of the good middle class homes who are not only among the "victims", but among the traffickers, and consumers as well. Regardless of the virtue of drug control, it is ultimately the punishment they must be concerned with. Our penal institutions grow increasingly notorious for degrading and criminalizing their inmates. Now these young statutory criminals are exposed to the same forces of personality destruction and criminalization.

More progress has been made in the area of treating those suffering from addiction to various drugs. Several states are developing programs for methadone therapy for heroin addicts, and New York City makes such therapy available to inmates of the city jail system.[77] The voluntary organization, Synanon, has also reported success with addicts through

[74] Cf. John Kaplan: *Marijuana—The New Prohibition,* World Publishing Company, Cleveland, 1970, pp. 28-29.

[75] Cf. *Congressional Quarterly Weekly Report,* "Drug Control Act," Vol. XXVIII, No. 5, August —, 1970, pp. 259-60, p. 259.

[76] Cf., *Time, loc. cit.*

[77] Cf. "City Council Overrides Lindsay, Orders Jail Methadone Program," *New York Times,* September 10, 1969, p. 57 : 1.

programs involving intensive mutually supportive group therapy and separate residence communities for addicts.[78]

One new program which has not been adopted in the United States, is the attempt in Great Britain to use public clinics which provide free drugs for addicts at maintenance levels. Recent reports of the apparent failure of this program so far has made it unlikely that such techniques will be tried in any jurisdiction in the United States.[79]

There are a variety of reasons why legislatures have not been more creative or responsive to drug problems. Foremost among them is certainly the strong public horror of drug use and drug "pushers." In fact the whole sense of the immorality surrounding any illicit use of drugs or marijuana, which was instilled in the public mind during the years when the crime syndicate was said to be "pushing" drugs to school children, has blinded them to the fact that today it is the school kids who are among the traffickers, "pushers", and consumers. But this same scare tactic is still used and reinforced frequently by such law enforcement bodies as the Federal Bureau of Narcotics.[80] In a recent associated press dispatch, for example, Dr. Thomas Price, the president of the National Coordinating Council on Drug Abuse Education and Information, which represents 99 organizations including such diverse members as the American Medical Association and the National Student Association, had this extraordinary complaint. A draft report then being prepared by the Bureau of Narcotics implies, he reported:

Smoking marijuana is the cause of criminal behavior, alienation, bad school grades, delinquency, and early or steady dating.[81]

Such a feeling also tends to lump all prohibited drugs and narcotics together in terms of their effect, and the results of their use and can inhibit or discount research which might gather more specific information especially about less harmful substances.[82] *The Uniform Narcotics Act*

---

[78] Cf. Lewis Yablonsky: *The Tunnel Back, Synanon,* MacMillan, New York, 1966, passim; cf. also Richard A. McGee: "New Approaches to Control and Treatment of Drug Abusers in California," in Wilner and Kassenbaum: *op. cit.* pp. 263-273.

[79] Cf. "Survey of British Legal Heroin System," *New York Times,* March 31, 1970, p. 25 : 1.

[80] Cf. Harry J. Anslinger & William F. Tompkins: *The Traffic in Narcotics,* New York, Funk & Wagnalls, 1953, passim.

[81] AP dispatch: "Blasts Narcotics Bureau Report on Marijuana Use," *Warren Tribune Chronicle* (Warren, Ohio), 18 January 1971, p. 8 : 7-8.

[82] Cf. "Hallucinogens," *loc. cit.,* p. 545.

of 1932, for instance, places marijuana in the same category as heroin. As a result of this, it is difficult to separate a less harmful drug, such as marijuana, for regulation in other ways.

Ongoing myths support this confusion. Many people believe that all drugs are addictive. The feeling that drug addicts are mentally ill is widespread. There is often a loose association made between marijuana users and drug addicts. And, while the use of marijuana is within the means of most people, the regular use of "hard drugs" is still prohibitively expensive in the United States. So addicts are practically obliged to turn to lives of crime in order to support their drives. There is also concern on the part of many that drugs destroy an individual's morality, turning addicts into sexual menaces, or dependent members of society. In addition, there is a widespread resignation that narcotics addicts cannot be rehabilitated.[83]

There are some efforts being made to counter such misinformation and myth, but they are often ineffective in the face of official pronouncements. Organizations, such as LEMAR are lobbying actively to end the restriction of marijuana use by adults, but if the California Legislature's response in firing its advisory commission which recommended reform is any indication, change, in that state, at least, is a long way off.

In the immediate future, the most likely changes lie in the area of reducing penalties for possession of various drugs, particularly if the party has no previous convictions. With the federal administration now advocating such changes, and with the fact that sons and daughters of the respectable middle-class—including those of some prominent political leaders—are now being arrested under such provisions, there is a growing public and official concern for such a reform.

C.   OBSCENITY AND CENSORSHIP

If there is any one area in the criminal law which arouses the most basic sensibilities of the keepers of public morals, it is the area of controlling obscenity and deleterious publications. But the moral outrage of free thinking Americans once they consider themselves deprived of their fundamental constitutional rights of free expression is also a formidable force to reckon with. With just words discerning the advancing threat of censorship Mr. Justice Douglas framed his dissent to the opinion of his colleagues in *Roth v. United States*:

---

[83] Cf. Eldridge: *op. cit.*, the author presents these myths in detail in pp. 16-34.

...if the First Amendement gurantee of freedom of speech and press is to mean anything in this field, it must allow protests even against the moral code that the standard of the day sets for the community. In other words, literature should not be suppressed merely because it offends the moral code of the censor.[84]

Yet, despite the not infrequent utterance of such tolerant sentiments, there has been a kind of tradition of self-censorship, or, let us say, self-control, in the United States, of all kinds of materials, including books, pamphlets, paintings, plays, and more recently, radio, television, and film. For, the simple truth of the matter is that a lot of what is published in this way offends. The media are somewhat monopolistic but still react to the market and to the interpreters of the public's moral sensibilities. They contribute to changing the moral sensibilities of the public as well, but that takes time and the change is never uniform. So in a country of puritans and free thinkers, and a market economy, there are tendencies for moralistic condemnation, liberal tolerance, and anarchistic "liberation"; there are moralists who believe they can improve us by offending us, and there are relatively conservative media anxious about losing a market if they offend, but eager to capture the market once the legal, moral restraints are removed.

One great Victorian moralistic crusader who probably did more than anyone else to reinforce American "reserve" in the field of publication was Anthony Comstock, the leading self appointed censor of the 19th Century in the United States, and founder of the New York Society for the Suppression of Vice. Comstock's single-minded efforts were responsible for banning of certain questionable materials from the United States mails in 1873.[85] Obscene literature had already been excluded from the mails in 1857.[86] And by his time, cities and states already had an array of anti-obscenity statutes and regulations, for, the first prosecution and suppression of an obscene book had occurred in Massachusetts in 1821.[87]

The question of defining what is obscene was apparently left unanswered, however, until the adoption of the English definition developed

---

[84] 354 *U.S.* 476 (1957), 513.

[85] Cf. Norman St. John-Stevas: *Obscenity and the Law*, Secker and Warburg, London, 1956, p. 161. See also James Murray, O.N. Paul, and L. Schwartz: *Federal Censorship*, Free Press of Glencoe, New York, 1961, pp. 18-24.

[86] Present formulation in 18 *U.S.C.* 1467, 1462-63; *U.S. Tariff Act* (1930), 19 *U.S.C.* 1305.

[87] *Commonwealth v. Holmes*, 17 *Mass.* 336 (1821).

in *Regina v. Hicklin.*[88] In that case, Cockburne, C.J., declared the following all inclusive standard:

... the test of obscenity is this, whether or not the tendency of the matter charged as obscenity is to depress and corrupt those whose minds are open to such immoral influences, and into whose hands a publication of this sort may fall.[89]

This test was naturally quite restrictive since it was relatively easy to assemble a group of sufficiently outraged witnesses to claim a particular publication was obscene, and then to establish the possibility that it could fall into the hands of someone who would suffer the prophesied corruption. This standard lasted until a new rule was promulgated in 1933 in a case over allowing James Joyce's *Ulysses* into the United States. In *United States v. One Book Called Ulysses,* Judge Woolsey indicated that such materials must have been intended to be obscene, and failing this:

...tend to excite the sex impulses or lead to sexually impure or lustful thoughts... for a person with average sex instincts.[90]

As this formulation was construed, however, it did not work as much of a limitation as it might have seemed to because the entire work in question had to be considered, and consequently over-all characterization was not as easy.[91] Under this test, *Ulysses* was allowed.

In 1951, the formula was altered when the Supreme Court adopted in *Dennis v. United States*[92] the rule developed in Pennsylvania by Judge Bok in *Commonwealth v. Gordon.*[93] Judge Bok stated in that decision that materials once established as obscene must also present:

... reasonable and demonstrable cause to believe that a crime or a misdemeanor has been committed or is about to be committed as a perceptible result of the publication and distribution of the writing in question.[94]

Yet this doctrine, which became known as the clear and present danger rule, had only a short life.

---

[88] *LR* 3 *Q.B.* 360 (1868) adopted in the United States in: *United States v. Bennet,* 24 *Fed. Cas.* No 14,571 (*CCSP. N.Y.*) (1879).

[89] *Ibid.* at 371.

[90] 5 *F. Supp.* 182 (1933) 184.

[91] *Ibid.* at 185.

[92] 341 *U.S.* 494 (1951).

[93] 66 *Pa. D. & C. R.* 101, (1949).

[94] *Ibid.* at 156.

In 1957 in *Roth v. United States,* the Supreme Court ruled that obscene materials, once established as such, did not enjoy the protections provided by the first amendment.[95] The court dropped the *Dennis* rule and attempted instead to adopt a definition of obscenity measured against the social value of the entire work. First, the Court determined that the clear and present danger test had no relevance.[96] Second, they indicated that the material in question must appeal to prurient interest,[97] and third, the material must have no redeeming social value.[98] The question to be asked was, in part, whether the average person, applying contemporary community standards, would consider the dominant theme of the material taken as a whole, to appeal to prurient interests.[99] In *Memoirs v. Massachusetts,* a trial regarding the book, *Fanny Hill* (which had also been the subject of the first obscenity in literature trial in the United States back in 1821) the Court provided a more succinct formulation of the *Roth* rule:

... Three elements must coalesce: it must be established that (a) the dominant theme of the material, taken as a whole, appeals to a prurient interest in sex; (b) the material is patently offensive because it affronts contemporary community standards relating to the description or representation of sexual matters; (c) the material is utterly without redeeming social value.[100]

In *Jacobellis v. Ohio,* a decision which applied this standard to decisions at the state and local level as well, the Court ruled that the community standard applied must also be a national community standard, rather than the reflection of some parochial tendency.[101]

At least one commentator believes that the Court has already departed from the *Roth* standard, however.[102] In *Ginsberg v. New York,* the Court expounded a variable obscenity doctrine.[103] It held that what is

---

[95] 354 *U.S.* 476.

[96] *Ibid.* at 486-87.

[97] *Ibid.* at 489.

[98] *Ibid.* at 484.

[99] *Ibid.* at 489. The A.L.I. *Model Penal Code* provides a similar definition at Section 251.4 (Proposed Official Draft, 1962).

[100] 383 *U.S.* 413 (1966) 418.

[101] 378 *U.S.* 184 (1964) 186n2.

[102] See D.E. Engdahl: "Requiem for Roth: Obscenity Doctrine Changing", 68 *Mich. Law Rev.* 185 (1969), p. 197.

[103] 390 *U.S.* 629 (1968).

not obscene for an adult, may be obscene for a child.[104] In other words, what may in one instance be within the protection of the First Amendment, in another instance is outside it.[105] But primarily, they upheld language in a New York statute which states that such material must be found harmful to minors.[106] In other words, the old *Dennis* test was given a significant role, although it had been specifically discarded in *Roth*.[107] The description of what was harmful for minors was an almost word for word inclusion in the statute of the obscenity definition given in *Memoirs*.[108] This gave an initial sense of consistency with judicial opinion—it apparently satisfied the Court—still what is accepted as a measure of harm in *Ginsberg*, had been intended only as a definition of obscenity in *Memoirs*, and in this instance the harm was established in advance by the state legislature, rather than being found to apply by the Court itself.[109] Finally, the ruling also departed from the national standard rule developed in *Jacobellis*, and would seem to allow each state legislature to decide independently what is harmful.[110]

Stanley v. Georgia is an even more striking departure from the *Roth* decision.[111] In this instance, three films were seized in a private home during an illegal search. The Court proceeded to apply First Amendment safeguards to what was clearly obscene under the *Roth* rule. But the Court attempted to distinguish the situation in *Stanley* from that in *Roth,* since it involved only the possession of obscene materials, and not their publication and sale: [112]

... (he) is asserting the right to read or observe what he pleases—the right to satisfy his intellectual and emotional needs in the privacy of his own home. He is asserting the right to be free from state inquiry into the contents of his library .... If the First Amendment means anything, it means the state has no business telling a man, sitting alone in his own home, what books he may read, or what films he may watch. Our whole constitutional heritage rebels at the thought of giving government power to control men's minds.[113]

---

[104] *Ibid.* at 634-35.
[105] *Ibid.* 637.
[106] *Ibid.* at 641.
[107] 354 *U.S.* 486.
[108] 383 *U.S.* 418
[109] Cf. Engdahl, *Loc. cit.,* p. 197.
[110] *Ibid.*
[111] 394 *U.S.* 557 (1969).
[112] *Ibid.* at 561. See also Engdahl, *Loc. cit.,* p. 199.
[113] *Ibid.* at 565.

The Court also pointed out that the state's attempt to prove danger from such materials was based on insufficient evidence.[114] In *Roth,* this had been ruled irrelevant.

Although the Court may maintain its strained distinction that *Stanley* is not the same as *Roth* because it involves a private home, a rather confused and conflict ridden situation exists. Under *Roth,* materials with appeal to prurient interest which were established as obscene—without redeeming social value according to a national community standard—do not come within the First Amendment's protection. In *Ginsberg* the Court seems to have said that some materials acceptable for adults are not acceptable for children if they are reasonably found harmful by the state legislature; now in addition, and as the results of *Stanley,* all these materials are still really protected by the First Amendment if one can just get them home safely. Or, what is obscene for the young may not be obscene for adults, and obscene things are not protected by the First Amendment, except that sometimes they are.

In the latest round of the controversy, the Supreme Court confounded its liberal critics, who had welcomed *Stanley v. Georgia* by ruling in *United States v. Thirty-Seven Photographs* that customs officials could still seize materials they deemed to be obscene, without a court hearing.[115] The Court indicated that *Stanley* would apply only to the home, but that transportation of materials to the home, where they could be viewed legally, might still be illegal.

The Court has been unable to develop a coherent rule for the suppression of certain materials or performances. This is hardly surprising since there are strong pressures from those on both sides of the issue of censorship either to suppress a large amount of material, which in the eyes of many people, is obscene, or to maintain a completely tolerant attitude. The situation is not made simpler by the huge number of local statutes and ordinances which allow the police to act in various instances. There is also the possibility to end certain practices obliquely through licensing boards or other administrative agencies. The California Alcoholic Beverages Control Board, for example, has revoked liquor licenses for bars whose entertainment is considered too risqué. The entire area of obscenity remains, therefore, another center of issues in which there is no wide and strong agreement on moral, social, or legal standards.

---

[114] *Ibid.* at 567.
[115] 402 *U.S.* 363 (1971).

Recently the President's Commission on Obscenity and Pornography recommended that all restriction on such material be dropped for adults.[116] That change still seems unlikely in the United States despite the often glowing reports of those who claim to see a drop in sex crimes, for example, as the benefit of this reform in Denmark.[117] And in fact within days the report, which had been commissioned by President Johnson, was condemned first by President Nixon's only appointee (who was later joined in his criticism by several other members of the Commission), condemned by the Vice-President, and then rejected by the President, all in the course of election year 1970.[118] With unsettled public attitudes on this matter, and lingering prudishness, both on the part of the public and various political leaders, legislative reform in this area may be a long time in coming. This presents a very confusing and unsettling situation where what prevails may in the end be what the pornography marketeers can get away with rather than any rationally defined and administered policy. The debate is only muddled and prolonged, we believe, by those who try to pull us between "prudery" and "permissiveness" on the basis of abstract social or moral propositions. The logical consequences seem clear if we are adherents of one party or another. The breakdown or reversal of these same positions seems to follow when adherents of these propositions—or their children— change camps. But in a pluralistic society it ought also to be possible to determine a legal test of offensiveness without going to first principles as to whether we ought or ought not to be offended. When that is possible it should allow a clearer distinction between what is offensive in public, although it may afford no public concern when it occurs in private.

D.   HOMOSEXUALITY: CONTROLLING PERSONAL MORALITY THROUGH THE CRIMINAL LAW

A study of the psychology of Americans, which in translation has been included in a popular German pocket book series has been a favorite source of European self-justification vis-a-vis the American "masculinity complex":

[116] "Panel's Draft Urges Liberal Pornography Laws," *The New York Times,* 9 Aug., 1970, p. 31 : 1.

[117] *Ibid.*

[118] "Federal Commission on Pornography Is Now Divided on Easing Legal Controls," *The New York Times,* 6 Sept., 1970.

Among the generality of Americans homosexuality is regarded not with distaste, disgust, or abhorrence but with panic; it is seen as an immediate and personal threat.... In America, as opposed to Western Europe, the homosexual is a threat, not to the young and immature, but above all to the mature male; nobody is sure that he might not succumb.[119]

Times have changed markedly since Gorer wrote about his impressions in the American Army during the second World War; and homosexual marches, protests, and picket lines would amaze any returning visitor from World War II days, about which Gorer wrote. Partly this new attitude may be the result of a more indifferent public, or a tolerance learned by resignation parallel perhaps to the eased restrictions on obscenity. Partly, however, this new attitude may be just a fashionable demonstration of "radical chic" for such causes as homosexuals, Black Panthers, and women's lib,[120] or perhaps, again just a new sense of tolerance for what a generation of writers has made more familiar and less foreboding. Judging by some of the discussion surrounding the

---

[119] G. Gorer: *American People: A Study in National Character*, Norton, N.Y., 1948, pp. 125, 127; *Die Amerikaner: Eine völkerpsychologische Studie*, Rowohlt, Hamburg, 1956, p. 85.

[120] Tom Wolfe wrote a satirical account of a party to raise funds for the unusually high bail demanded for Black Panthers accused of plotting to blow up department stores in New York City, calling it: "Radical Chic: That Party at Lenny's," *New York Magazine*, 8 Jun., 1970, pp. 26-56 (now included in *Radical Chic and Mau-Mauing the Flak Catchers*, Farrar, Strauss; Bantam, New York, 1971).

Fashionable society has not always been as generous, but has often taken a strange delight in the deviant exhilaration of encountering the more intriguing members of outsider groups in the non-commital public view of society receptions. In the German version of her *Origins of Totalitarianism*, Hannah Arendt captures something of this exotic taste by expanding on Proust's discussion of the first appearance of Jews and homosexuals in the salons of Paris:

> From the Jews one expected likewise the sensation of the strange-erotic, un-natural-beyond the normal, the sensation of enjoying a vice, after one was no more capable of higher or more serious feelings.

(*Elemente und Ursprünge totaler Herrschaft*, Europäische Verlagsanstalt, Frankfurt/Main, 1955, p. 143).

It is not surprising that this new cause of homosexual activism has also found sympathy among student activists (and now party "liberals") once it identified itself as one of the oppressed classes. What is surprising, on the other hand, is that, outside Berkeley, the movement has been most successful on the campuses of the major Middle American state universities: Buffalo, Wisconsin, Michigan, and Minnesota (cf. W.A. Sievert and E.R. Weidlein: "Special Report: Student Activism 1972—Beneath the Surface Calm: What?" *The Chronicle of Higher Education*, 13 Mar., 1972, p. 6).

reform of this same section under the German law, however, (see Chapter V: C. (2) below), one wonders whether the "panic" was not in fact a more general phenomenon shared in common with Europe's own Puritan strains.

The origin of the moral prohibitions against various kinds of homosexual behavior is usually traced to the Old Testament.[121] But the Anglo-Saxon statutory prohibition of buggery dates only from the time of Henry VIII.[122] And Coke who later defined the offense in his *Institutes* has left us the rhetoric which underlies the moralistic outlook that went into many American statutes. In the section on sodomy and buggery of the *Institutes* he exclaims:

Buggery is a detestable and abominable sin, amongst Christians not to be named, committed by carnall knowledge against the ordinance of the creator, and order of nature, by mankind with mankind, or with brute beast, or by womankind with brute beast.[123]

Despite this extensive moralistic elaboration, however, a historical legal issue has arisen concerning whether other further associated acts also fall within the definition of buggery and sodomy. As English law developed, the offense of buggery was construed narrowly including only the types of carnal knowledge specified by Coke. In 1817, for instance, in *Rex v. Jacobs,* the court ruled that the common law definition did not include fellation within buggery and sodomy.[124]

In the United States this question was not resolved until the 20th Century, however. At first, courts followed the direction provided by English courts in cases such as the one cited above. In *State v. Johnson,*[125] decided in 1913, a Utah court indicated that a statute which prohibited sodomy did not include in the prohibition the act of fellation. Apparently, other jurisdictions did not feel that the grant of such license was tolerable. In *State v. Cyr,*[126] a decision rendered in Maine in 1938, the court held the opposite, indicating that somehow fellation had really always been part of the common law definition of sodomy, and all American jurisdictions now accept the broader definition.

---

[121] Cf. e.g. *Leviticus,* 20 : 13.

[122] 25 *Henry VIII* c. 6, 1533.

[123] Edward Coke: *Institutes of the Laws of England,* Third Part, Clark & Sons, London, 1817, Cap. X, p. 58, "Buggery & Sodomy".

[124] 1817 *Russ. & Ry.* 332, 168 *Eng. Rep.* 830.

[125] 44 *Utah* 18, 137 *P. 632* (1913).

[126] 135 *Me.* 513, 198 *A. 743* (1938).

Perhaps in an excess of prudery, definitions provided in state statutes have been exceedingly vague. In one comprehensive study it was observed:

Modern labels unfortunately are neither explicit nor definitive, and the states have combined multiple titles to describe the generic term "sodomy"; thirteen states employ exclusively the term "sodomy"; nineteen states use the amorphous label "crime against nature"; one state relies on the term "buggery"; another six use a combination of "sodomy" and "buggery". The remainder have selected other designations which add to the already distended list of denominations.[127]

Only Minnesota, New York, and Washington define specific acts in their statutes.[128]

Penalties for the various homosexual acts which are now included in the statute's definition cover a wide range. The same study which categorized the statutory language above, continues:

In all states but four, a person convicted of private, consensual adult sodomy is guilty of a felony. Yet despite this uniform designation, the various legislatures have provided penalties which defy simple categorization because of their almost total individuality. Thirteen states have maximum penalties which are less than life, but at least twenty years, while the maximum sentence in another twenty jurisdictions is between ten and fifteen years. In seven states there are statutory alternatives that may exclude a jail sentence, requiring only that the defendant pay a fine, and in two others, there are provisions for both a monetary assessment and a jail term.[129]

Kinsey is cited by most authors on this subject for his illuminating studies in sexual practices. According to him:

59 % of American men have some experience with mouth-genital contacts . . . , 37 % have some homosexual experience . . . , 17 % of the farm boys have animal intercourse.[130]

These statistics are rather dramatic, and require some qualification. Edmund Bergler suggests the caution that one or two incidents do not

---

[127] "The Consenting Adult Homosexual and the Law: An Empirical Study of Enforcement in Los Angeles County," 13 *U.C.L.A. Law Revue.* 643 (1966), p. 659, "Part 11. Statutory Sex Offenses". See also Morris Ploscowe: *Sex and the Law,* Prentice-Hall, New York, 1951, pp. 195-216.

[128] Cf. *Minn. Crim. Code,* 690; *New York Penal Code,* Art. 135.00; *Wash. Rev. Stats.* 2456.

[129] "The Consenting Adult Homosexual . . .", *loc. cit.,* p. 689, "Part III. Enforcement Techniques".

[130] A. Kinsey; W. Pomeroy; C. Martin: *Sexual Behavior in the Human Male,* Saunders, Philadelphia, 1949, p. 392.

indicate that an individual is necessarily a practising homosexual.[131] It is not also less likely that such an individual could be arrested, however. While Kinsey's statistics are perhaps only partly indicative of occasional practices the extent of which were not always foreseen by lawmakers or the public, it is always an act, not an abstract condition or frame of mind, which is subject to prohibition. But again the figures can only verify the "peril" to society which the moralist legislator had already pointed out. In any case, figures estimating the number of practising homosexuals in the United States range between 4% and 17% of the population.[132]

Confronted with what is ostensibly such a significant proportion of the population which has engaged at some time or another in these acts, it is hardly surprising that enforcement of statutes in this area generally ignores acts done in private between consenting adults.[133] Nonetheless, surreptitious enforcement techniques are widely used to ferret out the unlucky. And these often include such devices as policemen in "drag" or behind peepholes in public restrooms.[134]

Considering the fact that a significant reform proposal has been made by the American Law Institute,[135] it is a little surprising that only one state in the United States has adopted it. In Illinois, homosexual acts done by consenting adults in private are no longer prohibited.[136]

---

[131] Cf. Edmund Bergler: *Counterfeit Sex, Homosexuality, Impotence and Frigidity,* New York, 1962, p. 27. See also Bernard J. Oliver: *Sexual Deviation in American Society,* College and University Press, New Haven, Conn., 1967, p. 123: "In general, the number of homosexuals varies according to the interpretation of what degree a person must have experiences of homosexuality to be so designated. These estimates vary from 4 to 17 per cent of the population of America."

[132] *Ibid.*

[133] See "The Consenting Adult Homosexual...," *loc. cit.,* p. 689, "Part III. Enforcement Techniques". See also no. 23 below.

[134] *Ibid.,* p. 686.

[135] A. L. I.: *Model Penal Code* (Tent. Draft No. 4, 1955) § 207.1-6; Interestingly, the A. L. I. members rejected the Reporter's recommendation for this draft section. An explanation at the time was given in a, "Special Note Re Consensual Sodomy Between Adults," § 207.5, "...The Council of the institute, at its March 1955, meeting, voted in favor of criminal punishment. Some members believe that the Reporter's position is the rational one, but that it would be totally unacceptable to American Legislatures and would prejudice acceptance of the Code. Other members of the Council oppose the position of the Reporters and the Advisory Committee on the ground that sodomy is a cause or symptom of moral decay in the society. . ."; In the Proposed Official Draft of 1962, the recommendation was accepted (see § 213.1).

[136] *Ill. Rev. Stat.,* Chap. 38, 11-6, 11-2, 11-9.

This is parallel to the recommendations made by the now famous *Wolfenden Report* in England.[137] It is interesting to note that that *Report* dismissed the main historical objections to such a reform—e.g., a menace to the health of the society, damage to family life, and a danger to youth—considering these aspects of social life would probably be unaffected by the change.[138]

Although prohibitions remain in all states except Illinois, fourteen states have altered their penalties for this offense, six increasing them, and eight decreasing them.[139]

Two, Minnesota and New York, have attempted to follow the lead set by Illinois in eliminating the prohibition of acts done in private by consenting adults, but they were unsuccessful in this attempt.[140] Four other states: Connecticut, Colorado, Oregon, and Hawaii, have reform laws under consideration.[141]

There are definite reasons for the slow change in this area of the law. Attitudes concerning homosexuality have not altered all that rapidly, although some embarrassment may be noticeable among lawmakers hesitant to be too far out ahead of most people's ways of thinking. One long range measure of change is for example the fact that, while at their 1955 meeting, the members of the American Law Institute refused to accept recommendations of their reporters, to include a section in the draft of that year which would have allowed acts in private between consenting adults, in 1962 this minor reform proposal could be accepted with less fear of jeopardizing the reputation of the whole *Model Penal Code* (see note 135, above). This is a reflection, perhaps, of the fact, as many students of the subject report, that public attitudes towards this offense are somewhat ambiguous.[142]

---

[137] Great Britain, Home Office/Scottish Home Dept., Committee on Homosexual Offenses and Prostitution, *Report . . .*, Cmd. No. 247, H.M.S.O., London 1957, p. 25.

[138] *Ibid.*, pp. 22-24.

[139] Cf. "The Consenting Adult Homosexual and the Law . . ." *loc. cit.* p. 663, "Part II: Statutory Sex Provisions."

[140] *Minn. Crim. Code* § 609.30 (Prop. Draft, 1962); *New York Penal Code*, Art. 135.50 (Prop. Draft, 1964).

[141] Cf. "Homosexuals Win Capital Agreement That Eases Curbs," *New York Times,* 1 June, 1972, p. 30C : 6-8. The article also refers to "an agreement worked out in Federal District Court" in the District of Columbia whereby the local sodomy statute "does not apply and cannot be applied to private consensual sexual acts involving adults."

[142] Cf. e.g. Edwin Schur: *Crimes Without Victims,* Prentice-Hall, Englewood Cliffs, New Jersey, 1965, p. 109.

There are a variety of reasons for public and official intransigeance on an issue such as this. The following reasons were listed as most often utilized by opponents of more liberal legislation in this area:

The prohibition of homosexual activity rests on numerous assumptions relating to the nature of homosexual conduct. Although vigorous disagreement exists over their validity and applicability, these assumptions include the incidence of adult-child sexual contacts; the possibility of offensive displays of homosexual behavior; the utilization of force or violence in homosexual contacts; the interrelationship between homosexuality and other forms of statutory criminal activity; and the possibility of curing or detering homosexual conduct. In addition, those who support the legal *status quo* further argue that homosexuality constitutes a menace to the health of a society, and that repeal of existing legislation would "open the floodgates" for an increase in existing homosexual behavior.[143]

Curiously, the one place where the "floodgates" seem to have been opened widest is in the prisons themselves. Studies by criminologists and official investigators report that in the jails, prisons, and many similar state institutions homosexual assault is a constant threat not only from inmates but from guards as well.[144] But if this condition is a concern to the public at large at all it has obviously been pretty well satisfied with a formal prohibition, and while it may be concern enough for law enforcement officers to use stake outs and entrapment, even the simple precaution of segregating prisoners by age and nature of offense often seems to be passed over inside most institutions.[145]

Another commentator explores the subconscious psychological reasons for resistance to change in this area of the law, and indicates that in addition to more visible reasons, there exists a general fear of homosexuality stemming from an inner anxiety that one might have such tendencies oneself, the association of homosexuality with the excretory function and a general rigidity in cultural definitions of sex roles.[146]

---

[143] "The Consenting Adult Homosexual . . . ," *loc. cit.* pp. 653-54, "Part I: Introduction".

[144] See references in Chapter I: A, n. 34, and Chapter II: C, n. 138.

[145] *Ibid.*

[146] Cf. e.g. S.D. Ford: "Homosexuals and the Law: Why the Status Quo?" 5 *Calif. Western Law Rev.* 232 (1969), p. 271. Not long ago the story of the rapid rise of newly graduated lawyer made national news. He was reported very successful in pornography cases in conservative areas. His tactic was to tell the jury: "Psychologists tell us that these pictures are arousing to homosexuals and people with sexual repressions. They don't effect you, do they?"

Along a more conventional line, the same writer indicates that homosexual activism—through various homophile groups—is distasteful to many, the government reinforces negative feelings by maintaining a discriminatory policy towards such individuals, and the ambivalence of physicians and psychiatrists over whether such practices are a disease or not, contributes as well.[147]

Whatever reasons one chooses, resistance to change in the law remains strong, particularly in more isolated sections of the country. Wholesale reform along the lines of the measure adopted in Illinois has not yet begun, and appears unlikely in the immediate future. The situation here is so far noticeably different from that which led to an easing of resistance on the question of abortion. In that case popular discussion already had accepted the idea—if not solved the question of the ultimate morality of it—in consideration of such questions of social concern as family planning, fear of deformed births, and ethical reasons for performing abortion. One should not dismiss the effects, the pressure and demonstrations of womens' organizations either, although they contributed more to the dramatization of the cause than to the substantive matters of the discussion itself.

Certainly the cause of "women's lib" reopens the discussion of many inequities which the feminist movement had not been able to project into the public awareness with such vigor since the days of the women's suffrage movement. However, rational or irrational the means the new feminists employ there are plainly signs of action to change appearances of discrimination today that go far beyond the problem of inequities, and all women will share in the benefits (and removal of protections, where they occur) regardless of their persuasion on feminism itself. "Gay liberation" is one of the same types of numerous "people's liberation" movements which arose in the wake of the Vietnam war resistance in the United States, where members of the administration and the partisans of the right overeager to justify themselves by labeling dissenters probably are most responsible for ideologizing a whole generation of causes into identifying themselves in Marxist/Leninist terminology. This particular cause which traces its activist conversion to a sudden turnabout in customary expectations when the occupants of a "gay bar" in Greenwich Village in New York City turned on the police during

---

[147] *Ibid.*

a raid in 1969.[148] Unlike "women's lib", however, *this* "people's movement" does not have the advantage of the same "consciousness-raising" effect on the public in which—regardless of what the public may think of the movement's tactics—they are reminded of principles which supposedly they already accept. In this case—as Gorer doubtlessly correctly perceived for World War II years—the public is not basically persuaded that they are not threatened. What is more in cases like this the "people's movements" are surely correct in perceiving that Americans have not universally "integrated" the tolerance of the liberal spirit of Locke and Jefferson. But the status of any reform proposal similar to either that of the *Wolfenden Report* or the *Model Penal Code,* i.e. removing the prohibition on private acts between consenting adults, is perhaps rather a political one. Legislators have so far had no constituency to whose political claim they could politically afford to yield on this question. No matter how embarrassing the absurdity of some of the arguments in defense of public control of personal morality through the criminal law may become, it is a rare politician who will allow himself to get too far ahead of what the public already accepts.

Under these circumstances the "movement" has undoubtedly done the right thing politically in joining the array of "people's" causes from the anti-draft, anti-war movement to the welfare mothers. That way the candidate of the peace and social welfare causes can be handed a ready made platform of demands. The difficulty with this "new politics", however, is that, although it can lend conglomerate political power or recognition to a host of splinter groups and causes, unless something of the old, also American, ideal of Lockean-Jeffersonian liberal tolerance revives, instead of there being people who are in favor of this or that, or advisedly dissent from this or that, and who are also white, or black, or "ethnic", the new ideological perception of things allows no such individual chance preferences: There are then "poor people", "black people", "minority-ethnic peoples", "people in favor of legalizing marijuana", "health-food people", "Jesus people", "gay people", female "persons", etc. The trouble is, if that is what it takes to be an effective political person nowadays, the old-fashioned Lockean-Jeffersonian individualistic, idealistic "people" have not much of a chance of being one of "the people" at all.

---

[148] Cf. "The Militant Homosexual," *Newsweek,* 23 Aug., 1971, pp. 45-48. As in the case of all the other "movements" mentioned, reference is made only to their own claims to represent.

CRIMINAL LAW AND REFORM IN WEST GERMANY

CHAPTER IV

HISTORICAL AND THEORETICAL PROBLEMS: ISSUES IN THE "GENERAL PART" OF THE CODE

A. FULL-SCALE RECODIFICATION: THE BACKGROUND OF THE GERMAN CRIMINAL LAW REFORM

(1) Passage of the German Criminal Law Reform Acts

After nearly one hundred years, in June, 1969, legislation attempting the first comprehensive reform of the German criminal code was finally acted upon. Thus the late "grand coalition", the first co-alignment of the conservative Christian Democrats (CDU) with the social-democratic opposition (SPD) in the history of the Federal Republic, and a succession of effective ministers of justice, managed to secure agreement on a compromise reform, which single party government had until then been unable to accomplish. The current effort at reform had been under way for over ten years. The proposals had been widely debated and even during this relatively short period—so far as the law is concerned—the attitudes of both jurists and the public had undergone considerable change.

As might be expected in a code dating essentially from the mid-19th Century, the most passionate public debate had been over the matter of morals legislation. But here the German popular press, as well as many legal scholars, had been divided over the necessity for the steadying hand of the state in moral affairs.[1]

---

[1] Generally we might assume that a reform attempt would serve to reduce the extent of moralism woven into the existing law. But in the instance of the German government's proposed draft criminal code of 1962, this was not the case. Instead the draft of 1962 appeared to be considerably more moralistic than the Code adopted nearly 100 years ago. According to the count of Horst Woesner, Justice of the Supreme Court of the federal state of Bremen, whereas the code of 1871 listed only 30 forms of violations of decency, and in the subsequent laws this had grown to only 80, the proposed reform would have distinguished 190 separate forms of violations of decency. (Cf. "Reform ohne Erneuerung," in *Der Spiegel,* 10 April, 1967, p. 57.)

However, the most significant contribution of the reform appears to lie elsewhere. The abstract principles of the "general part" of the code may offer far more in the abolition of the distinction between a prison sentence (*Gefängnis*) and imprisonment in a penetentiary at compulsory labor (*Zuchthaus*), and in the gradual shift from short term prison sentences to fines and other penalties. The "reform", if there is to be a reform and not simply a revision, is by no means complete in the several new law reform acts, however. Above all, it contains no unifying new conception of the penal goal—something that is considered important for systematic treatment by German jurists—although the general desire for resocialization, whatever else the penal process may serve, is growing. But the full development of a resocialization program will have to wait for a further reform of penal institutions and the laws governing the execution of sentence.

The reform of the political section of the code, which was completed several months earlier than the main reform law act, is significant for its new description of offenses against the state. One must realize that most of the political section of the code of the Nazi period, in the version of 1934,[2] had been abrogated by the Allies [3] after the war. This gap was filled, once the Federal Republic was constituted, by Art. 143 of the Basic Law (*Grundgesetz—GG*), which governed the employment of military forces against an internal threat. This law was replaced by the penal code amendment (1st *Strafrechtsänderungsgesetz—* 1. StÄG) of 30 August, 1951, in which political provisions were reintroduced in up-dated form. Because of the cold-war climate of those years, the section may be considered excessively conservative and state protectivist by today's standards. German political conservatism is not entirely understandable in terms of the world situation of such recent times, however. There was—and remains—a certain distrust of pure liberal democracy in Germany, justifiable perhaps to some extent by the experience in which liberal democratic institutions were abused in the outright political wars of the 1920's and 30's and in the manipulation of liberal laws in the courts of the Weimar Republic.[4]

---

[2] I.e. Sections I-III and 102, 103 of Section IV of the "special part" of the code, dealing with various forms of treason, attacks against, or defamation of the Fuehrer, hostile acts against friendly states, etc.

[3] Cf. *Control Council Law* No. 11.

[4] Concerning the fears of a "self-destructive democracy" see: Theodor Maunz; Günter Dürig; Roman Herzog: *Grundgesetz Kommentar*, Beck, Munich, 1968, Vol. I, pp. 18 4-5. Cf. also Hermann von Mangoldt; Friedrich Klein: *Das Bonner Grund-*

Many of the offenses recognized by the 1. StÄG are somewhat dated, however. And their repeal or temporary removal, was construed as a means towards promoting new contacts with East Germany or at least keeping the possibility of contact with the East alive.[5]

Finally, among the provisions relating to public morals and decency and to the protection of religious sensibilities, which have afforded the most strenuous public debate, the following have been entirely eliminated: the provision concerning adultery (including prosecution upon application of the injured party in a divorce by reason of adultery); provisions against male homosexual acts done in private between consenting adults (without exploitation or compensation); and the prohibitions of bestiality; and of trickery in procuring consent to extramarital intercourse.

The question of morals protection in the law is far more complex than the superficial attempt at regulation of private moral behavior suggests. The temptation in any great work of legislation or of legislative reform is to legislate not only for what people need, but also for what the legislator thinks they ought to be. Of all branches of the law, the criminal law is perhaps the most susceptible to modelling after political and philosophical [6] as well as religious moral ethical outlook. And the question

---

gesetz, 2nd ed., Vahlen, Berlin, 1955, pp. 113-16. See also such works as Lutz Lehmann: *Legal & Opportun: Politische Justiz in der Bundesrepublik*, Voltaire, Berlin, 1966 esp. pp. 7ff. which illuminate the temper of judicial (and bureaucratic) opinion as formulated by judges (and officials) of the Weimar period who had been, for the most part, appointed under the former imperial regime and remained dedicated to its principles and perhaps to its restoration. How much this period still represents the breakdown of liberal democracy in political memory, even in the United States, was recently dramatized to the present authors by the remark of a liberal American sociology professor at a great American private university. After being vilified during a student protest, perhaps not entirely unjustifiedly, but so that he is now often openly abused on the street: He proclaims "It's the Weimar Republic!"

[5] Some may remember the legalistic debates of the press as to whether an American could conscientiously allow an East German border guard to stamp his passport with the seal of a government which his country did not recognize—a debate which continued at least until Robert Kennedy visited East Berlin in 1962. The restrictions on West Germans, who were then particularly concerned with trying to maintain contacts with Germans in the East, were much more far-reaching, though often no less dubious. The logic of this is considered in Lutz Lehmann: *Op. cit.,* pp. 168-89.

[6] Clearly there are matters governed or regulated by law which are simply results of convenience and custom, or disinterested attempts at rational solutions.

of the intrusion of designs for moral ethics in the law applies to all aspects of the code: to either a "rehabilitative" or "retributive" penal goal for the "general part"; to insistence on a strictly individualistic liberal or a state protectivist social attitude in the political section; as well as to legislation in the area of private and public morals.

A law providing only bare procedure and usage as recourse has time and again shown itself to fall short of the prevailing sense of justice or social propriety. Thus the institution of equity arose early as a com-

On the other hand when whole areas are newly organized or rationalized, conceptualization of the problems of law or social control itself may introduce a kind of design and ambition, which goes beyond simple convenience or analysis of the traditional system's structure. There is often good reason for allowing or encouraging this. But there is perhaps also hope for a realization of the limits upon one's ability to change people by legislation when one examines the extent that lawmakers develop social philosophy in the law, and the extent to which even legal philosophers may bind themselves in paradoxes of their own making.

The late German socialist legal philosopher, Gustav Radbruch prepared a collection of maxims on the law from notable philosophers and literary figures (*Kleines Rechtsbrevier: Spruchbuch für Anselm,* F. von Hippel (ed.) Vandenhoeck & Rupprecht, Göttingen, 1954). He maintains that "only in their arrangement is a conscious intention easily recognizable" (p. 5). Yet the distinguished socialist's maxims of social ethics provide in the abstract—material for the conservatives social ethical claims as well (see e.g. page 184 n. 25 below). Perhaps no one as much as Immanuel Kant contributed to establishing the liberal idea of the "state under law" (*Rechtsstaat*), the nearest German equivalent of the English expression "rule of law", as a legal political ideal in Germany. Yet he too could be subject to a curious kind of pedantic legalism which we may possibly attribute as much to legal moralism and the dictatorship of his own abstract conceptualization of the justification for legal penalties as to a sense of the human political social need for the certainty of "rule of law":

> Even if a civil society resolved to dissolve itself with the consent of all its members—as might be supposed in the case of people inhabiting an island resolving to separate and scatter themselves throughout the world—the last murderer lying in prison ought to be executed before the resolution was carried out. This ought to be done in order that everyone may realize the desert of his deeds, and that blood guiltiness may not remain upon the people; for otherwise they might all be regarded as participators in the murder as a public violation of Justice. (*The Science of Right,* Part II "Public Right." Basically Hastie transl. with minor revisions, quoted in: Morris R. Cohen and Felix S. Cohen: *Readings in Jurisprudence and Legal Philosophy,* Prentice-Hall, New York, 1951, p. 322.)

An excellent study of how the conceptual logic of legal and political thought has contributed not only to the advance of legal philosophy but also its abuse (though one may not agree with the judgment of the author on all points) is Chapter XVI, "The Decline of the Law" in F. A. Hayek's: *The Constitution of Liberty,* Univ. of Chicago Pr., Chicago, 1960, pp. 234-49.

plementary judicial mechanism to the procedural recourse of the common law. More recently in the question of *mens rea* the German Supreme Court for civil and criminal matters rebelled against the long standing doctrine that ignorance of the law does not excuse:

(So far as) the greatest number of felonies punishable under the Reich's criminal code (was concerned), the opinion that excusable error about what was against the law was pretty well inconceivable, may have had some justification in the politically and socially well balanced times of the second half of the 19th Century . . . . For those penal provisions which the legislature has become accustomed to attaching to the ever further reaching administrative regulations of the various areas of social life, the presumption that everyone knew the law was not accurate then, and is even less so today. For these restrictions are not very often derived from general moral principles, but rather from considerations of social or national [*staatlicher*] convenience [*Zweckmäßigkeit*]. The number of these administrative penal provisions [*strafrechtliche Nebengesetze*] has for a long time far exceeded the amount of pure criminal law.[7]

---

[7] *Entscheidungen des Bundesgerichtshofs in Strafsachen*—BGHSt 2, 202f, (1952).
    It is still problematical to what extent one can argue the non-applicability of the principle *ignorantia juris nocet* in the German law. Rather, the highest federal court decided in 1952 (cf. BGHSt 2, 194-212) that "awareness of unlawfulness" is an essential element of the complete picture of the criminal act (cf. interpretation of R. Maurach: *Deutsches Strafrecht: Allgemeiner Teil,* 3rd ed., Müller, Karlsruhe, 1959, 39 II, p. 410). The principle in question is thus not so much one of "ignorance of the law" as such, for which we would for the positive law at least generally have to accept the common understanding as enunciated for example by Kelsen:
    That ignorance of law does not exempt from obligation is a principle which prevails in all legal orders and which must prevail since otherwise it would be impossible to apply legal order. (Hans Kelsen: *General Theory of Law and the State,* 1949, p. 72)
What is required by the above decision is rather *mens rea,* or wrongful intent, for which a certain knowledge or "awareness" of the particular law may be essential. This is a flat acknowledgement of the fact that for many situations a particular knowledge of prevailing regulations is not a foregone conclusion and, far less, that which is generally accepted as expectable of a *sense of right* or social sensibility. We find this sense of law codified, at least in the instance of the law regarding violations of public order of the 24th of May, 1968 (*Gesetz über Ordnungswidrigkeiten*—OWiG):
    . . . should a violator act without the awareness of doing something not permitted, namely because he does not know of the existence or applicability of a legal provision, and if this is not his fault, it is not (considered) a violation in his case. (OWiG 6,3)
Similarly, according to the commercial violations act of 1954 (*Wirtschaftsstrafgesetz*—WiStG) we find that all violations are regarded as "violations of public order" [*Ordnungswidrigkeiten*] (WiStG 3,2), and thus subject to the limitation in OWiG (1968) 6,3 above, unless they are:

A new difficulty arises, however, when one attempts to apply the apparent "moral" of equitable reinterpretation of culpability under the law, "no guilt where there is no moral guilt" [8] in the general sense which the authors of the draft code of 1962 attempted. For despite

> ... in their extent or result capable of effectively hindering the realization of the norms [*Ziele*] of the economic system, especially of the prevailing market economy or price system, (WiStG 3,1 (1))

or where the violation is:

> blatantly repetitious, by trade, on the basis of disreputable self interest, or otherwise irresponsible... showing lack of concern for the public interest in protection of the economy... etc. (WiStG 3,1 (2))

This means, simply put, that there is a public moral resistance to imposing legal guilt in violations of public order or commercial regulations where there has been no intent to commit a violation or where the violator did not and could not be expected to know the regulation in question. To want to apply the maxim "no guilt without moral guilt" may sound generous at first when applied to the violations here concerned. Transferred to the criminal law at large, however, as the draft code of 1962 (*Entwurf eines Strafgesetzbuches*—EStGB 1962) attempted, this principle does not serve so prominently to limit excessive punitive measures against offending parties acting without criminal or wrongful intent or fore-knowledge of the illegality of their actions. Rather, among a moralistic and moralizing people with a strong public law, mission sense of the state, this attitude or rule supports a tendency to read-in a moral to give sense to the *mission* of the law. The result is plainly not so much a limitation on exessive regulation-mindedness of the law. Rather, a special moral meaning is given to all laws, indeed to everything provided for by the state to fulfill its moral purpose.

The conservative or social-liberal ideas of the state already maintain a purposive-corporate, as opposed to a purely functional sense of law and society. The addition of a further moral sense, to the ostensible higher purposes of law and state, lends these social theories what amounts to a social-theology of their own.

For a description of the role of wrongful intent, or *mens rea*, as a necessary attribute in determining what is a penal offense according to the accepted German criminal law doctrine of analysing the elements of a criminal act (the *Handlungslehre*), see page 187f. below.

[8] This appears to be the attitude of the authors of the draft code of 1962 (*Entwurf eines Strafgesetzbuches*—EStGB 1962), and is set out in the principles of guilt and punishment contained in the Introduction:

> The draft accepts the theory of criminal law based upon guilt [*Schuldstrafrecht*]. This means that punishment, which entails a moral judgment upon human behavior, and is always felt to express one, may only then be imposed, and in principle only to that degree, that one can morally reproach the perpetrator for his action. (p. 96)

(Deutscher Bundestag: *Verhandlungen des Deutschen Bundestages*, 4, Wahlperiode, Vol. 80 *Druchsache* IV/650: "Entwurf eines Strafgesetzbuches (EStGB 1962) mit Begründung" Bonn, 1962. See also *Bundesratsdrucksache* 200/62.)

As Professor Würtenberger has pointed out in his foreword, a leading theoretical study on the idea of guilt, by Arthur Kaufmann, has been written from the point of the nobility of this ambition, the philosophical and doctrinal result for the criminal law is often a specious reading-in of moral guilt to otherwise morally indifferent actions. Thus not only is the much discussed carrying over of morals offenses to control by the secular arm in question,[9] everything from a simple traffic violation to the breach of administrative procedure is susceptible to interpretation in moral terms. Thus all guilt becomes moral guilt. And the state is clothed in an aura of moral purposiveness, which, if theologically, or ideologically, correct is, in an aspiring pluralistic, liberal democracy, politically intolerable.

All nations harbor a sense of public propriety. But it may not be necessary to legislate for propriety, as long as traditional ideas of what propriety is are generally respected. It is precisely when the principle is not universally upheld, however, that its legislation becomes an issue.[10]

view that guilt is essentially a moral question, or it is not properly speaking guilt. (Arthur Kaufmann: *Das Schuldprinzip,* Winter, Heidelberg, 1961, esp. ch. 4, "The Idea of Guilt as an Absolute Moral [*sittlicher*] Principle" (*"Das Schuldprinzip als absoluter sittlicher Grundsatz"*). The difficulty with such a proposition for the law is plainly that it represents a moral philosophical stand within an orthodox tradition. There is an assumption, perhaps, that all moral philosophical systems have basic principles in common; but even within the Christian tradition there is a history of discord when one goes from the general to the particular on many issues. And many defensible legal prohibitions are morally indifferent. To use an example of the new radical rhetoric, which would have seemed absurdly unreal in 1961, surely few of us would accept, one logical expansion of the proposition that only moral guilt may serve as a proper basis for legal guilt, the notion that "moral" causes may be pursued "by any means necessary". We may believe that this latter suggestion is a rejection of morality altogether, but that is not the real issue here. For the logical, theoretical formulation of one system instructs the adherents of its rival system, regardless of how poorly they learn or understand the substance of its meaning. But even in Europe in 1961 there were significantly different moral ethical systems between political blocs. When similar differences exist within a liberal democratic society, however, it is probably more certain to ask for legal justice under laws which are hopefully made by men of moral intention, but without intending to impose their particularistic moral views. We recognize that this does not always occur; but the recognition may serve to spur the effort to improve.

For an earlier, somewhat different approach to the same problem see: Walter O. Weyrauch: "Das psychologische und das ethische Schuldelement," Jur. Diss., Frankfurt/Main, 1951, typescript.

[9] For a discussion of the literature on this subject see: Horst Woesner: "Strafrechtlicher und sittlicher Schuldvorwurf," 17 *Neue Juristische Wochenschrift* (NJW), (1964).

[10] The customary law of the traditional societies of South and East Asia appears, for example, to have been upheld without extensive means of sanction. One explana-

However, the question can not always simply be reduced to the form, "Whose moral standard is to be enforced?" For, those who seek this role for the state often do not claim the moral standard is at all dependent upon their own behavior. For them, the very legitimacy of "moral law" lies in its absolute applicability and, they may quite readily accept the doctrine of the "fallen nature" of man, which to them only appears to corroborate the necessity for the protective legislation they demand.

Yet, while there are few who would insist on the strictures of Calvin's Geneva to protect us against our sinful natures, there are many who talk of absolute moral law as if it were ascertainable by the judicial authorities out of the nature of things [11] as the supreme civil and criminal

tion of the writing of such a book as the *Laws of Manu* is that either some laws were not so firmly respected as formerly, or in fact an invocation to a more pious (if perhaps fictitious) past was necessary. Sir Henry Maine is very eloquent on this point:

> ... without the most violent forcing of language, it is impossible to apply these terms, *command, sovereign, obligation, sanction, right* to the customary law under which the Indian communities have lived for centuries. ... It would be altogether inappropriate to speak of a political superior commanding a particular course of action to the villagers. The council of elders does not command anything, it merely declares what has always been. ... In the almost inconceivable case of disobedience to the award of the village council, the sole punishment, or the sole certain punishment, would appear to be universal disapprobation. (*Village Communities*, p. 67f.)

This style of life is not necessarily outmoded today for the internal affairs of a small community which knows how to live according to humane sensibilities —although if the group shares many fixed notions, it can become oppressive for free-thinkers. Walter O. Weyrauch has written a study of what he calls the "behavioral constitution" of such a group of Berkeley young people who were paid to take part in a nutrition experiment which required them to live together for three months under close observation in a laboratory "penthouse": "The 'Basic Law' or 'Constitution' of a Small Group," 27 *Journal of Social Issues* 49 (1971). Like many others of their generation, they rejected the notion of imposed rules, and even tried to make the procedures of the experiment subject to discussion. And yet the internal self-adjustment pattern of the group seemed to be guided, where tensions arose, by reaction to loss of status with the others. These observations are not surprising, considering what we know of customary law societies. What is interesting here is that this social response continued among a group committed in principle to free development of the individual unhindered by rules or convention.

[11] It has been argued that that decision would not have been made again later in quite the same way. Cf. e.g. Max Güde: "Man darf den Souverän nicht reizen." *Der Spiegel*, 16 Sept., 1968, pp. 59-64. But laws and precedents are often harder to unmake than to make in the first place. There was considerable disappointment that this precedent survived the first reform law. But the point of law at issue in that decision—that parents who permitted their engaged children to lodge together

court of the Federal Republic (*Bundesgerichtshof*—BGH) did in an important decision (which although it survived the first reform act, has now been eliminated by the fourth in the fall of 1970).[12]

Political liberalism favors another "ethic", however, the "moral resistance" to any undue imposition upon one's private freedom. In Germany, as everywhere else, however, there are many who adhere far more readily to the notion of liberalization in the realm of personal behavior than to the liberalism of political and social tolerance.

Socialist theory which may appear to parallel individualistic liberalism in its rationalism, has habitually reverted to various kinds of moral protectivism, once in power.[13] But in these cases, this result does not arise out of socialist rationalism but rather out of the conservative moral protectivism of the leading class of the movement. In Germany, the liberal and socialist forces have carried the liberalizing tendency, so far as the rationalization of reduced protectivism in the realm of traditional morals is concerned. But although the apparent force of the rhetorical battle among jurists, journalists, and student groups seems more and more to favor looser construction of the law these days, one should not underestimate the political resistance of morally conservative labor, conservative rural Catholics, and a conservative middle class.

In this discussion, "moralism" may, therefore, appear to be used in different senses. But all of these refer to the resort to different kinds of moral legal protectivism. Equity arose to balance what often appeared to be lack of justice in the common law procedure; certainly the German

---

under their roof were guilty of pandering—has now been eliminated by the fourth reform law.

[12] BGHSt 6 (1954), (46-59), p. 52ff.:

> ... The rules of simple morality [*Sitte*], or convention, derive their (weak) binding authority only from the acceptance of those who voluntarily recognize and follow them. They are no longer in force when they are no longer recognized and followed. They change in content, when the conception of what propriety demands changes. The norms of moral law [*Sittengesetz*], to the contrary, are valid in and of themselves. Their (strong) binding authority rests upon the prevailing [*vorgegebenen*] and unchallengeable [*hinzunehmenden*] order of values and the proprieties and obligations [*Sollensätze*] which govern human society. They apply independently of whether those upon whom they look with the right of being followed really recognize and follow them or not. Their content can not change for that reason, that the attitudes about that which applies changes."

[13] H.-H. Jescheck discusses the retreat from free love (which seemed to go hand in hand with the Revolution at first) to moral propriety in the socialist countries in: "Die Behandlung der mänlichen Homosexualität im ausländischen Strafrecht," 19 *Studium Generale*, 339 (1966).

high court's action in their rejection of formal guilt, where moral culpability or intent is lacking seems to reflect this as well. Obviously moral legislation to protect us against our "sinful nature" or even because we are "sick" [14], is deliberately protective. There may be the same attitude in the "ethic" of individual self-reliance against an elitist conservatism;

---

[14] Concentration on single branches of social-psychological research—often to the exclusion of consideration of the methods, results, and experience of other areas—has led in recent years to rather fixed notions about social and psychological preconditioning and determinism. There has been a considerable indulgence of these theories in the law, as elsewhere in public life, with the result of a significant occurrence of diminished responsibility and a reaction against the defense of insanity. An interesting general review of the sociological and psychological literature of criminology is contained in G.O.W. Mueller: *Crime, Law and the Scholars: A History of Scholarship on American Criminal Law*, Heinemann, London, 1969, esp. pp. 176-99. It may be enlightening to refer to two attitudes discussed: "... one psychiatrist writes that 'no one would maintain that *all* criminals are mentally ill or abnormal', and another maintains that all are ill or abnormal [opinions attributed to D. Stafford-Clark: *Psychiatry To-Day* (1952) p. 221, and B. Karpman: *The Sexual Offender and his Offenses* (1954) p. 562, respectively]" (p. 197). These new sciences, where the language is only developing, seem to rely more on personal reaction and personal terms than many investigators, who attach special meaningfulness to their use of "scientific methods" are often prepared to acknowledge. This phenomenon in itself is relatively harmless if the practitioner has a general command of the literature of his field and a good sense of logic and linguistic usage. Otherwise it is not unexpectable to see either the misguided practitioner, or the misguided court which relies on him, reaching conclusions or giving advice which proceeds from the logic of his own language, or his special understanding of it, as much as from any professional observation. In an editorial in the *Journal of Offender Therapy* (quoted by Mueller in an earlier draft), Melitta Schuldeberg seems to refer to just such occurences:

> In the case-record of a juvenile murderer who attempted a second murder within the institution, the supervising psychiatrist tells us that he regards this as indicative of therapeutic progress, since, "his aggression was coming out." No "research" can correct such thinking. The doctor's intellectual confusion is the inevitable consequence of his moral confusion. In our effort to "be non-judgmental," some of us have lost all judgment and fear of values is becoming a disruptive force. (Melitta Schuldeberg: "Editorial,", *J. Off. Therapy*, 1,12, (1962)).

See also: J.L.J. Edwards: "Diminished Responsibility: A Withering Away of the Concept of Criminal Responsibility," (pp. 301-41); Glanville Williams: "Automatism." (pp. 345-54), in G.O.W. Mueller (ed.): *Essays in Criminal Science*, Rothman S. Hackensack, N.J.; Sweet & Maxwell, London, 1961. A recent article by Norval Morris contains an appendix (compiled by G. Lowenthal) with a "Summary of Several Arguments Advanced for Abolition of the Defense of Insanity" (in "Psychiatry and the Dangerous Criminal," 41 *Southern California Law Rev.*, (1968) pp. 514-47).

and ultimately in an "ethical" "critique of pure tolerance" [15] out of impatience with the same liberal pluralism; manifestly in the protectivism of "social relevance", one may even say "social realism", to conserve the expression of moral force for the work of social reconstruction. Any effort, in short, to insure the moral-ethical content of the law— without which it might well be considered only a hollow set of standard operating procedures—can grow to a kind of "moralism" the more the effort to fill that hollow: the greater the determination to form the law in the image of any such particularistic ideal—the more "moralistic" the legislator, regardless of the specific "moral content" of his law.

The present authors are well aware of the fact that various American state codes may be far more "moralistic", in the sense of containing more morals legislation, than the German code of 1871.[16] And while the description of German protectivism may have a peculiar ring to the American ear, it is partly because the provisions of the American codes, where they are known to exist, are often taken to be dead letter and so the reasoning behind them is considered to be of no concern.[17] But this opinion is no guarantee against enforcement of morals blue laws from time to time by authorities who do not see it that way. For while this type of legislation may die a kind of formal death on the books by way of disuse, it might take just the same kinds of rhetorical argument in the United States, as lately in Germany, to get these laws repealed. The protectivist contends that elimination of morals legislation would be misunderstood by the public to imply that certain things were not only legally, but, also morally permissible,[18] and that such legislation should be left for the prosecutor's use at his discretion. Yet a conservative pragmatist may share the same moral position, and still regard it the more important question, whether it is supportable, in view of the current

[15] Cf. R.P. Wolff; B. Moore; H. Marcuse: *Critique of Pure Tolerance*, Beacon Pr., Boston, 1965.

[16] Cf. e.g. American Law Institute (ALI): *Model Penal Code*, Tentative Draft No. 4, Philadelphia, 1955, *(passim)*. Refers extensively to morals blue laws.

[17] Cf. e.g. H.L.A. Hart: *Law, Liberty, and Morality*, Vintage, New York London, 1963, Hart comments:

> No one, I think, should contemplate this situation with complacency, for in combination with inadequate published statistics, the existence of criminal laws which are generally not enforced places formidable discriminatory powers in the hands of the police and prosecuting authorities. (p. 27)

[18] Cf. e.g. EStGB 1962, *Bundestags (BT) Drucksache* IV/650 of 4 Oct., 1962, 193 *(Begründung)*.

rate of violent and destructive crime, to concentrate our primary law enforcement efforts on making private behavior a public issue.[19]

(2) Origins of the German Criminal Code and of the Present Reform: Contending Versions of Social Ethics in the Federal Republic

German criminal law today consists of the penal code (*Strafgesetzbuch* —StGB) first adopted in 1871 (plus additions and modifications) now reformed by the law reform acts of 1969 and 1970. The juvenile court law (*Jugendgerichtsgesetz*—JGG) of 1953, contains not so much material criminal law provisions as criminal procedure applicable to juveniles. The German law of criminal procedure (*Strafprozessordnung*—StPO) dates in its present form from 1965. There are in addition, a series of relevant penal regulations in the so-called *"Nebenstrafrecht"* and *"Ordnungsstrafrecht"* which list the penalties to be awarded for vio-

---

[19] The simple answer of the "moralist" is, however, that it is precisely in the undisturbed examples of "moral decline" that violent crime has its origins. And he very often promises himself salutary effects against crimes of violence from attacking loose morals. In a recent example in ordinarily more tolerant San Francisco, the director of the vice detail led several raids on nudie film theaters taking not only operators but patrons also into custody. In his words:

> We're going to continue to make arrests where arrests are indicated in the pornographic entertainment racket despite certain adverse developments in our campaign. . . . People here have always inclined to go along with sophisticated pleasure facilities on the basis that San Francisco was a cosmopolitan community; the Paris of the West, that sort of thing. But recently the pendulum has swung too far in the direction of organized perversion, vice and the proliferation of cash-and-carry filth. We believe that this expansion of the field of vice is a major contributant to heavier crime and violence. It is from the ranks of the pimps, prostitutes, pushers, and sex freaks that the perpetrators of more vicious crimes are recruited. We aim to deplete these ranks through arrest and presecution. (*San Francisco Examiner,* 19 August, 1969, p. 29:1)

However sincere this kind of reasoning may be, plainly there is also a good measure of political moral, social criticism involved. Deviation as a deliberate pattern in comfortable circles seems to manifest much more of a threat to the defenders of society than that same deviation associated with outright criminality in an arm of society less meaningful to the defenders social—or political—aspirations. The *Buffalo Evening News* of 24 January, 1970, carries two articles, carelessly juxtaposed, which illustrate the problem. In one, the new sheriff says he requires 40 to 50 people for a narcotics task force, apparently to increase the number of undercover agents he claims are "necessary to preparing a case" working at the State University, which he calls: "the real source of marijuana and psychedelic drugs in our area" (p. A3). In another article, members of Negro neighborhood organizations complain that far from a need for cover, they have to keep their children at home to avoid pushers and junkies on the street (p. A5).

lations which arise in other areas of German law. Despite these additional penalties for violations of administrative and legal orders it is intended that the principles of the "general part" of the criminal code shall govern penal liability clearly and comprehensively for all areas.

The StGB adopted in 1871 was based upon the Prussian state StGB of 1851 which became the criminal code for the Union of North German States (*Norddeutscher Bund*) in 1870.

There was some dissatisfaction with the code from the first and since the 1880's there have been a series of attempts to reform it. These were held up at first principally because of the so called "*Schulenstreit*", a philosophical debate over the intent and basis in law for the proper exercise of penal authority by the state. The sociological school proposed a goal directed resocialization of prisoners, referring to a "specific prevention" through this process. The classical school adhered to the traditional ideas of retributive justice and "general prevention" through deterence. These differences became less noticeable after the turn of the century, and a number of reform proposals were developed at the instance of the Justice Ministry in 1909, 1913, 1919, 1922, and 1927, none of which succeeded. Two further proposals appeared during the Nazi period in 1934 and 1936. On the other hand, noticeably successful single reform measures, inspired by the sociological school, include the juvenile courts law, *Jugendgerichtsgesetz* (JGG), the introduction of the measures of "safeguarding" (*Sicherung*) and "resocialization" (*Besserung*), and the general tendency to restrict the practice of awarding short term prison sentences for minor offenses.

Work on the reform was taken up again after the formation of the Federal Republic. In 1954 a commission (*Große Strafrechtskommission*) was appointed which prepared the first draft of what became the government proposal of 1962. The first half, the "general part" (*Allgemeiner Teil*), elucidating the legal definitions of crime, punishment, and controls in criminal law, appeared in 1956. The second half (*Besonderer Teil*) with the specific titles was presented in 1958. After many changes, these appeared as the government draft of 1962 (*Entwurf eines Strafgesetzbuches* —EStGB 1962). In reaction to the government proposal—which was long seen as excessively conservative by many jurists—an alternative proposal for the "general part" (*Alternativ-Entwurf eines Strafgesetzbuches*—AEStGB)[20] was completed by 14 well known German and

---

[20] Jürgen Baumann *et al.*: *Alternativ-Entwurf eines Strafgesetzbuches* (AEStGB): *Allgemeiner Teil*, Mohr (Siebeck), Tübingen, 1966, *Besonderer Teil:* "Politisches

Swiss law professors in 1966. The section on political crimes of the "special part" appeared in 1968 shortly before passage of the revised section of the criminal law governing political offenses (8th *Strafrechts-änderungsgesetz*—8. StÄG of 25 June, 1968). The further sections on sexual offenses; violations against marriage, family, and personal status; and violations against religious sensibilities appeared in late 1968, just prior to the meeting of the German jurists association, *Deutscher Juristentag* (DJT), which considered the necessity for reform of the sexual offenses provisions of the code in the meeting of the criminal law section.

The main emphasis of the government draft lay, the official reasoning went, in a new policy goal in the regulation of crime within a framework of a newly rationalized system of penalties and controls. It attempted to differentiate the scale of penalties while at the same time respecting the principle of equality before the law, civil liberties, and the dignity of man.[21] From such statements it may begin to become clear that the authors of the proposed reform saw their work far less in the matter of substantive reform than in the ambition for a new approach to doctrine, uniformity, and the systematization of established judicial opinion. Professor H.-H. Jescheck of Freiburg, a member of the commission, explained the traditionalistic position, which prevailed among the authors of the draft of 1962, by rejecting the liberal, neutralistic, and value-indifferent notion of the state. For Jescheck, this is particularly important considering the disillusionment of many Germans in both politics and the moral authority of the state as a result of the not too distant German past.

A state which would restrict itself to being a well-functioning, general-purpose apparatus would sacrifice any integrating function and would always be the morally weaker in the confrontation with the East, if it did not collapse by itself in the first great economic crisis.[22]

Law becomes then an instrument of moral rearmament in the struggle against destructive forces, foreign or domestic. How close the logic of traditional conservatism and radical socialism are to one another should

---

Strafrecht," 1968; "Sexualdelikte; Straftaten gegen Ehe, Familie und Personenstand; Straftaten gegen den religiösen Frieden und die Totenruhe," 1968.

[21] Th. Würtenberger: "Strafrecht," in *Staatslexikon*, 7th ed., Vol. 6, p. 770.

[22] H.-H. Jescheck: "Das Menschenbild unserer Zeit und die Strafrechts-reform," in *Recht und Staat*, Nos. 198-99, Mohr (Siebeck), Tübingen, 1959, p. 8.

be apparent from language such as this. They share the search for moral purpose in the state and society. The unprecedented growth of American radicalism in the Vietnam war years frequently assumes a similar aspect. Both conservatives and radicals share the conviction that if the society or the state acknowledges a higher moral purpose, its members, or citizens, will become moral, and, with officials acting in accordance with the higher moral purpose of society, acts of state will also be moral. For the individualistic liberal—who is not necessarily the person referred to as a liberal in American usage at all—this is logic in reverse: For him it is indivdual moral action which contributes to a moral society. For him an institution functions only through the actions of individuals. And only an individual can make a moral decision.

It is not difficult to understand that there should be concern for moral renewal in post-war Germany. Aspects of this same quest could be recognized to some degree in the United States and elsewhere and, as a result of the Vietnam war, is current in the United States again. The greater question posed by such a moral position is, however, how exactly the state should assume such moral authority, and whether the criminal law is the proper forum for its expression. For, once we take this moralistic position we must confront the further question of whose morality should be manifested in the state and the law. That question is also clear to Jescheck, who answers:

If one asks where the state should acquire this new and surely very necessary moral authority, the answer can only be: through the way of life of us all, and especially also of us jurists.[23]

This attitude ascribes to the function of law that it reflect the general social values, and in particular those of a leading group. Jescheck is well aware of the problems entailed, but faces them squarely. He admits that the social values of a leading group may be in a minority, but maintains that it is these values which uphold the character of the existing society, particularly in view of the political disinterest and disillusionment of the citizens of today.

... It may be perhaps only a certain select group of the people who determine what the present order of values may be, for unfortunately we do not have as politically

---

[23] *Ibid.*, p. 8, (Jescheck also refers to Ernst Forsthoff: "Das politische Problem der Autorität," in 1 *Der Horizont* 1 (1956), Selbstverlag der evangelischen Akademie Baden, Herrenalb).

fruitful a time as a hundred years ago when public affairs were taken to heart by every citizen.[24]

But we cannot necessarily assume that the position of the minority party of those days, the Social Democrats, would have been much different on this basic issue, although they differed on particular doctrines and titles in the code. Jescheck calls the writings of Gustav Radbruch, the distinguished legal philosopher and socialist Justice Minister during the Weimar Republic, to his aid on this point. Jescheck borrows a Goethe quote from Radbruch, who had similarly sought to uphold the obligation of the social-state to provide moral leadership to its citizens. Radbruch's social-economic politics may have differed from those of Jescheck, but the notion of the social significance of moral authority, whether left or right, remains, and draws upon common cultural tradition.

If we treat men according to what they are, we make them worse. If we treat them according to what they ought to be, we will make them into that which they can become.[25]

In effect, both the traditional conservative and the social-democratic schools are operating on the notion of the "good of society". Yet, whereas among conservatives the idea of retributive justice remains prominent,[26] the Social-Democrats (officially) go over entirely to a rehabilitative rather than retributive penal goal.[27] As seen by its authors, the proposal of the

---

[24] *Ibid.*, p. 8f.

[25] *Ibid.*, p. 9. Jescheck quotes Goethe from Radbruch: *Kleines Rechts-Brevier: Spruchbuch fur Anselm*, F. von Hippel (ed.) Vandenhoeck & Ruprecht, Göttingen, 1954, p. 26. The *Rechts-Brevier* is not written as a treatise, but is rather a collection of maxims on the law which Radbruch used collectively to demonstrate attitudes towards law, and for which he says: "only in their arrangement is a conscious intention easily recognizable" (p. 5).

[26] H.-H. Jescheck: *Op. cit.*, p. 9f.: "The sense and value-content of the various legal descriptions of violations would also in the future be characterized in that the strong framework of punishments would be maintained, although from the standpoint of purposefulness it might be more advantageous if the criminal legal reaction were left entirely in the hands of the judge in each instance." And. p. 13: "Penal law does not strive towards a successful cure in the first instance, but rather towards the realization of the expectations of justice...."

[27] Cf. e.g. Gustav Radbruch: *Rechtsphilosophie*, Erik Wolf (ed.) Koehler, Stuttgart, 1963, p. 269. Radbruch aspires not simply to a better criminal law, but rather to a law of "safeguarding" [*Sicherung*] and "rehabilitation" [*Besserung*].

law professors (AEStGB) constituted a kind of social-liberal alternative,[28] taking account of modern criminological approaches without going as far in the direction of socialist law as Radbruch.[29].

Seen in this way, the issue seems to have become one of political and legal philosophy—depending on one's point of view he may choose to say ideology. To use Radbruch's own terms, it may seem to be a question of "individualistic" liberalism *vs.* the "supra-individualistic" philosophies of either (or both) the right and the left. In simpler terms, perhaps, it appears to be a question of whether one would join those who argue the rights of the individual first, or would prefer the argument of those who—regardless of whether they explain the role of the individual as subordinate to, or the fulfillment of the purposes of the whole of society—put the rights of the collective first.

For the ideologist, and for different reasons the Anglo-American who tends not to think in terms of fine philosophical distinctions, things often seem to be polarized between the individual and the system. This may well have some basis in the history of political, philosophical conflicts in England and America, and also for the ideologists in those countries, where they often are in fact "individuals" poised against the system. But, in England and America, political opposition has often been one of liberal conservatives pitted against conservative traditionalists on the right, or of conservative liberals pitted against social radical rationalists on the left. In Germany, this is really not the case. The political climate of the mid-Continent tends to be more extreme. Yet, while the serious contenders at the opposite ends of the political spectrum of the Federal Republic until today have been by no means extremists, an "individualistic" liberal on the German political scene can be regarded as quite an individualist indeed.

Since Bismarck, or perhaps since Frederick the Great, the somewhat patriarchal conservative has acted more or less to preempt the field of social legislation from the social rationalist and radical. Germany's "liberals ", on the other hand, in pursuing a course more of "economic liberalism", than of liberal democratic individualism, have gained for themselves more of a reputation for seeking their own economic, class,

---

[28] Cf. e.g. Jürgen Baumann: "Was erwarten wir von der Strafrechtsreform?" in J. Baumann (ed.): *Program fur ein neues Strafgesetzbuch: der Alternativ-Entwurf der Strafrechtslehrer*, Fischer, Frankfort/Main and Hamburg, 1968, see esp. pp. 21ff.

[29] Radbruch: *Rechtsphilosophie, passim.*

self interest than for representing a liberal democratic, free, competition of ideas, goods, and services. The "social market economy", the economic system devised by the ostensible successors to the conservative traditionalists, the Christian Democrats, offers more "social" benefits than many a more "liberal" system in the West. Thus, while the ambitions of their former cabinet colleagues and political opponents, the Social Democrats, may differ somewhat in content, they are agreed very much in form. The issues between the major German political parties, therefore, rarely figure as a conflict between private individual rights (i.e. argue the good of society can only arise from the sum of the good of its members) vs. the priority of the rights of society as a whole, but rather they are concerned with debating how best the aspirations of the individual can be satisfied in pursuit of the collective benefit of society. The issue is not one of individualism or liberalism vs. either conservative or social democratic notions of the "good of society", but of the "social" democratic version vs. the "Christian" democratic version.

This is not to say that all members of the major parties adhere to party philosophy, nor does it mean that there are no attempts at liberalization of the law with a primary view (in any single instance) toward the rights of individuals rather than because of some special good or benefit to society as a whole. The AE, for example, would seem to contain a great deal of just such an aspiration. Yet, in German politics, the success of these proposals depends upon their being accepted by the major parties, and the acceptance by the parties has usually meant— where it did not simply reflect a significant change of public moral outlook or opinion—that a major program change must be fitted into party doctrine first. One may probably argue that it was such a significant change of moral outlook and opinion, which had already come about, that made the provision for punishment of adultery by application of the injured party after a divorce granted for this reason seem vindictive and outmoded. Similarly, it would seem, the provision guarding women against men who prevail upon them to grant sexual intimacy by misleading them into thinking that a valid marriage has taken place—or by making them think that they are their real husbands—could be safely eliminated, not because public opinion has changed as to the extent of the outrage, where it may in fact legitimately be said to have occurred, but rather because awareness of this latter offense's occurring at all has declined with the rarity of actions taken under this provision, and also because the ridiculous situation which resort to this title entails, makes it of little use as a remedy.

B.   WHAT IS A CRIME?

*(1)   The Gravity of an Offense and the
Constituent Elements of an Offense*

Like the French Code Pénal, the StGB distinguishes three levels of gravity of an offense as measured against the severity of the penalty imposed for conviction. These are defined under the revised law as follows: A felony *(Verbrechen)* is a grave offense punishable with the newly defined uniform prison sentence *(Freiheitsstrafe)* of one year or more (§ 12,1). The extent of the reform this involves, at least in theory, is apparent when one considers that this penalty has been reduced from penetentiary at compulsory labor *(Zuchthaus)* or confinement in a fortress *(Einschließung* or *Festungshaft)* of more than one year. Since the gravity of the offense is defined according to the severity of the penalty, however, this must lead to some confusion. But the intent of the reform has been to give shorter prison sentences, in general, and to avoid giving short-term prison sentences, where possible, by giving sentences set out to probation, or by substituting per diem fines.

A petty offense *(Übertretung)* is one punishable with a jail sentence *(Freiheitsstrafe)* of up to six weeks, or a fine of up to 500 DM (§ 1,2). This has been modified from a light jail sentence *(Haft),* or a fine of up to 500 DM. (This provision is dropped in the second reform law [2, StrRG], which is to take effect on 1 October, 1973.)

Offenses of moderate gravity *(Vergehen)* are all other offenses which can be punished with a uniform jail sentence *(Freiheitsstrafe)* (of up to one year) or a fine (§ 2,2). The penalties here have been reduced from confinement in a fortress for up to five years, a prison term *(Gefängnis),* or a fine of more than 150 DM, or a simple fine. (Under the interim law see §§ 1, 1; 3.)

According to the established method of analysis of the criminal act *(Handlungslehre)* an offense under the criminal code has three necessary constituent characteristics: the combination of elements constituting a particular crime according to a specific title of the criminal code *(Tatbestand),* illegality *(Rechtswidrigkeit),* and guilt *(Schuld).* This analysis is not defined in the code (StGB), but has become established in a body of German criminal law concepts. The "General Part" of the Code defines the limits of the respective parts of this analysis.

The *Tatbestand* is what would correspond in Anglo-American law to the offense described under a particular title of the code. Given such an offense *(Tatbestand),* illegality *(Rechtswidrigkeit)* may be assumed if not excluded by reason of a justification *(Rechtfertigungsgrund)* such as: self-defense, consent, etc. Guilt *(Schuld),* in this system, means personal responsibility. Thus guilt cannot be established for an otherwise illegal act or the omission of a legally required act, where personal responsibility is precluded by: lack of intent, error, mental incapacity, or where the fulfillment of a required act would mean the assumption of an action above and beyond that which may be reasonably expected.

(2) The Concepts of Guilt and Mitigation

Guilt is the only consistuent of the analysis of an offense which appears to have been treated in a different manner in any of the proposals leading to the reform. In the alternative draft, (AE § 2, Para. 2) the concept of *Tatschuld* was introduced. This term attempted to attach guilt directly to the act of the offense to the exclusion of other surrounding circumstances.

What is said with the concept of *Tatschuld* is that only the guilt arising from the deed will be punishable, not guilt arising from manner of living [*Lebensführungsschuld*] or poor character [*Charakterschuld*].[30]

The benefit of this new expression was simply, and only, to assure that "the punishment fits *the crime*", i.e. that the degree of the penalty would be fixed only according to the degree of the offense. This issue probably would not have arisen had not the "criminal-type" theory found some resonance in certain branches of criminology and been accepted to some extent in the then existing law, as for example in the case of the treatment of the "habitual criminal" (the old § 20a StGB), a provision now repealed.

For the authors of the alternative draft, guilt should relate to the offense committed and not be calculated on the basis of the offender's criminal record and/or sociological and psychological background:

I am completely aware of the complex nature of the concept of guilt and the concept of guilt-in-the-act [*Tatschuld*]. It is also clear to me that it is always difficult, if it will not indeed be impossible, to establish adequately the degree of guilt-in-the-act. Any judgment of the degree of guilt remains an attempt, or at best an approach. That is even more the case for a guilt based upon how one has led his life [*Lebensführungsschuld*] or a guilt which is not strictly based upon the offense [itself].

... Let me say again, by the way, that the concept of a guilt based upon what kind of life one has led [*Lebensführungsschuld*] or upon character [*Charakterschuld*]

[30] J. Baumann: "Die Reform des Allgemeinen Teils eines Strafgesetzbuches," in Leonhard Reinisch (ed.): *Die deutsche Strafrechtsreform,* Beck, Munich, 1966, p. 60.

sharply limits the freedom of the offender at the moment he commits the offense. If one sees guilt as I do as free, personal, self-determination in the possibility to act differently, one who sees the crime not as the necessary consequences of criminogenic factors, but rather as product of the human will, he will want to derive the guilt incurred from the invasion of legal interests [die rechtsgutverletzende Tat] and from nothing else.[31]

Baumann had introduced this concept in his own counter proposal (Gegenentwurf—GE) in 1963.[32] The idea was substantially incorporated in the alternative draft of the 14 law professors.

As incorporated into the alternative proposal of 1966, the provision (AE § 2, Para. 2) reads: "The penalty may not exceed the degree of guilt attaching to the act of the offense [Tatschuld]."

Yet, according to the established analysis of the act of the offense described above (the Handlungslehre), or under the general principle of nullum crimen, nulla poena, sine lege (§ 2 StGB), one might have assumed all along that guilt (although not sentence) had on no account to have pertained to anything other than the act of the offense itself. Schmidt[33] and Lackner[34] considered this point at length in discussion of Baumann's earlier counter proposal (GE) and concluded that in effect no significant change in the concept of guilt was involved.

Guilt-in-the-act [Tatschuld] is even according to the GE not the result of the isolated evaluation of the facts of the case and the basis for the charge [Schuldvorwurf] arising from them . . . . Guilt-in-the-act can, therefore, not be essentially different from what judicial opinion has long understood as "guilt" [Schuld] as the basis for the determination of sentence [Strafzumessung]. Since our criminal law system is built around circumscribed offenses [Tatbestände] and all sentences without exception are tied to the "acts" [Taten] "guilt" in a general sense can always only be guilt-in-the-act. A loosely formulated "guilt based upon the life one has led" or "guilt based upon character" is already excluded for the reason that the law [Rechtsordnung] does not recognize punishment for the anti-social attitude of the offender. This is not the place to consider the problem of guilt based upon how one has led his life which is discussed in the literature, but receives very little consideration in judicial opinion; it is fundamentally only a question of to what extent the personal circumstances,

[31] J. Baumann: in Kleine Straitschriften zur Strafrechtsreform, Gieseking, Bielefeld, 1965, p. 47. This article was also published as "Zum Entwurf eines StGB" (in answer to criticism of Baumann's GE by Eberhard Schmidt in MDR 629 (1963), in Monatschrift für deutsches Recht 802 (1963).

[32] J. Baumann: "Entwurf eines Strafgesetzbuches, Allgemeiner Teil," in Recht und Staat 274/75, 1963 (referred to as Gegenentwurf—GE).

[33] Eberhard Schmidt: in Monatschrift für deutsches Recht 629 (1963).

[34] Karl Lackner: "Der Allgemeine Teil des künftigen Strafgesetzbuches in der Auseinandersetzung: ein kritischer Beitrag zum GE Baumann," Juristenzeitung (JZ) 617 (1963).

namely, the whole past of the defendant, carry weight as the basis for the charge in a specific offense [*Schuldvorwurf*] .... The legal attachment of guilt to guilt-in-the-offense in my opinion contains only the danger that the courts will understand it as a rejection of their established practice and the personality of the offender will no longer receive its proper weight in the passing of the sentence.[35]

Thus Lackner felt that Baumann was not only guilty of semantic obscurity, but also that his term *"Tatschuld"* could only serve to inhibit judges later from properly considering the personality of the offender before passing sentence.

Baumann himself, was, however, very much concerned with the sociological and psychological background of the offender and believed these circumstances should be considered in passing sentence. Consequently, in his counter proposal (GE § 42.II) he listed conditions for determining the extent of the sentence: "insofar as these indicators are not already a part of the legal act of the offense [*Tatbestand*]" (GE § 42.I). Furthermore, if his sentencing rules (GE § 42.II) can be interpreted as excluding social and psychological circumstances from the determination of the offender's *"Tatschuld"*, this is certainly not true in the instance of the repetition of an offense within three years (GE § 43) for which he calls for twice the penalty for a first offender.

Yet the same concern for consideration of surrounding circumstances (as in GE § 42.II) for determining the extent of the sentence appeared in the government proposal of 1962 (EStGB 1962 § 60 Para. 2). In the alternative proposal (AE 1966), on the other hand, the authors —including Baumann—adhered more closely to an unmixed concept of *Tatschuld* in which, although not excluding consideration of these conditions, they maintain: "Behavior before and after the fact is only to be considered insofar as it allows one to determine the extent of *Tatschuld*." Thus, in effect, what Baumann and his colleagues tried to counteract with the concept of *Tatschuld* was not a provision of the then existing code (except such tacit predisposition as the now repealed § 20a StGB), of the government proposal, or of established judicial practice, but rather a possible inclination to judge guilt according to a sociological, criminological approach such as the theory advocated by Lambroso, which suggested that there is an identifiable criminal-type.[36]

---

[35] *Ibid.*, p. 618.

[36] Baumann: *Kleine Streitschriften*, p. 152. Baumann writes:
> The idea of guild as a result of "how one has led his life" [*Lebensführungsschuld*] has currently, in more recent criminal law concepts, received some stimulation through the theorics of "blindness to the law" [*Rechtsblindheit*] and

The debate over the concept of guilt has born fruit in the reform, however. A new provision (§ 13) has been introduced into the StGB designating that: "The guilt of the offender is the basis for determining the punishment." This would seem to satisfy the reservations of Baumann and the authors of the AE, without the introduction of the term "guilt-in-the-act", which, as Lackner pointed out, would really have added nothing to the established theory. The sociological, psychological effects of punishment receive a new formal consideration too: "The effects which may be anticipated from the punishment for the offender's future life in society are to be considered" (§ 13,1). The new provision goes on to stipulate what socio-psychological considerations "for and against" the offender are to be weighed in passing sentence (§ 13,2).

C.   APPROACHES TO CRIMINAL LAW REFORM

(1) *The Theory and Form of Correction*

The most significant departure in the reform of the "general part" of the code would appear to be the elimination of the distinction between forms of long-term imprisonment; the introduction of a new milder scale of imprisonment, fines, and penalties; and the wider use of probation and fines to avoid short term prison sentences. The removal of the distinction between sentences to *Gefängnis,* prison, and *Zuchthaus,* penitentiary with compulsory labor, serves principally to eliminate a major psychological barrier to the already difficult task of assisting former prisoners to return to society. The milder scale of sentencing, although considerably less than revolutionary, is a compromise between the very liberal AE proposals and the beginnings in this direction already a part of the government's draft. The new system makes use of the Scandinavian model of *per diem* fines in place of short term jail sentences for certain lesser offenses. The wider use of fines and probation and such innovations as social therapeutical treatment for compulsive offenders indicates not only a tendency to a more liberal attitude in ideas of penology, but also a general disillusionment with the socially profitless system of the inherited form of correction for the ambitions of modern, liberal democratic society. But despite the considerable discussion in this area, which has surrounded the work of reform, and has led to these changes, one

"hate for the law" [*Rechtsfeindschaft*] and through the treatment as experienced in the cases both in the modified theory of intent (e.g. Mezger), and in the concept of guilt as taken from the leading theory of guilt in judicial opinion.

major German criticism of the reform law seems well taken: there is as yet no new or clear cut conception of what the goal of penal correction should be.

In a country where theory and legislation are traditionally expected to work together, this kind of criticism is perhaps more strongly felt, though there is naturally considerable relief at the passage of a compromise reform at all after so many years. But awareness of this lack of harmony is felt by both conservatives and social liberals. Writing some time before enactment of the new law, Professor Th. Würtenberger, who had taken a fairly conservative position on the reform as a whole, as member of the Catholic criminal law reform council, stressed the social considerations necessary in the design of a system of penal correction today:

The future legislator must, therefore, make a binding and clear value determination, both as to the substance and purpose of the penal system in general as well as the intent and method of the execution of sentence in particular. . . . The EStGB 1962, which should contain the clear and definite outline of modern thinking in penal law remains almost completely colorless in answering the significant question as to the real mission and purpose of the exercise of the penal function by the state. It is a significant step forward, on the other hand, when the AE 1966 declares; "punishment serves the protection of legal interests and the resocialization of the offender into the law-abiding community" § 2.1. Yet the determination of the objective of the execution of sentence is not completely identical with the legislative determination of the aims of the penal system as a whole. Even in this last respect, the EStGB contains no directive.[37]

The AE (§ 37.1) attempted to formalize in law the idea that one specific purpose of penalization is the resocialization of the offender into the community. It may be asked, however, whether the explicit inclusion in law of this concept would mean any change in practice. The point of this discussion lies in the fact that in the traditional legal notion the sentence is the method of carrying out "legal justice", which is to say retribution.

In this connection, Würtenberger (writing in 1967) reminds us that a matter which should not be forgotten during a criminal law reform is the need for a reform of the penal institutions themselves; and in particular if a new penal goal, such as resocialization of the offender, is to be given new emphasis. He points out that at no time in the last hundred years have reformers managed to combine their attempt at criminal law reform with a parallel institutional reorganization. The matter is becoming more crucial, however. The first reform law dealing with the "special part"

---

[37] Th. Würtenberger: "Reform des Strafvollzugs im sozialen Rechtsstaat," *Juristenzeitung,* 233 (1967), p. 238 (now also in English, see page 257 below).

of the code already in effect and the bulk of the second reform law dealing with the "general part" to take effect in 1973.

Today we must reconcile ourselves to the situation that the reform of the code has gone so far that the draft of 1962 is before the special Bundestag Committee without the equally necessary institutional reform anywhere in sight. There are a few important consequences for the future modernization of the penal process which derive from this development of criminal law reform. Since the alternative draft (AEStGB 1966) contains sophisticated proposals for the creation of a complicated system of punishments apparently the basic and essential ideas for a system of punishments will be fairly generally laid down when the reordering of the institutional side of the penal system should be just about to begin. Therefore, there is the danger that the new criminal code will determine much about such punishments that institutionally speaking will later be scarcely or not at all realizable.[38]

This imbalance between the legal and the institutional reform could quite seriously inhibit any attempt at achieving a new approach to resocialization, assuming that that ideal expressed in one form or another is regarded as one ambition of the reform law now enacted. It is in the penal institutions where the reform will ultimately be measured for its success or failure. This is the decisive fact which Baumann too, recognizes when he declares: "What we need is not so much a new criminal code, as a new law governing the carrying out of sentence." [39]

Even the most hardened legal moralist adherent of retributive justice is more or less prepared to accept the resocialization theory to some extent today. The residual difficulty with a system of resocialization—if the case for resocialization remains based on a rejection of a penology of pure retribution—is that there is also an implicit moral position taken by the state in resocialization to an established norm. This can certainly become as much a form of moralism as retributive justice ever was. For the prisoner not only loses his liberty but also his freedom to shape his own civil values, when, and if, he returns to society.

This could be restated as the question of whether a prisoner has any civil rights left, or which rights remain, and which are taken away. It could be asked what form of resocialization could avoid setting up moral norms which would serve as substitute goals for prisoners. But, if resocialization is finally desirable, the stand against its implicit moralism seems to carry the principle of non-moralistic value-indifferent criminal law to its logical absurdity.

---

[38] *Ibid.*, p. 231.

[39] J. Baumann: "Die Reform des Strafvollzuges," in Reinisch (ed.): *Die Deutsche Strafrechtsreform*, Beck, Munich, 1966, (pp. 89-105) p. 105.

Of all reports on the success of resocialization, and the reconstruction of moral values, the most illuminating, so far as these goals are concerned, comes from the advocates of the New China.[40] Here the measure of success is not simply "resocialization", but plainly "re-education", not only to society, but to what society itself is and ought to be. This particular ideological danger does not appear to be especially imminent in the West at the moment, but keeping the ultimate logical consequences of this idea in mind does the most to guarantee its limited employment. No less a partisan of the resocialization theory than Gustav Radbruch has warned that an unrestrained "social improvement" theory can be ultimately as damaging as the most draconic conservative, deterrent, or retributive justice:

The improvement and assurance theory when pursued to its logical conclusion would in fact lead to these same results [i.e. contravention of the principle: *nullum crimen, nulla poena sine lege*] if it were not cut off by the third element of the idea of law, by the *security of law*.[41]

It may be worthwhile, in view of the missionary social zeal both in Germany and America today, to examine the implications of the principles of the resocialization theory more closely. When we consider what appears to be the hopelessness of the human condition for inmates of most of our prisons, and while there are model low security prisons, even most new facilities are only new versions of the same old thing, there will certainly be considerable agreement on the objective of resocialization. We should take care, however, to distinguish between the need, or obligation, to provide opportunity for inmates to improve themselves to be able to make their own way in society, and the enthusiasm to want to turn this into re-education. Frankly we might all be a lot happier if the criminal element of our society could be converted to social-minded citizens. The problem is rather that our prisons are not centers of liberal education. We have to consider that the idea of resocialization as a principle begins with basic education and instruction in a trade, and continues with re-education to the values of civil society. We must realize what such an assignment of authority to discipline minded prison officials can entail. And here we do not have to ask ourselves what would happen to the inmates of the idealistic Peking jail, Felix Greene describes, if they did not develop social conscience. It is enough to remember the battle

---

[40] Cf. e.g. Felix Greene: *Awakened China: The Country Americans Don't Know*, Doubleday, Garden City, N.Y., 1961, ch. 20, "Prisons: Bad and Good," pp. 209-18.

[41] Radbruch: *Rechtsphilosophie*, p. 268.

of principles between the warden and the bird man of Alcatraz. No matter what the accomplishments of the inmate, the institution, which already has the fate of the inmate in its hands, wants his soul too, in acceptance of its values. Require the institution to provide opportunity, and we can at least see to what extent the obligation is carried out. Require the institution to educate, and we have no idea what they may be doing.

We are confronted today with the new prospect for Americans of more and more persons facing prison for what are certainly for many quite legitimate moral political reasons. Should the heat of controversy continue, many of us may even be forced to join them. Considering the gravity of the situation, it was no great surprise to hear that the Defense Department had established a crisis center for internal disorders. Again, considering conditions which will be more thoroughly treated in the political justice section, they might even have been remiss in not doing so. What follows, however, is far from the assuagement of civil or political distrust: the prospect of the Pentagon's maintaining dossiers on not only ringleaders of disturbances, but also on all the bizarre political ideas of the student press, and all published utterances of dissent or even pro-administration declarations. If we can manage to be concerned about the fact that this center exists not for the purposes of sensitivity as to why the crises arise, but for controlling them when they do, if we have doubts about who should be able to evaluate such material at the high level of the administration, the question becomes more meaningful when applied to the prisons, no matter how progressive they become. Do we really want moral, political re-education in our prisons? Or in any other public institution, for that matter?

We want to offer the opportunity for basic education, even higher education for those who would benefit, and for learning a trade. But our educational ideals in this part of the world are dedicated to the ambition of building the integrity of character to accept the responsibility for our moral decisions. How then could we properly expect re-education of those who have faced the prospect of prison for their convictions, to accept the values of the government, whatever they may be, and accept re-education to the moral, political consequences of those values, before qualifying for release. There is no need for a constructive prison policy to take on such a menacing perspective. But we must realize that they are already the most self-justified institutions in society. We owe ourselves that much—to be concerned about the rhetoric and principles we add to their mission.

The moral principles themselves are generally very exalted. But the rhetoric is often curiously interchangeable for other principles, when the regime changes. Professor Paul Lin has very eloquently captured the spirit of the ambition of re-education in achieving the ideal of socialist man as inspired in the writings of Mao Tse-tung:

The heart of the problem is to root out selfishness and to bring into existence selfless, dedicated man with a new outlook whose first happiness should be in the service of his fellow man in the largest sense of human community. This is the ideal socialist man, whose greatest joy is to be producer rather than consumer, giver rather than receiver.... Now, orthodox empirical philosophers of the human scence would immediately ask, "Isn't this sheer quixotism?" "How can human nature be changed?" The Chinese response [i.e. Maoist response] would be that there never has been any abstract "human nature", but only the human nature of different classes of people in social history. There is no theoretical or even empirical reason why all men in all times must be selfish. There is no reason why unprecedented methods in an unprecedented social situation cannot produce a new man. This would not be done overnight or even in one generation or two, but the Chinese feel that it can be done in the long run, and what is required is to apply the Promethean attitude to man himself, just as he has applied it to nature. Like the old man who moved a mountain, putting his faith in succeeding generations to follow his example, so also can this inspired generation pioneer the way to the ultimate self-transformation of man. Such is the grand, long-range conception behind the cultural revolution.[42]

It is difficult not to be impressed by such winning devotion to an ideal, and to mankind itself. But it is equally difficult not to find the same rhetoric of conviction many times over in the history of moral and social ideas. Originality, or the lack of it, is certainly not the test of moral-political ambition, however. For these perhaps class-bound authors, the question is rather one of the enforced imposition of ideological or sectarian moral authority. Again, this is no rejection of moral politics as such, but rather the question as to whether there is any specifically moral content to any action which does not derive from personal moral

---

[42] Paul Lin: "Historical Perspective on Contemporary China," in a paper delivered at the Canadian Institute of International Affairs / University of Guelph: "Seminar on the Promotion of China Studies in Canada," April, 1968, MS, p. 23f. These papers have since been published in *Contemporary China*, C.I.I.A., Toronto, January, 1969. This description is a general summary of the social political philosophy of Mao Tse-tung. The reader can refer to these ideas in Chairman Mao's own words as they arise in the *Quotations from Chairman Mao Tse-tung*, Foreign Languages Press, Peking, 1966, which is itself a selection from the writings of Chairman Mao dating from the early 1930's through the 1960's.

decision. Whether it is a question of the "new man", of "Christian man", or a choice of any other specifically moral-political ideal:

> There are some with whom we may study in common, but we shall find them unable to go along with us to principles. *Perhaps* we may go on with them to principles, but we shall find them unable to get established in those along with us. Or if we may get so established along with them, we shall find them unable to weigh *occurring events* along with us.[43]   (Confucian *Analects:* IX. 29)

(2) *The Grading of Punishment*

The most significant departure of the government's draft proposal from the old law, and an ambition pursued by the AE as well, was the introduction of a new scale of proportionality of degrees of imprisonment, fines, and penalties. A glance at the accompanying comparative table reveals that there the differences between the StGB and the EStGB 1962 were considerably less than revolutionary, although the shift in proportionality was probably fairly much in line with the prevailing judicial attitude in the Federal Republic. The AE developed a certain restructuring: a single form of imprisonment and a new scale of fines and penalties, which indicated far more an attempt at reform—if that is desirable here—rather than a simple revision.

As has already been indicated, a new uniform classification of prison sentences has been adopted and a new scale of fines and penalties has been incorporated into the law. Thus the AE concept ultimately prevailed in this respect. To understand just how much of a reform this may entail, it is necessary to consider briefly the older forms of sentencing. A comparative chart showing the development of the concepts of uniform prison term sentence and preference for probation and fines has been prepared to facilitate this examination.

Einschliessung (the old § 17 StGB) was until 1953 designated confinement in a fortress (*Festungshaft*), and this probably gives a far better idea of the form of "confinement" than the literal translation of the word itself. This mild form of major prison sentence was heretofore reserved for a variety of offenders from duellists to political criminals "whose motives were recognized as honorable." [44] Already largely in

---

[43] James Legge: *The Four Books: Confucian Analects, the Great Learning, the Doctrine of the Mean, and the Works of Mencius,* Paragon, New York, 1966 (reprint of Shanghai 1923 ed.), p. 120f.

[44] R. Maurach: *Deutsches Strafrecht: Besonderer Teil,* 3rd ed., Müller, Karlsruhe, 1959, p. 636.

disuse, this provision was dropped by the EStGB 1962. Although Baumann had provided for a similar form of confinement (*Festungsstrafe*) in his own draft of 1963 (GE §§ 30, 31) this was not taken over into the AE.

Zuchthausstrafe, penitentiary with compulsory labor, a designation which has now been eliminated, the severest form of imprisonment, under the old law, was designed to punish the worst forms of criminality and repeated offenders of middle range crimes. It was carried over from the StGB (the old § 14) to the EStGB (§§ 43, 44, 45). Under both the old law and the EStGB, where the law provided, there was provision for confinement for life. But, in the interest of separating out those lesser criminals who might well be given ordinary prison (*Gefängnis*) sentences, the EStGB raised the maximum and minimum limited-time sentences from 15 to 20 years and from 1 to 2 years respectively. Again, Baumann had provided for a *Zuchthaus* penalty in his GE (§§ 27, 28, 29), but, as he explains, out of resignation to the argument that this heavy penalty must remain for crimes such as murder, in order that the cry for the return of the death penalty not be lent any further strength (p. 67).

Part of the penalty associated with the old *Zuchthausstrafe* was the loss of certain civil rights and honors and the right to practise in certain professions (the old §§ 31-36 StGB). While § 36 StGB fixed a limit to many of these secondary penalties, however, this did not seem to be the case in EStGB § 45. Baumann, despite his insistence that the very existence of distinct *Zuchhausstrafe* hinders resocialization—and despite his exceptions to the concepts of *Lebensführungs-* or *Charakterschuld*— is quite explicit in withdrawing these privileges without limit of time (GE § 29). Since the AE did not distinguish a separate *Zuchthaus* form of imprisonment, there was to be no corresponding form of loss of civil rights and honors. But, as pointed out in the AE commentary, in many cases regulations governing certain professions, the status of officials, and university degrees may in effect bar the offender from the exercise of these previous rights automatically.

For major crimes considered to require a lesser form of punishment than *Zuchthaus* (penitentiary at compulsory labor), *Gefängnis* (prison) has been the usual form of confinement. Under the old § 16 StGB, such a sentence could extend from one day up to a maximum of five years. Those sentenced to *Gefängnis* might be employed in ways appropriate to their skills, and *had to be* upon their own demand. (That was the law, but it would take a brave prisoner—like a brave soldier—to resist any imposed voluntary employment on grounds that it were not lawfully required.) The loss of certain civil rights and honors and the right to practise in certain professions could also occur here, but in this instance the sentence had explicitly to include such a penalty. This was usually the case when a person guilty of a severe crime was for some reason sentenced to *Gefängnis* rather than *Zuchthaus*. The loss of these rights had not, however, to be permanent, as in the case of those sentenced to *Zuchthaus*.

The government proposal (EStGB § 46) raised the minimum sentence for *Gefängnis* to one month and the maximum to ten years in line with the attempt to reserve the most severe form of imprisonment—*Zuchthaus*—for only the most severe crimes, and at the same time limit the number of short-term prison sentences for minor offenses. The AE provided for only a single form of imprisonment *(Freiheitsstrafe—AEStGB §§ 36-39)*, which corresponded generally to the existing *Gefängnisstrafe*. It employed a minimum of six months to a maximum of fifteen years. The object of the increased minimum was, again, to eliminate *Gefängnis* as a punishment for minor crimes.

Haft (the old § 18 StGB) or a light jail sentence, might range from a minimum of one day to a maximum of six weeks with no special work provisions. The EStGB (§ 47) extended the maximum to six months, in line with the overall attempt at a new scale of proportionality, the extended form of light jail sentence was redesignated *Strafhaft*. The AE absorbed this form of punishment either into the uniform *Freiheitsstrafe* or into a system of probation and/or fines. The obvious difficulty in both cases was that this could result in longer short-term sentences in order to secure a more severe form of punishment.[45]

The court was able to substitute probation for a sentence to *Gefängnis, Einschliessung,* or *Haft* of not more than nine months (the old § 23 StGB). Probation was only allowed when the offender's personality, past life, or behavior since the offense led one to believe that there was promise of a favorable change in his way of life. The EStGB allowed for essentially the same thing. In the AE (§ 40) probation was possible for a prison term of up to two years. In all the above forms of probation certain formal and financial obligations were to be imposed *(Auflagen—* § 24 StGB; EStGB § 74; AEStGB § 41).

---

[45] K. Lackner: "Der Allgemeine Teil des künftigen Strafgesetzbuches in der Auseinandersetzung: ein Kritischer Beitrag zum GE Baumann," *Juristenzeitung* 617 (1963), p. 619.

The old law (§ 27 StGB) did not usually foresee the use of fines as a substitute for imprisonment, but rather in addition to imprisonment. The EStGB (§ 51) continued in this spirit, but allowed for the substitution of a fine for a *Freiheitsstrafe* (jail sentence) of up to three months. The AE (§ 50) would have extended this to include sentences up to a year.

The EStGB adopted a form of the Scandinavian per diem fine (*Tagessatz*) in the new fine system. The per diem fine would be caculated according to the financial condition of the offender. The number of daily rates would be calculated according to the gravity of the individual offense.

Alongside the fine and probation system, the EStGB had, however, introduced a new form of short term confinement (*Strafhaft*). Assuming the object of the new proportionality system were devised to empty the prisons of small time criminals and lesser offenders, who might be learning something worse in prison, this latter introduction could only serve, as Baumann pointed out, to pick up even more petty offenders into the penal system:

If the EStGB becomes law, we will have for example just as before, the petty second offender thieves and confidence men in security cells; and in the work houses sit the common nuisance people (beggars, bums, and prostitutes) for some bagatelle crime.[46]

In this sense then, Baumann's point seemed well taken. For, whereas the proportionality principle was introduced in order to restrict heavier penalties for severer crimes, the persisting treatment of a second offense petty crime as equivalent to a crime incurring a severer form of imprisonment might satisfy the instinct of retributive justice, but could hardly work to facilitate the more effective resocialization of the offender.

---

[46] J. Baumann: "Die Reform des Allgemeinen Teils eines Strafgesetzbuches," in L. Reinisch (ed.): *Die Deutsche Strafrechtsreform*, Beck, Munich, 1966, (pp. 56-71), p. 64.

COMPARATIVE TABLE

showing shift in emphasis of proportionality from various degrees of imprisonment to fines and penalties.

§ StGB (prior to reform laws)	§ EStGB	§ AEStGB
14 *Zuchthaus*—penitentiary at cumpulsory labor	44 *Zuchthaus*	
17 *Einschliessung*—preferred confinement under observation	(No Provision)	36 37 *Freiheitsstrafe*— 38 uniform prison 39 sentence
16 *Gefängnis*—imprisonment	46 *Gefängnis*)	
18 *Haft*—short-term jail sentence	48 *Strafhaft* (or *Gefängnis*)	
23 *Strafaussetzung zur Bewährung*—probation	71 *Strafaussetzung zur Bewährung*	40 *Strafaussetzung zur Bewährung*
24 *Bewährungsauflagen*—conditions of probation	74 *Bewährungsauflagen*	41 *Bewährungsauflagen*
	75 *Weisungen*—special orders	42 *Weisungen* 43 *Anweisungen an behörden*—official supervision
31 *Unfähigkeit zu offentlichen Amtern*—inability to hold public office (result of *Zuchthausstrafe*)	56 *Verlust der* 57 *Amtsfähigkeit* 59	(No Provision)
32 *Verlust der bürgerlichen Ehrenrechte*—loss of certain civil rights, honors, and right to practise in certain professions	*Verwirkung der bürgerlichen Ehrenrechte*	
42m *Führerscheinentzug*—loss of driver's licence	58 *Fahrverbot*	55 *Fahrverbot* 79

§   1. StRG
(Reform Law)

14 *Freiheitsstrafe* —
Uniform prison sentence; sentence under 6 mos. only under special circumstances, otherwise fine if possible.

15 Where the court may fix penalty as it sees fit, the minimal uniform prison sentence or fine in its place are permissible.

17 Minimal uniform prison sentence for recidivist.

---

23 *Strafaussetzung zur Bewährung* —
Probation

24 Probation not over 5 years, nor under 2 years.

31 Inability to hold public office, be elected, or vote while serving a prison sentence.

32 (Repealed)

42m *Führerscheinentzug*—Loss of driver's license

37 *Fahrverbot*—Driving prohibition

---

§ StGB (prior to reform laws)	§ EStGB	§ AEStGB
27 *Geldstrafen*—fines	51 *Tagessätze*—per diem fine *Geldstrafe neben Freiheitsstrafe*—fine in addition to jail sentence	49 *Geldstrafen*
27b *Ersatzfreiheitsstrafe*—jail sentence for failure to pay fine	55 *Ersatzfreiheitsstrafe*	53 *Ersatzfreiheitstrafe*
	53 *Geldstrafe anstelle von Freiheitsstrafe*—fine in place of jail sentence	50 *Geldstrafe anstelle von Freiheitsstrafe*
		56 *Anordnungen neben Geldstrafen*—court orders besides fine or loss of driver's license
		57 *Verwarnung unter Strafvorbehalt*—mild probation

§   1. StrRG
       (Reform Law)

14 Substitute fine (instead of prison term of less than three months) is replaced by only a fine in the first place.

29 If the fine is not collectable, the penalty reverts to the uniform prison sentence.

CHAPTER V

CURRENT ISSUES AND THE
REFORM OF THE "SPECIAL PART" OF THE CODE

A. POLITICAL OFFENSES

(1) *Constitutional Questions*

With the opening declaration of the Basic Law (*Grundgesetz—GG*) of the Federal Republic that "human dignity is inviolable" (*Die Würde des Menschen ist unantastbar.*"—Art. 1,1 GG), the German state is committed [1] to an ideal close to that expressed by the American Declaration of Independence in its recognition of "certain unalienable rights".

In a sense, all the Western democracies have come to share very much of these same political ideals, expressed in the rhetoric of the British parliamentary tradition, the liberal political philosophers of the Renaissance and the Enlightenment, and the constitutionalism and democratic formalism which followed the American and French Revolutions. The substantive force these expressions assume in the political realities of their respective governments is, however, considerably more dependent upon the momentarily dominant strain in the political interpretation they are given, whether liberal, conservative, social-democratic, or otherwise. And then it is quite another matter to what degree one reads these same lines, proclaiming "human dignity" and "unalienable rights", as affirming them for the individual, first, or, properly speaking, for society, and for the individual only in the sense that he enjoys these benefits, as a member of society.

The issue here is not one of anarchism *vs.* social organization; traditional liberalism, the most individualistic of the political philosophies considered here, never questions the necessity of the existence of the

---

[1] For a summary of legal opinion that Art. I, 1 GG is not simply to be regarded as an ethical declaration but also as a basis of substantive, positive law cf.: Hermann von Mangoldt and Friedrich Klein: *Das Bonner Grundgesetz,* 2nd ed., Vahlen, Berlin and Frankfurt/Main, 1957, Vol. 1, pp. 145ff.

For a summary of opinion especially to the contrary, see: Theodor Maunz; Günter Dürig; Roman Herzog: *Grundgesetz Kommentar,* Beck, Munich, 1968, Vol. I. pp. I-3-26, esp. p. 53.

state, and affirms most clearly that not only society but also government is essential before political liberty and political rights become meaningful concepts or can be secured at all.[2] What is at issue between the philosophies of interpretation is rather the nature of their constitutional and legal outlooks. Radbruch characterizes the nature of the argument most clearly according to the relative importance that these three most dominant political, legal philosophies assign to the role of private and public law:

For liberalism, private law is at the heart of all law; public law has a narrower protective compass which supports private law and above all private property.

For the "supra-individualistic" philosophies on the other hand:

... private law appears only as private initiative, a temporary and recallable area of flexibility in the midst of an all-embracing public law, given in the expectation of dutiful exercise, removable whenever that expectation is not realized.... The motivation for the prominence of public law is different: on the one hand, the preeminence of the state above the individual, on the other, the state as the protector of the economically weaker individual.[3]

This is not the place to discuss these philosophies further, except insofar as they are useful to understand the legal-constitutional outlook of the Federal Republic. The Weimar Republic was Germany's experiment with liberalism. Until today the roots of its downfall are looked for in the supposed constitutional inability of the state to restrain the political activities of its sworn enemies.[4]

---

[2] To compare both a historical and a recent view cf. e.g.: John Locke: "An Essay Concerning the True Original Extent and End of Civil Government," § 171: "Political power is that power which every man having in the state of nature, has given up into the hands of society, and therein to the governors whom the society hath set over itself, with this express or tacit trust that it shall be employed for their good and the preservation of their property." cited from *Treatises of Civil Government and A Letter Concerning Toleration,* ed., by Ch. L. Sherman, Appleton-Century-Crofts, New York, 1937, p. 116.

cf. also e.g.: Ludwig von Mises: *Omnipotent Government: The Rise of the Total State and Total War,* Y.U.P., New Haven, 1944, p. 48: "Liberalism is not so foolish as to aim at the abolition of the state. Liberals fully recognize that no social cooperation and no civilization could exist without some amount of compulsion and coercion. It is the task of government to protect the social system against the attacks of those who plan actions detrimental to its maintenance and operation."

[3] Radbruch: *Rechtsphilosophie,* p. 226f. Compare also G. Gurvitch: *L'Idee du Droit Social,* 1931, pp. 154ff.; Duguit: *Les transformations du droit privé depuis le Code Napoléon,* 2nd ed., 1920.

[4] Concerning the differences with the Weimar Constitution and the fears of "self-destructive democracy" see: Maunz; Dürig; Herzog: *Op. cit.,* Vol. I, pp. 18= 4-5. Cf. also: von Mangoldt; Klein: *Op. cit.,* pp. 113-16.

Against the possibility that the basic rights guaranteed by the constitution of a liberal democratic society should be used by persons or groups opposed to that form of society, in order to undermine it the Basic Law includes three provisions which would limit or supend certain rights to those persons or groups when the Federal Constitutional Court (*Bundesverfassungsgericht*—BVerfG) decides that the form of society itself is threatened. The broadest of these limitations is Art. 18 GG, which provides that:

Whoever misuses the right of free expression of opinion, especially as guaranteed in the freedom of the press (Art. 5,1 GG), academic freedom (Art. 5,3), freedom of assembly (Art. 8), the freedom to form associations (Art. 9), the privacy of postal and telephone communication (Art. 10), the security of private property (Art. 14), or the guarantee of political asylum (Art. 16,2), in order to fight against the liberal democratic form of society, forfeits these basic rights. The forfeiture of these rights and the extent to which they are forfeited is to be determined by the BVerfG.

This provision has been invoked only once, but then to overturn a state law in North-Rhine-Westphalia under which a communist editor had been prohibited from publishing because of alleged activity in connection with the banned communist youth organization, FDJ (*Freie Deutsche Jugend*). The BVerfG upheld its exclusive right to decide the forfeiture of these basic rights which are otherwise guaranteed under the GG.[5]

Two further provisions prohibit organizations,

---

[5] *Entscheidungen des Bundesverfassungsgerichts (BVerfG)* 10, 118-24. For a summary of opinion on the origins and application of Art. 18 GG see: Maunz; Dürig; Herzog: Vol. I, pp. 18=1-36; von Mangoldt; Klein: pp. 113-16.

Until the passage of the "emergency laws" in June, 1968, it had become widely feared that the government was making use of the residual treaty right of the occupying powers (Art. 5, 2 *Deutschland-Vertrag*)—which the allies agreed to relinquish only upon passage of "emergency laws"—to control postal and telephone communications where a threat to allied security was thought to exist by referring their own security cases to the allied authorities for their control and report. (A *Bundestag* investigating committee reported in March, 1964, that they had uncovered insufficient evidence, though considering improper conditions in both the Federal Office for Protection of the Constitution and the Interior Ministry, that conclusion could not be excluded—cf. *Der Spiegel*, 15 April, 1964, p. 23f.) N.B.: Under § 136a StPO it is prohibited to force individuals to give evidence against their will or to use evidence obtained by illegal means when the accused has not agreed to it.

For a discussion of the role of residual authority of the occupying powers, see e.g.: Konrad Hesse: *Grundzüge des Verfassungsrechts der Bundesrepublik Deutsch-*

... whose purposes or activities run counter to the criminal laws or are directed against the constitutional order or the idea of understanding among nations. (Art. 9,2)

or political parties,

... which according to their goals or the behavior of their members are designed to disturb or destroy the liberal democratic basis of society or endanger the existence of the Federal Republic. (Art. 21,2)[6]

Both provisions require a decision of the BVerfG to be implemented. Art. 21,2 has been invoked twice to ban both the neo-Nazi *Sozialistische Reichspartei* (SRP) in 1952[7] and the communist party (KPD) in 1956.[8] In the case of political parties,

... their internal organization must correspond to democratic principles. (Art. 21,1.3)

One difficulty the court is faced with in these decisions on whether to pronounce the forfeiture of the basic rights of citizens is that they have not only to decide whether the persons or groups may be acting in violation of the laws and the constitution; they must also decide the more philosophical question of whether these activities are directed "against the liberal democratic form of society" itself. But, where the concept of liberal democracy is based as much on what it is not as what it is,[9] the danger of any decision on the part of the court is that it may be

---

land, Müller, Karlsruhe,, 1967, pp. 39f.; 265ff and Th. Maunz: *Deutsches Staatsrecht,* 13th ed., Beck, Munich & Berlin, 1964, pp. 389ff. (cf. esp. the latter for further literature, p. 389).

Compare the description of cases involving illegal methods for gathering evidence in F.A. Allen: *The Borderland of Criminal Justice,* Univ. of Chicago Pr., Chicago, 1964, esp. p. 10. This situation for American criminal legal procedure has been somewhat altered by passage of the "Crime Control Act" of June, 1968, and the subsequent authorization of the Attorney General to use wiretapping (with court permission) in some anti-racketeering investigations. Cf. e.g.: *New York Times*: Wed. 12 Feb., 1969, p. 1:3. See also discussion in pp. 109ff. above.

[6] For commentary on Art. 9 and 12 GG see von Mangoldt; Klein: pp. 80-85; 91-95, and on Art. 21 Maunz; Dürig; Herzog: Vol. I, p. 21=1-51.

[7] BVerfG 2, 1-79.

[8] BVerfG 5, 85-393. An English translation of this decision by W.P. von Schmertzing was published as: *Outlawing the Communist Party: A Case History,* The Bookmailer, New York, 1957.

[9] Cf. e.g. F.A. Hayek: *The Constitution of Liberty,* Univ. of Chicago Pr., Chicago, 1960, p. 19: "It is often objected that our concept of liberty is merely negative. This is true in the sense that peace is also a negative concept or that security or quiet or the absence of any particular impediment or evil is negative".

imposing restrictions which are themselves intolerable to popular notions of liberal democracy, which is assumed not to exist where these basic rights are not guaranteed. An ill-considered court action could thus provide aid to the counter charge that the defenders are the ones who are in fact undermining liberal democracy.

In this respect, the BVerfG had clearer support at the time of its ban on the SRP in 1952, since the arbitrary and destructive violence of the Hitler regime was still in people's minds and represented the living example of the negation of everything promised by liberal democratic idealism:

Thus the liberal democratic society is describable as a form of society, which precludes every kind of rule by force or arbitrary government. It is based upon the rule of law [rechtsstaatliche Herrschaftsordnung] deriving from the self-determination of the people according to the will of the prevailing majority, freedom, and equality. The fundamental principles of this form of society include at the very least respect for the rights of man as laid down in the constitution (GG), above all the rights of the individual to life and the free development of his personality, the sovereignty of the people, the separation of powers, the responsibility of the government, the adherence to law on the part of the administration, the independence of the courts, the principle of a choice between political parties, the equality of opportunity of all political parties with the constitutional right to form and exercise an opposition.[10]

In the prohibition of the KPD in 1956, the BVerfG carried the catalogue of positive liberal democratic attributes somewhat further, with the intriguing but problematical rejection of dialectical/historical materialism:

Liberal democracy rejects the notion that historical development is determined by a scientifically recognizable goal, and that consequently individual social decisions can in substance be defined as steps in the realization of such a final goal. Rather men design their course of development themselves through community decisions, which are always to be made only in the greatest freedom. That makes it possible, and requires, that every member of the community be a free contributor to communal decisions, however. Freedom of co-determination is only possible if the communal decisions—practically speaking the majority decisions—leave everyone the greatest measure of freedom, but remain at least always reasonable.[11]

---

[10] BVerfG 2, 1-79 (12f.).

[11] BVerfG 5, 85-393 (197). The above must be seen in light of two other points in the decision which at once qualify and re-emphasize the position cited: "A party is not already then unconstitutional, if it does not recognize the highest principles of a liberal democratic society; there must be beyond that an active belligerent, aggressive attitude toward the existing form of society [Ordnung]" (p. 85). "A party is already

Although historically the liberal democratic concept of society offers no philosophical basis for historical determinism, to insist on a dogmatic ideology for the liberal democratic position is just as mistaken, insofar as the implications of that ideal have always been much more restricted simply toward resistance to unnecessary coercion. Furthermore, however uncritical the Marxian terminology it has pretty well pre-empted the conceptual language of certain areas of social discussion. But in any case it would be inconsistent with the liberal democratic tradition of tolerance, for subtle or overt acceptance of ideology, so long as that does not imply acceptance of the use of force in political and social decisions, to require the exclusion of any group from participation in the political process on those grounds. Thus, however, else the party may have been at odds with lawful and constitutional behavior, it is questionable whether the BVerfG is also charged with illuminating the proper philosophical perspective of its fellow citizens. The anti-liberal attitude of communist governments had been known long before the BVerfG decisions of 1956. But the political and cold-war climate of Germany may have been sufficient in itself to support such a decision at that time. In the meantime, however, there has been considerable question as to whether that decision, however justifiable legally and philosophically, was politically necessary, since the communist party hardly represented an internal danger to the Federal Republic at that late date.

For this reason—and since under these circumstances the propaganda claim against the democratic spirit of the Federal Republic appeared far more invidious than the internal threat from communist party activity— there had been considerable talk in recent years as to whether that decision should have been made, or whether a similar decision might be expected if the KPD were to attempt to reconstitute itself today. That legal, philosophical dilemma was agreeably resolved with the opportune assistance of the communists themselves, and without action on the part of the authorities, when, pledging to adhere to democratic and constitu-

---

then unconstitutional, when it pursues another social and political variety of liberal democracy than that current in the Federal Republic today, in order to use it as a stage through which it is developing for an easier abolition of any form of liberal democratic society . . ." (p. 86).

For the opinion that the above rejection of historical/dialectical materialism contributed substantially to supporting the decision to ban the KPD see also: Günter Zehner: "Die Rechtsprechung des Bundesverfassungsgerichts zum Aufbau des Staates," in *Das Bundesverfassungsgericht* (published by the BVerfG), Müller, Karlsruhe, 1963, (pp. 195-267) pp. 212f.

tional principles, the party recently reorganized itself without official objection.[12] The reconstitution of the party was accomplished in part by the purely formal device of switching the letters of the "KPD", of the *Kommunistische Partei Deutschlands, to create* the "DKP", *Deutsche Kommunistische Partei.* The former Chairman of the party was also permitted to return from East Germany, where he had fled into exile, and the warrant for his arrest, dating from before the ban, was allowed to lapse in accordance with the statute of limitations, and no new proceedings were introduced.[13]

(2) *Treason, Betrayal, and State Secrets*

The political section of the criminal law contains the titles of crimes against the state and the government, and this is the one section of the reform, which, considering its place in the public concern, was debated and enacted (8th *Strafrechtsänderungsgesetz* of 25 June, 1968—8. StÄG)[14] many months before the main reform bill. Aside from occasional motives of personal gain or weakness, these crimes are obviously also inspired by political attitudes. The intensity of the pursuit, prosecution, and definition, of such crimes is itself a measure of the political climate. It is this kind of political atmosphere itself which a literal translation of the technical term *"politische Strafjustiz"* as "political justice" can call to mind,[15] to the great uneasiness of those who fear an over-protective "public law".

A sensitive point for all governments and the root of state protectivism of all kinds is secrecy and the question of state secrets. Indeed, the definition of what a secret is, is already an important political judgment. Part of the general issue of access to secrets, in the German reform movement, involves the freedom of the press—at least to the extent of their freedom to report what they believe the public have a right to know. Another aspect is the question of whether one ought not to have a special recourse

---

[12] Cf. *Der Spiegel*, 4 Nov., 1968, pp. 58f.: "DKP: Alter Wein"; *New York Times*, 28 Oct., 1968, p. 4:4: "Reds to Enter West German Elections".

[13] Cf. *New York Times*, 23 Oct., 1968, p. 41:2: "West Germany Abandons Warrant for Red in Exile".

[14] In force since 1 August, 1968, see *Bundesgesetzblatt* (BGB 1) I, pp. 741ff. ; see also major provisions in *Politisches Strafrecht,* collected by J. Burghardt with an introduction by Peter Cramer, Gehlen, Bad Homburg v.d.H., Berlin, Zürich, 1968.

[15] Cf. e.g. Otto Kirchheimer: *Political Justice,* P.U.P., Princeton, 1961, subtitled: "The Use of Legal Procedures for Political Ends". Ridder also makes this point in several places cf. e.g.: Helmut Ridder: *Grundgesetz, Notstand und politisches Strafrecht.* Europäische Verlagsanstalt, Frankfort/Main, 1965, p. 7 n 1.

when the government has secrets which may be considered to be against the interests of a free and democratic society. The former question was the central legal issue of the famous Spiegel afair of 1962.[16] In that case there was the further issue of whether it was permissable to publish assembled material and conclusions which had already been published separately, drawing new conclusions from it.

Under the *old* § 99 StGB (the concepts of state secrets and treason), state secrets were in part defined as those concerns: "facts, concrete things, or knowledge, especially writings, drawings, models or formulas, or news about them," for which secrecy was necessary "for the well-being of the Federal Republic. . ." (§ 99.I). And treason would be committed if they came into the hands of someone not entitled to know them, or if their publication, would "endanger the interests [*das Wohl*] of the Federal Republic. . ." (§ 99.II). The authors of the AE and the government's former proposed draft of 1966 (RegE 1966) had attempted to separate the issue of freedom of the press, and reduced the offense often referred to as "journalistic treason" [*"publizistischer Landesverrat"*] to a lesser category than outright treason. The RegE 1966 § 99a,1 introduced the title of "making state secrets public" [*Offenbarung von Staatsgeheimnissen*]; the AE version (§ A 15) refers simply to "making secrets public" [*Geheimnisoffenbarung*]. The AE also included a separate title for simple "release of secrets" [*Geheimnispreisgabe*] (§ A 16), where the secret had been passed on to a member of parliament or the press, for example, but not published. The advantage of these substitutions was a lesser penalty for a lesser crime than treason, and only the deliberate release of a state secret "to a foreign power", or the publication of a state secret "in the interest of a foreign power" (RegE 1966 § 99,1; AE § A 17) would be punishable as treason.

In the proliferation of paragraphs on state secrets contained in the 8. StÄG, the essence of these modifications seems to have been in-

---

[16] For extensive discussions of the *Spiegel* affair cf.: Jürgen Seifert (ed.): *Die Spiegel Affäre*, 2 vols., Walter, Olten and Freiburg i. Br., 1966; David Schoenbaum: *The Spiegel Affair*, Doubleday, New York, 1968. A brief discussion of the BVerfG decision on a complaint by *Der Spiegel* is contained in a Note by R.S. Storette, "Freedom of the Press. . . ." *Harvard International Law Journal*, Vol. 8, no. 2, Spring 1967, pp. 364-72. See also R.F. Bunn: *German Politics and the Spiegel Affair*, Louisiana State Univ. Pr., Baton Rouge, 1968. The decision of the BGH in the criminal prosecution of the *Spiegel* editors is reported in *NJW* 1965, 1187. The BVerfG decision on the legitimacy of the search and seizure at the *Spiegel* offices is reported in *NJW* 1966, 1603.

corporated. The new § 95,1 StGB speaks of state secrets being made public [*Offenbaren von Staatsgeheimnissen*] where "the danger of a severe disadvantage for the external security of the Federal Republic is brought about." If the danger is brought about through carelessness, the charge of "release of state secrets" [*Preisgabe von Staatsgeheimnissen*] (§ 97,1) is possible, and need only be prosecuted upon the decision of the federal government (§ 97,3). A decision of the government had been similarly required under the previous law (§ 100c) but had then to be prosecuted under the title "treason by carelessness" [*fahrlässiger Landesverrat*]. The penalty under the new law is much the same, and can be more severe, but the name of the crime is less onerous.

On one point, the recourse for unveiling supposedly improper secrets, the old law seems more liberal than the new, however. The former law (§ 100,III StGB) granted immunity to a member of parliament [17] who made such a secret known in committee or in the house in order to protest an action on the part of the government, or to attack the keeping of a state secret, which he conscienciously believed to concern or involve a violation of the constitution of a federal state or of the Federal Republic. The government's draft of 1966 (RegE 1966 § 99a,5) would have extended that immunity to prosecution to anyone acting to protect the constitution. The proposed change would, however, have made that person punishable for treason if it could be proved that his assumption of a violation of constitutional government or procedure were in error, and that he were responsible for that error himself. The difficulty involved in this departure from the rule for a concrete case to a general principle that should apply for all citizens and all cases becomes readily apparent. The tradition of parliamentary immunity is a safeguard for the representative over and above the special immunity of the original

---

[17] According to Art. 46,1.1 GG: "A representative can at no time be prosecuted or taken into custody [*dienstlich verfolgt*] because of his vote or because of a statement, which he has made in the Bundestag or one of its committees . . . ." Yet, even here no general license is intended. The removal of the old § 100.III StGB, therefore, involves loss of a by no means superfluous authority. Even under that provision, legal opinion has been extremely cautious: cf. Welzel: p. 414 also in JZ 55, 142, and in *Zeitschrift für die gesamte Strafrechtswissenschaft* 66, 41. Should the Bundestag find action against a member contrary to their established practice, however, they might still choose to invoke Art. 46,4 under which "every detainment or other restriction of the personal freedom [of a representative] is to be withdrawn at the request of the Bundestag." Failing that, the representative may still appeal to the doctrine of an unwritten reason of justification [*übergesetzlicher Notstand*], q.v. below page 228f. and cf. Welzel: p. 414.

§ 100.III StGB. But, since persons discovering improper secrets are more than likely government servants already, they are in danger of committing multiple violations, intimidated first by the possibility of reprisal from the agency upon discovery of the disclosure, and, further, by fear of being made out to be "in error" in order to save face for the agency. The penalty for the "error" would have been only slightly less than that for the charge of treason itself.

The AE (§ A 18) attempted to combine the provisions of both the former law (§ 100.III StGB) and the government's draft of 1966 (RegE 1966 § 99a,5). The AE introduced the concept of an "illegal state secret" which would have included knowledge of attempts against either the liberal democratic form of government or the peace among nations (AE § 18,1). Yet, this provision, too, would have remained more principle than practicality. For, it is just as conceivable, that the government might make a secret of an attempt to contravene or violate the law or constitutional government without intending anything so grave as the destruction of liberal democracy or world peace. On the other hand, AE § 18,2 would have in effect continued parliamentary immunity as in the original § 100.III StGB for a representative who revealed a secret in parliament.

The draft of the socialist (SPD) coalition partners of those days contained a similar provision (SPD-E § 99,5) against what the AE had called "illegal state secrets", excluding specifically those concerns, which would violate federal or state constitutions, from being classified as state secrets. A provision in the same sense has been incorporated into the new § 93 StGB definition:

Matters, which violate liberal democratic principles, or, being kept secret from the treaty partners of the Federal Republic would violate limitations on armaments, are no state secrets. (§ 93,2 StGB)

Yet, democratic ideals and moral obligations notwithstanding, the lawmakers realized that the betrayal of even those "non-state secrets" could afford considerable injury to the interests of the Federal Republic. For, under § 100a of the old law and § 100a,2 of the new, release of even fabricated secrets, where that could affect the interest or security of the Federal Republic, is punishable to the same extent as the betrayal of real secrets. How much more then is the interest in real substantive information even though it is not a "state secret". Accordingly, we find that:

Whoever informs a foreign power or one of their agents of a secret which according to the violations designated in § 93,2 is no state secret, and thereby incurs the danger of a severe disadvantage for the external security of the Federal Republic, will be punished like someone guilty of treason. (§ 97a StGB)

This should, nonetheless, not be interpreted to mean that that person who discovers that the government were keeping such improper secrets (which although not "state secrets"—according to § 93,2 StGB—are also not "illegal state secrets"—in the description proposed in AE § A 18) would have no legitimate recourse to counteract government action involving violations named in § 93,2. No specific corrective course is laid down in the new political justice section. But, reading the provisions of the new § 97b StGB concerning the liability from improperly publicizing or acquiring information regarding improper secrets, we may infer the acceptable means to expose them to be the opposite of the unacceptable means: and that is to infer little more than that what one may do is primarily to observe the proprieties of the chain of command of the agency to secure verification of one's suspicions. The proper steps to that end would appear to be—reading positively from the negatively phrased provisions of § 97b:

1st—verify that one is not himself guilty of a misapprehension concerning the nature of the secret;

2nd—attempt to work against the violations (specified in § 93,2) which may serve as the substance of any improper secret of state;

3rd—according to the circumstances, apply the proper means to that end;

4th—making the secret public, or gathering information relative to what one believes to be an improper secret is generally no suitable course, if the agent has not first called upon a member of the Bundestag for support.

If the secret were entrusted to the person concerned, or available to him in his capacity as an official or as a soldier in the *Bundeswehr,* he will be punished even then, if he does not first call upon his superior in rank, or, if a soldier, his superior officer for support.... (§ 97b,2 StGB) (The BGH seems to affirm this recourse in principle, while reserving judgment on whether it may not even then be illegal—BGHSt 20, 342.)

It should be noted, however, that although a member of the Bundestag is independent of the administration, and possibly of the government, the special guarantee of immunity in releasing supposedly improper secrets which was contained in the original § 100,III StGB has now been removed. And the reservations against release of secrets which are not state secrets, contained in § 97a StGB, is a stern warning against free use of the recourse presumed in § 97b.

Surely the new law admits that there may sometimes be things that the government ought really not to be doing, and therefore, should not have in their inventory of state secrets. Yet, if they are doing these things—however improper that may be—if the disclosure can hurt the Federal Republic (the "well-being" [*Wohl*] protected by § 99.I is not to be "identified with" [or limited to?] "security" or "striking force" according to BGHSt 17, 50,60 para .1) the damage is done. This does not preclude, however, that making public an improper activity on the part of the government, or one of its agencies, may not necessarily work to the "severe external disadvantage" of the Federal Republic, and may possibly well deserve to be revealed in order that it can be counteracted. Still, one must be careful to exhaust the limits of review within the agency itself—prudence any civil servant or military person should already know, and which in any event the administrative regulations of all agencies ought to detail sufficiently. Finally, one ought to call in still higher proper authority (a member of parliament or a superior officer) who—being unprotected himself—may properly decide whether he wants to take the risk of revealing the secret upon himself. This double expansion and tightening of the former state secrets provisions does provide a residual recourse of sorts, certainly, though it may sound more like a meek confession that even in a democracy someone in government may still have undemocratic thoughts. But, the whole concentration on channels more than substance or correction cannot escape the ring of a "public law" mentality, described by Radbruch, which would far rather be crying out for the administrative doctrine of "the King can do no wrong"!

What conclusion can one come to concerning the "reform" in this area of state secrets? Certainly the tendency in former judicial opinion, and the inclination of protectivist political outlook, seem to have been continued in the present "reform". In the area of treason and the protection of state secrets, there has been some readjustment as described above, where a nominal distinction is made between certain crimes that were formerly all called treason. Thus the motive—or the lack of one in the case of the loss of a secret, for example—is taken into account, so that it is plain that not all those who have passed along secrets are, therefore, traitors. In another respect, however, there is still a question whether one were not freer before, since formerly, at least, a member of parliament might protest a supposed abuse on the part of the government, and where necessary reveal a "state secret". When that was the case even under the "severer" political section instituted in the cold-war days of 1951 (StÄG of 30 August, 1951), one might have expected to have retained that benefit in a reform designed to respond to more liberal times.

Despite the concrete reality of the violations of the principles of liberal democratic constitution which occured in the Nazi era, and perhaps in East Germany today, the effect of such provisions against reported administrative or governmental abuses against freedom or democracy can serve as little more than confessions of liberal democratic principle, and certainly as no real guarantee against further abuses. In the end, individual citizens must be more concerned about defending their beliefs than they are about reprisals. But, this argument—without adequate personal legal safeguards—can be better used by a revolutionary than a liberal democrat. To the legalistic mind, the protest of legal recourse, however vague, may be of considerable moral value, under the circumstances, and all the more reason for providing more recourse, it would seem. Yet only in the original § 100,III StGB and in AE § 18,2 was any concrete recourse with legal immunity provided.

So far as freedom of the press to inform the public in the area of so-called state secrets already published or known in part is concerned, the general provisions of § 93,2; § 97b,1-2 may well have created more problems than they have solved. The authors of the reform have done a great service by at least severely limiting the liability of newsmen who may put together secrets from known facts.

The basic legal difficulty in this regard is the doctrine known in judicial opinion as the "mosaic theory". The fear often expressed by supporters of this doctrine is best put in words like those of Jescheck:

This theory is based . . . on the assumption that the systematic combination of already known bits of information could result in a new [previously] unknown recognition which ought to be kept secret.[18]

The theory has been the subject of much contention as to whether a combination of material and formal prohibitions is admissible under the fundamental legal doctrine of *nullum crimen . . . sine lege,* regardless of the fact that the substance of the theory can hardly be denied. An eloquent demonstration from a Swiss military court decision is quoted by Jescheck:

Whoever knows the location of a fortification because he lives in the vicinity of it, still knows, to that degree, nothing about the continuity of an entire fortification

---

[18] H.-H. Jescheck: "Zur Reform des politischen Strafrechts," *Juristen Zeitung,* 6 (1967), p. 9. Compare decisions in: RGSt 25, 45; BGHSt 7, 234; BGHSt 15, 17; *Bayerisches Oberlandesgerichtshof* (Bay ObLG) in Wagner in *Goltdammer's Archiv für Strafrecht* (GA) 1966, 67, No. 70. Cf. also H. Woesner: "Das Mosaikgeheimnis im strafrechtlichen Staatsschutz," *NJW,* 19 (1966), pp. 910ff.

system. On the same account anyone [acting] in a restricted circle to bring together [the] single known facts in order to make possible the determination of the way they fit together is concerned with the uncovering of secrets.[19]

The implication of this reasoning must be faced. This is a way that secrets may be uncovered. In fact, it is perhaps the most fundamental underlying premise of all our educational and scholarly ideas. Not only is it possible, therefore, for students and scholars to make what is commonly known as a "contribution to knowledge" without ever going outside their respective laboratories, institutes, or libraries, the possibility of a revealing conclusion based on data already published is open to anyone. Therefore, while it may be necessary to control areas of sensitive information more closely, an imprecise combination of material and formal prohibitions designed to prevent disclosure of secrets so inexact they cannot be circumscribed, must be tantamount to censorship of whole areas of discussion.

Considerable discussion of the problematic "mosaic theory" led to attempts on the part of some legislators and members of the legal profession to see this legal concept rejected altogether in the new law. That formulation did not succeed. But a kind of compromise was struck in the formulation of the definition of state secrets:

state secrets are facts, [concrete] things, or knowledge, *which are accessible to only a restricted circle of people* [emphasis added] and must be held secret from a foreign power in order to avert the danger of a severe disadvantage for the external security of the German Federal Republic. (§ 93,1 StGB)

The one problem of the use of previously published and accessible material is thus eliminated from consideration, it is hoped; for, by definition, secrets "are accessible only to a restricted circle".[20] The assumption is, that the "mosaic" is laid together only from published or available information which is not "accessible only to a restricted circle". The difficulty with this assumption is that it reveals a very rigid notion of how thought and research processes operate. It is as if it were possible to arrive at a completed picture by piecing together only certain specific facts. This law will doubtlessly relieve the fears of most journalists who might be endangering themselves by practising their profession in repeating "old news" with "new news". But, knowledge

---

[19] (Switzerland) *Entscheidungen des Militärkassationsgerichtes*, 3rd vol. No. 89, p. 189. Cited by Jescheck: *ibid.*, p. 10, n. 26. Cf. also Jescheck: *Pressefreiheit und militärisches Staatsgeheimnis*, de Gruyter, Berlin, 1964, 24f.

[20] Cf. e.g. P. Cramer in *Politisches Strafrecht*, p. 29f.

is hardly so exclusive a thing as to be broken down into a few separate parts which can be kept secret or restricted. And even if the parts were individually secure, there is nothing to keep them from being discovered, separately, analyzed together, and arranged in the secret "mosaic" pattern.

B.   OFFENSES AGAINST RELIGIOUS SENSIBILITIES

It is clearly indicated that where the approach to law in general, and the criminal law in particular, is so strongly influenced by traditional religious attitudes, the protection of religious sensibilities would enjoy a favored place in the code. As a matter of course, we might have expected the question of the right to protection of religious sensibilities to arouse some concern in post-war Germany, since the whole history of religious and racial persecution had left a legacy of extreme self-consciousness. The issue at hand is, however, far less a question of intolerance and persecution of other religions, although outbursts of desecration of synagogues and Jewish cemeteries have occured from time to time[21]— than it is a reaction against religious intolerance and the position of religion altogether.

Three titles of the code applied expressly to offenses against religious sensibilities. In their old form these provisions were essentially as follows: § 166, blasphemy [*Gotteslästerung*]; § 167, prevention of, or disturbance of a religious service; and § 168, grave robbing or desecration of a grave. The old § 166, on blasphemy, included provisions against three separate offenses: public abuse (verbal, written, or pictorial) against God, "causing an annoyance" whereby the religious feelings of *someone* [22] were injured; public abuse against a Christian church or *recognized* religious society, its institutions, or usages; and abusive mischief in a place of

---

[21] For. comparative statistics relating to such acts punishable under the law —particularly the "new wave" of outbursts in 1959 following the example of two young men who painted Nazi slogans and swastikas on the new synagogue in Cologne—see: Peter Paepcke: *Antisemitismus und Strafrecht*, Diss. jur., Freiburg i. Br., 1962. For the most part, however, these offenses where they occur are classified as "public disturbances" under the title "attacks on human dignity [*Menschenwürde*]", § 130 StGB (newly formulated in 1960), rather than as "violations of religious sensibilities".

[22] Cf. e.g. Hans Welzel: *Das deutsche Strafrecht*. 8th ed., de Gruyter, Berlin, 1963, p. 384: "Not God himself, but rather the religious sensibility is the object of protection of § 166. Therefore, someone must really have taken offense at the blasphemy."

religious assembly. It is this title, § 166, in its first two provisions which were the subject of issue for the reform-minded resistance to the even stronger provisions contained in the EStGB 1962.

The Germanic drive towards perfecting the law to account for all possible abuses sometimes gives the appearance of devising regulations for every occasion on which the irritable citizen may cry out, "there ought to be a law ... !" The constitutional basis, and necessity, for the above provisions is traced today to Art. 4 (1) GG, the guarantee of freedom of belief, conscience, and religious confession or philosophic persuasion.[23] In fact, however, the guarantees of the criminal code have, formerly, applied to the traditionally established, organized religions and their institutions.[24] The proposals of the EStGB of 1962 would ostensibly have strengthened the privileges of the religious sensibilities of established tradition, not only against positive annoyance, but even against possible arousal. Thus the "causes annoyance" of the old § 166 StGB became in EStGB 1962: "capable of injuring the general religious sensibility". This extension is explained by the authors of the draft in their "justification" [Begründung] as follows:

According to § 166 StGB (first provision) anyone who annoys another by means of a public, abusive expression against God is guilty of blasphemy. This version has shown itself to be unsatisfactory primarily because the chance circumstance of whether someone really takes annoyance at the blasphemy is included as a constituent of the prohibition. Besides the fact that the verification of this essential element often creates difficulties in providing evidence, it also disguises the basic idea of the provision, which is intended to see that public pronouncements about God are held within the limits which consideration for religious sensibility requires.[25]

True as it may be that far less offensive pronouncements may lead to prosecution while major abuses go unnoticed, the tendency of the Begründung (EStGB) would be to make a legal offense of a pronounce-

---

[23] Cf. e.g. Werner Schilling: *Gotteslästerung strafbar?*, Claudius, Munich, 1966, p. 93f. See also the historical attitude toward these provisions described by Renate Hüttemann: *Gotteslästerung und Beschimpfung religiöser Gemeinschaften, ihrer Einrichtungen und Gebräuche im geltenden und kommenden Strafrecht*, Diss. jur., Marburg, 1964.

[24] Cf. e.g. *Entscheidungen des Reichsgerichts in Strafsachen* (RGSt) 64, 121; 56, 128; Binding: *Lehrbuch des gemeinen deutschen Strafrechts, Bes. Teil*, 2nd ed., 1902-06, I, p. 179; Schönke-Schroeder: *Strafgesetzbuch, Kommentar*, 9th ed., 1959, § 166 (II); Welzel: op. cit., p. 384.

[25] Deutscher Bundestag: "Entwurf eines Strafgesetzbuches 1962 mit Begründung," in *Verhandlunges des Deutschen Bundestages*, 4. Wahlperiode, Vol. 80, *Drucksachen* IV/631-90, Bonn, 1962.

ment which causes no annoyance, and might only then annoy when one shares certain "orthodox" sensibilities. In this provision, the authors of the EStGB 1962 adhered to judicial opinion so far as it was expressed by the *Reichsgericht* (RG) decision in 1931 in which they declared:

it is immaterial what purpose the accused was pursuing, when ascertaining the outward facts of the case ... for the law intends also to protect the plain feeling of the simple religious-minded person.... It is sufficient for the title § 166, that a picture is capable of being taken as an abuse of the church or its institutions and customs by such a person.[26]

However, the draft of 1962 did not take into consideration the far more liberal decision of 1961 in which the *Bundesgerichtshof* (BGH) rebuffed the tendency during the years between 1958 and 1961, when a number of charges were brought against students for alleged blasphemous writings in student newspapers.[27]

The BGH decision of 1961 proceeds from the constitutional guarantee of a "freedom of art" deriving from the "right of free expression of opinion" (Art. 5, para. 3 GG). This, according to the courts, "requires evaluation in consideration of the canons of contemporary art:"

... judging a work of art in proceedings under the criminal law requires a consideration of the canons [*das Wesen*] of contemporary art, even when this is not easily understandable. It is sufficient, [the BGH acknowledges,] to proceed as the *Landgericht* [the lower, state court] has done, on the basis of the impression of a work of art which a person has, who is open to the arts, or at least attempting to understand them, even if that person is not especially versed in the literature.

The decisive break with past usage is contained in their conclusion:

What impression this makes on such a person, must be decided by the judge himself; if necessary, he can have the work explained to him by an expert. It was not proper to examine specific individual men and women as "witnesses" as to reactions which the work produced in them.[28]

With that decision, the individual is guaranteed, as far as blasphemy is concerned, against accusation under a doctrine as general as that used in Nazi Germany where the "wholesome feeling of the people" ["*gesundes Volksempfinden*"] was the legal basis for enforcing conformity.

As laudable as the decision of 1961 was for the protection of the

---

[26] RGSt 64, 121-30 (esp. pp. 125f).

[27] For citations of the offensive material and a brief review of the proceedings see: Ansgar Skriver: *Gotteslästerung?* (Das aktuelle Thema, Vol. II), Rütten & Loenig, Hamburg, 1962.

[28] *Goltdammer's Archiv für Strafrecht*, 240 (1961).

individual against fear of prosecution as a result of actions by other individuals, or groups, who had only to claim injured religious sensibilities to effect legal remedies, the question then became: what remains of the "protection of sensibilities theory" ["*Gefühlschutztheorie*"]? "The object of protection under these provisions," the Schönke-Schroeder commentary maintains, "is the religious peace, and the religious sensibilities of the individual; religion as such is not the object of protection."[29] Yet how is the premise to be supported at least in the case of the supposedly injured sensibilities of "individuals", if the fact of injury must be decided in the abstract by the judge?

Further difficulties have long been recognized in the text of the old law, which was directed against blasphemy in an age where traditional notions of God are not only questioned by large segments of the population but where the same reservations are common among both Catholic and Protestant theologians. Only the "established religious societies" were protected, while equal protection of the law might also be expected to apply, for example, to thousands of foreign students and foreign workers, among others, now living in Germany, and to smaller sectarian or philosophical groups as well.[30]

In a country where so much weight is attached to upholding legal form, and where the separation of church and state is at least one of the prevailing theoretical constitutional premises, the whole issue of particularity in the protection of religious sensibilities is naturally problematical. But to judge by the attitude of the Federal President Heine-

[29] A. Schönke and H. Schroeder: *Strafgesetzbuch Kommentar* 13th ed., C.H. Beck, Munich & Berlin, 1967, p. 840.

[30] For a discussion of these latter points see: Werner Maihofer: "Die Gotteslästerung," in Leonhard Reinisch (ed.): *Die deutsche Strafrechtsreform*, C.H. Beck, Munich, 1967, pp. 171-89. Far different is the viewpoint of K. Panzer: *Der Katholik und die Strafrechtsreform*. Volkswartbund, I/64. He maintains that because the concordats and state-church treaties continue to be recognized, both greater Christian churches enjoy a special legal status "not *under* the state but rather as genuine partners with equal rights *alongside* the state, and, indeed, on the same level with it" (p. 61). For this reason, he maintains, because of the special privileges which the two churches enjoy, "they cannot be even constitutionally regarded as the same as other religious groups" (p. 62). "Thereby it ought to be adequately demonstrated that a differentiated treatment of religious groups is constitutionally admissible" (p. 62). Yet, even accepting these claims based upon the historical position of the established churches and their existing treaties, this would not necessarily oblige further privileges. Whether the church is "at the same level" or not is immaterial. The church does not claim to be a liberal democracy within, the state does.

mann (SPD), who was then Justice Minister, it is possible that the "grand coalition" may have made a certain secularization of the protection of religious sensibilities politically possible by freeing the government from all too much concern for the reactions of its more conservative Catholic constituencies. In a careful statement as to the CDU-SPD coalition government's thinking, he wrote:

> While it is not contested that the penal code provisions against blasphemy and the abuse of a religious society should protect neither the honor of God nor of Christianity, but rather the religious peace. Still this attribute must be more strongly worked out than it has been. Under our constitution the churches can have no more of a guarantee than philosophical [*Weltanschauung-*] associations. On the other hand, the proposal to relinquish all penal provisions in the area of the contest of religious or world outlooks is not unquestionable.[31]

But the political role of confessionalism is considerably older than the democracy, and there have been calls for an even stronger formulation of the blasphemy provision than was foreseen in EStGB 1962, and versions which would protect, at least formally, more than mere temporal sensibilities, were not lacking. As mentioned above, the years of the *Große Strafrechtskommission,* years of unquestioned CDU majority, were also years of notable blasphemy cases brought mostly against students for writings ranging from political satire on the Christian Democrats in Gospel form: *"Deutscher Gruß* 1959" ["Heil Hitler 1959"], *"Glaubensbekenntnis* 1960" ["Apostle's Creed 1960"], *"NATO Unser"* ["Our NATO ... "], to an unceremonious criticism of churchgoing Christianity *"Missa Profana"* ["Profane Mass"], in which case the important decision of 1961 [see above] was given, and to a phantasy beyond what is normally possible for a priest and a young woman in a confession booth, *"Paradiesgeschichte"* ["A Tale of Paradise"].[32] It is little wonder that with the religious sensibility curve of those years, that the Catholic *Strafrechtskommission* within the CDU/CSU found the

---

[31] Gustav Heinemann: "Grundgesetz und Strafrechtsreform," *Bulletin des Presse- und Informationsamtes der Bundesregierung,* No. 4, 1968, Offprint p. 5f. By comparison with the government's draft, the AE eliminated the provisions against blasphemy and the abuse of a religious group. For the case of disturbance of religious services it introduced a new clause to the anti-trespassing provision, § D 1. (2), making prosecution dependent on a complaint (3), however. The AE preserved a provision against grave robbing § D2. Cf. J. Baumann *et al.* (eds.): *Alternativ Entwurf eines Strafgesetzbuches, Besonderer Teil: Sexualdelikte: Straftaten gegen Ehe, Familie und Personenstand; Straftaten gegen den religiösen Frieden und die Totenruhe,* Mohr (Siebeck), Tübingen, 1968.

[32] Cf. Skriver: *op. cit.,* pp. 96-134.

draft code's guarantees "insufficient" and called for specific protection of "the honor of God as an objective value".[33] In a much more recent statement in an influential Catholic journal Joseph Listl, S.J.,[34] notes that the violations in the area of religion are serious moral delinquencies, but, in words not unlike those of Justice Minister Heinemann in 1968, he recognizes that in a pluralistic society it is another question whether religious people are entitled to more protection of their sensibilities. In conclusion he accepts the proposals of the criminal law commission of the Protestant study group as fulfilling the expectations of the Catholic criminal law commission.

In principle, the three point proposal of this group [35] is very much in the spirit of the EStGB. Their proposal had a distinct advantage. It extended applicability of the section generally to "the substance of the religious or philosophical creeds of others". The philosophical, theological problem is reduced here by having no specific mention of God, but "institutions and practices" would still have been protected. Certainly the generality of such a provision makes it less susceptible to attack because of particularism in a democratic, pluralistic society. The question remains, however, whether formal guarantees to particular groups has generally speaking more justification than the guaranteed rights of individuals. The law can provide recourse against libel and slander, perhaps against insult and abuse, but it is hardly effective in securing immunity from disrespectful discussion altogether. Formalistic claims may be satisfied with formalistic guarantees, but that does not create tolerance. If there is any moral to be drawn from more recent blasphemy cases, one might suggest that the litigious insistence on formal guarantees has produced even more unqualified abuse in counter claims of legal rights:

[33] Schilling: *op. cit.,* p. 100, cites the "Niederschrift der Eichholzer Tagung, 'Strafrechtsreform'," of 24-26 September, 1962, duplicated by the Arbeitskreis für Allgemeine- und Rechtsfragen of the CDU/CSU. Panzer: *op cit.,* p. 58, considers the "honor of God" a legal interest of society, hence within the provisions of then existing and proposed provisions without making God himself the object of legal protection.

[34] Joseph Listl: "Strafrecht und Moral: Umstrittene Fragen der Strafrechtsreform," *Stimmen der Zeit,* 257 (1967).

[35] "Gewissensfreiheit und Religionsdelikte, Stellungnahme der Evangelischen Studiengemeinschaft zur Behandlung der sogenannten Religionsdelikte bei der Strafrechtsreform," 10 *Zeitschrift für Evangelische Ethik,* 177 (1966). See also the discussion of the above by Maihofer, *loc. cit.,* p. 184f.

the hour cometh, that whosoever killeth you shall think that he offereth service unto God. (John: 16.2.)

The resolution of this problem, as it appears in the new law, perpetuates the protection to religious sensibilities. The sphere of protection is somewhat democratized, however, to include the sensibilities, not only of members of the established churches, but also of members of any other religious or philosophical or confessional group existing in the country. The new reading eliminates the specific mention of blasphemy, but is directed against any public or published written, verbal, or pictorial expression, which "insults the content" of the beliefs of the above named groups, "in such a way as is capable of disturbing the public peace". The protection is extended to cover the institutions and usages of those groups as well.

In principle, the new version of § 166 preserves the spirit of protection of religious sensibilities aspired to by the old law. The problem of determining the limits of freedom of artistic expression, or of determining what is offensive in public or published written, verbal, or pictorial expression, remains for the courts to decide, as in the BGH decision of 1961.

C.   OFFENSES AGAINST PUBLIC MORALITY

(1) *Abortion and Birth Control*

In his description of the attitude of the members of the *Große Strafrechtskommission,* the authors of the EStGB 1962, Professor Jescheck maintained:

> The declaration of [*Bekenntnis zu*] certain standards [*Gütern*] and values, which we hold to be essential will have, furthermore, the result that—in contradistinction to the reform of the Swedish criminal code—certainly no changes in principle in the judgment of those offenses involved in the debates of world outlook: like abortion, homosexuality, and adultery, will come into effect. The tragedy of the fate that so many must bear, cannot be removed by giving way in the area of the criminal law.[86]

Of all offenses under the law, however, those named are easily the most actively debated in the persistent controversy between moralistic reformers and liberal reformers. Of the three, abortion might seem the most serious of the offenses, from its religious, and moral-ethical asso-

---

[86] H.-H. Jescheck: "Das Menschenbild unserer Zeit und die Strafrechtsreform," in *Recht und Staat,* Nos. 198-99, Mohr (Siebeck), Tübingen, 1959, p. 9.

ciation with willful murder. Along with the increased interest in birth control methods in the last few years, however, there has also come an increased tolerance for the idea of abortion—medical reasons aside— where it did not seem ethically justifiable to force a woman to bear an unwanted child, particularly where the pregnancy was the result of a criminal attack. Similarly, the argument that the moment of conception cannot be looked upon as the beginning of what we regard as human life is used against the moral attitude that the interruption of pregnancy is murder.

But traditional religious, ethical, and moral objections have not been satisfied by this line of argument. Perhaps this is because these reservations are directed against persons engaging in sexual relations while disregarding the only traditional religious sanction for such relations, the intent—or at least readiness—to beget offspring and carry on the line of human life. By extension, the prohibition against interruption of pregnancy was given added meaning during the Nazi period, to include the prohibition of the sale of or instruction in the use of birth control devices, although more out of political concern for uninterrupted population growth than for religious or moral-ethical reasons. Whatever the origin of this interpretation and the corresponding regulations, conservative groups have been able to call this legal ammunition to their support in the intervening years [see the discussion of § 184.I.2 StGB below].

The laws governing the prosecution for abortion are grouped together with murder and manslaughter in the StGB under the heading "crimes against life". The specific titles include: *Abortion*, § 218—A woman who induces an abortion on herself or procures one through someone else is punishable with a prison sentence of up to five years [para. 1]. (Previously the sentence of penetentiary at compulsory labor could be applied for severe cases, but this sentence is precluded by the present reform's general elimination of the provisions distinguishing between sentences to *Zuchthaus* or *Gefängnis*.)—A person who performs an abortion for someone else is punishable with a prison term of up to five years, in severe cases, up to ten [para. 2]. The attempt is punishable [para. 3].— A person who provides the means of carrying out an abortion to a pregnant woman is punishable with a prison term of up to five years, in severe cases, up to ten [para. 4].

Means of Abortion, § 219—constitutes a ban on making information regarding means of abortion public, and on recommending means or displaying any instrument for this purpose [Para. 1], except in medical or pharmaceutical journals or among doctors or persons who have professionally to do with medically admissable cases of abortion [Para. 2]. (N.B.: This latter indirect reference to medically admissable cases is the only indication in the criminal code that such cases exist.) *Services for Abortion,* § 220—Whoever offers his services, or recommends the services of another, for the purpose of carrying out an abortion is punishable with up to two years imprisonment or fine.

As suggested, German courts do recognize one justification for carrying out an abortion where the child could conceivably be born alive. That is where the action is called for on medical grounds (the so-called *medizinische Indikation*) to prevent severe adverse effect on the health of the mother, or to permit a necessary operation to save the mother's life. Failing any law specifically allowing this action, in light of the general prohibition in § 218 StGB, the courts recognize the applicability of § 14, para. 1 of the Law for the Prevention of Hereditarily Diseased Offspring (*Gesetz zur Verhütung erbkranken Nachwuchses*—Erbges G), a eugenics law dating from July 14th, 1933,[37] and otherwise abrogated by the military government after the war. The accompanying regulations for carrying out this law (*Ausführungsverordnungen*) of July18th, 1935, and August 31st, 1939 provide that the abortion requires the assent of the woman; must be performed according to the established medical practice; must take place in a hospital or clinic; and requires the approval of a medical board.[38] The federal states of Bavaria and Hesse have refused to allow the application of this residual law for their own territory.[39] Yet even where the provisions of § 14 of the Erbges G are no longer in force, the courts go back to a decision of the *Reichsgericht* in 1926

---

[37] Cf. *Reichsgesetzblatt* (RGBl) 1933, I, p. 529; see also revised version RGBl 1936, I, p. 773.

[38] Cf. e.g. Paul Bockelmann: "Das Problem der Zulässigkeit von Schwangerschaftsunterbrechungen," in *Universitätstage* 1964 (of the Free University of Berlin): *Gesellschaftliche Wirklichkeit im 20. Jahrhundert und Strafrechtsreform,* de Gruyter, Berlin, 1964, pp. 211-39.

[39] A description of the prevailing law is contained in Werner Kienzle: "Schwangerschaftsunterbrechung, Sterilisation und Kastration nach geltendem Recht," *Goltdammer's Archiv für Strafrecht,* 1957, pp. 65-77.

For a comparison of abortion laws in Germany, Austria, and Switzerland with a general historical background, see: L. Breitenecker and R. Breitenecker: "Abortion in the German-Speaking Countries of Europe," in David T. Smith: *Abortion and the Law,* Pr. of Western Reserve Univ., Cleveland, 1967, pp. 206-223. This article is not up to date, however, and does not cover cases permitted by the courts.

(RGSt 61, 242) which recognizes an unwritten reason of justification (literally a state of necessity above the law: *übergesetzlicher Notstand*), to save the life of the mother. The provisions of the Erbges G still in use, in effect, amounts to only the codification of the accepted judicial opinion since RGSt 61, 242. Where the Erbges G does not apply, however, the BGH has determined that its provisions " . . . constitute no more stringent conditions . . . than those principles contained in judicial opinion relating to necessity beyond the law," [40] and that "the stipulations contained in § 14, para. 1. Erbges G . . . must be given as the minimal condition even if the interruption of pregnancy is allowed under the perspective of necessity beyond the law."[41]

In short, in Germany, as elsewhere in the modern world, it is generally considered intolerable to oblige a woman to continue a pregnancy which she cannot survive, or can, only at the cost of severe impairment of her health. At the same time it is generally acknowledged as insupportable [*unzumutbar*] both to oblige a physician to act to save a woman's life or face charges of failure of a duty to act (an *Unterlassungsdelikt*) where it is reasonably expectable that he should, and then to hold him guilty of bringing about an interruption of pregnancy, a prohibited act (a *Verbotsdelikt*), where that is the inevitable consequence of his action in accordance with the ethics of medicine and the law.

Bockelmann considers the consequences of the papal encyclical *Casti Connubii* (of December 31st, 1930) at some length, since according to Catholic doctrine any interruption of pregnancy, including that done on medical grounds[42] is morally rejected on the basis of the inviolability of life. Yet, here, a woman is not obliged to forego an operation which could save her life, even if that would mean the termination of pregnancy, since that operation is undertaken for the sake of saving the woman's life and not with the intent of abortion.[43] In other ways, however, the encyclical does not provide such an easy answer.

Where there must be a specific choice made between saving the life of the mother or the life of the child, for example, there is no concrete answer given by application of the principal of the sanctity of life.[44] Even where, waiting out the crisis, not both lives, but only one is lost, the principle is no answer if one does not look upon deliberate inaction as

---

[40] BGHSt I (1951), (pp. 329-32) p. 330f.
[41] BGHSt 2 (1952), (pp. 111-16) p. 111f.
[42] Bockelmann: *loc. cit.*, p. 218.
[43] *Ibid.*, p. 225.
[44] *Ibid.*, p. 219.

more in accord with natural law than considered action. All the more intolerable is the situation for the physician, where he is bound by professional ethics and the law to act to save the mother, where he is acknowledged to act in exceptional circumstances by RGSt 61, 242, and yet the moralist advocates the legal device that he be looked upon not as having acted on grounds justifying exception to the law (*Rechtfertigungsgrund*) but rather on grounds only legitimating exclusion of penalty (*Strafausschliessungsgrund*).[45] Where not life itself but a severe danger to health is at stake, there is again no answer. Here, in fact, medical attention is weighted theologically differently from the hand of fate, in what is generally looked upon as the natural course of events. The cost of this enforced inaction is the apparent sacrifice of the life of the mother in refusing to allow any act deliberately inhibiting the further course of pregnancy.[46]

This difficulty—which has been by no means unknown to the Protestant denominations [47]—is one well known to the law and not uncommon to theology. It arises when the effort to legislate a fixed just or moral answer for the hypothetical situation on the basis of general principle leaves no room for moral choice or equitable decision where no logically defensible answer is given for the specific circumstances at hand.

The failure to effect a reform in this area in the new law is significant. But one must wonder whether the matter can really be considered closed, even for the immediate future. Under the circumstances, there does not appear to be any advantage in adding to the extensive debates over the proposed introduction of a so-called "ethical indication", or what has been advocated as the supposed ethical grounds for the interruption of pregnancy. But the reform law does not even go so far as the EStGB 1962 to codify the grounds for the long accepted "medical indication". Instead the medical profession is still dependent on the morally and politically tenuous ErbgesG or the legally exceptionable doctrine of necessity beyond the law (*übergesetzlicher Notstand*). Yet, regardless of what moral position one takes on the law, one has also to consider the social and psychological effect of what people are in fact doing.

The reform of the abortion titles anticipated in the EStGB 1962 was to go only so far as to incorporate the existing judicial opinion into the code. In place of §§ 213, 219, 220, StGB considered above, the EStGB listed: § 140, Abortion; § 141, Aggravated Abortion; § 142, Procuring

---

[45] *Ibid.*, p. 216.
[46] *Ibid.*, p. 219.

Means of Abortion; § 143, Publicizing Means for Procuring Abortion; § 144, Offering Services for Procuring Abortion. With EStGB 62 § 157, however, the "medical interruption of pregnancy (by a doctor only) because of danger to the pregnant woman" was to be recognized. EStGB § 157 would have eliminated dependence on either the morally and politically objectionable ErbgesG or the tenuous doctrine of necessity beyond the law *(übergesetzlicher Notstand)*, a distinct improvement from the point of view of legal sensibilities which try to produce an adequate law for all circumstances. Along with this proposed new title were provisions against its possible abuse: § 158, Medically unfounded interruption of pregnancy; § 159, Failure to observe the established forms when carrying out a medically founded interruption of pregnancy.

What are advocated as the ethical grounds for interruption of pregnancy *(ethische Indikation)* [48] are, in a way, an extention of the medical grounds. Here the ethical concern is not to oblige a woman to continue a pregnancy arising from criminal attack—this is a concern not only bound to the notion of a rising criminality, but also to reflection on the conditions in the years immediately following the war. Insistence on the obligation to continue pregnancy in such cases was a frequent cause of suicide. The imminent danger of suicide is, however, perhaps the most common of *medical* grounds for the interruption of pregnancy—and was the specific grounds in the case originally resulting in the doctrine of "necessity beyond the law".[49] The simple threat of suicide, where it does not appear a real and present danger is, however, expressly rejected as justification, where the patient still retains the capability for responsible action [*Zurechnungsfähigkeit*] (BGHSt 3, 10); and in BGHSt 2, 383, the concept of "ethical indication" is expressly rejected. This attitude was taken over by the EStGB 1962 in the "justification" [*Begründung*] of the section on medical grounds.[50]

[47] A general review of the problem—relative to the "ethical indication"—is contained in Dietrich Lang-Hinrichsen: "Betrachtungen zur sogenannten ethischen Indikation der Schwangerschaftsunterbrechung," 18 *Juristen Zeitung* (JZ), 721 (1963), p. 726ff.

[48] The most complete history of this question is contained in Lang-Hinrichsen: *loc. cit.*

[49] RGSt 61, 242-58.

[50] *Bundestags* (BT) *Drucksache* IV, 650 (4 Oct., 1962); see also in F. Bauer et al. (eds.): *Sexualität und Verbrechen*, Fischer, Frankfurt/Main, 1963-65, p. 390. The draft codes of 1959, I and II, and of 1960 included provisions for recognition of the "ethical indication", but these were later stricken in the cabinet and *Bundesrat* debates. Cf. e.g. Lang-Hinrichsen: *loc. cit.*, p. 725.

The section of the AE which was to deal with control of abortion had not yet appeared as this chapter was written, but from the tone of numerous articles [51] it could be assumed that the AE version would recognize not only medical grounds for the interruption of pregnancy, but probably ethical grounds, and possibly others as well. Yet, the distinctions in recognizing any general grounds are often only a matter of degree. In the case of the "ethical indication", for example, one can talk of rising criminality, the disorder in Europe after the war, the chaos in the Congo uprising, and attacks on children, and still there is no satisfactory means for determining the legitimacy of the claim of rape for most cases until the birth of the child. Even if the courts were to undertake an evaluation of such evidence, there is the danger that by the time of decision, it might well be too late for an abortion without danger to the life of the woman. If the matter were handled expeditiously, there is all the more chance for abuse. Certainly the claim cannot be made contingent upon filing charges against the attacker, since unless he is apprehended he may not be known, and if he is known, the publicity of a trial may be as distressing as the pregnancy which the recognition of these further grounds is designed to avoid.

Since cases of documentable personal and familial distress can arise under many circumstances, however, the immediate question becomes, if there were to be recognition of grounds for interruption of pregnancy, why not a law adequate to cover all "legitimate" cases, without inviting abuse of the system provided to make the decision. Such a law can be, of course, as broad as that of Japan (Eugenic Protection Law of 1948), or as controlled as that of Sweden.[52] Swedish law recognizes, beyond the medical and ethical grounds: eugenic grounds, in the case of severe inheritable diseases or debilities; social-medical reasons, where the circumstances of the woman's life may impose physical or psychological difficulties and reduce her capacity to look after the children; since 1963 a further reason is recognized in the case of anticipated deformity of the unborn child as the result of drugs.[53]

---

[51] Cf. e.g. Armand Mergen: "Die Indikationen," in L. Reinisch (ed.): *Die deutsche Strafrechtsreform,* Beck, Munich, 1968, pp. 106-26. For an extensive coverage of the opposite point of view cf. Lang-Hinrichsen: *loc. cit.*

[52] For a discussion of the operation of these laws in Sweden cf. Gerhard Simson: "Die legale Schwangerschaftsunterbrechung in Schweden und ihre Praxis," in F. Bauer et al. (eds.): *Sexualität und Verbrechen, op. cit.,* pp. 199-217.

[53] *Ibid.,* pp. 207ff.

Yet, there are not only moral reservations which speak against the toleration of abortion. The dependence of the legal interest and definition upon ethical, religious, or philosophical ideas, so far as the legal personality or interests of the unborn child is concerned, is frequently inescapable. Under German law, for example, an as yet unborn child can inherit (§ 1923.II. *Bürgerliches Gesetzbuch*—BGB). Although the law provides that only a person living at the time of the death of the testator is eligible (§ 1923. I. BGB), provision is made for that person, "who at the time of the death was not yet living, but had already been conceived" (§ 1923. II. BGB). Judicial and legal opinion also extends certain civil and personal protections to the unborn child (under § 823.I BGB guarantees against intentional or careless injury to life, body, health, etc.).[54] By extention, Art. I GG, the protection of human dignity, [*Menschenwürde*] may also be conceived to apply to the unborn child [55] —as it may also be construed that "it is the embryo as a personality *in nascendo* which is . . . the object of protection [*Schutzobjekt*] of § 218." [56]

The extention of the abortion control laws in Sweden was accompanied by further measures of sexual education and promotion of means of birth control.[57] The abortion laws themselves were not designed to fulfill

[54] Cf. e.g. Rudolf Schmidt: "Der Schutz des Leibesfrucht gegen unerlaubte Handlung," *JZ* 167 (1952).

[55] Cf. e.g. K. Panzer: *op. cit.,* p. 21: "On this point one can proceed on the basis of what modern biology and medicine recognizes that it is not first with birth that human life is formed; rather already from the moment of conception on everything that we consider bodily and mentally-spiritually [*geistig-seelich*] as the essence of man is present—if at first only in its essence [*keimhaft*]."

[56] Hans Welzel: *Das Deutsche Strafrecht,* p. 260. Lang-Hinrichsen (*loc. cit.,* p. 732f.) and others also urge the same social concern to provide for the victims of rape whom the law allows no recourse other than bearing unwanted children, "to guarantee by law all forms of relief for the woman *during* the time of pregnancy; especially it should be made possible to give birth to the child at public cost and in another locality" (p. 733). "The community should stand by the woman, the state should help materially, and, at her wish, take over the education of the child . . . . the mother should have the right provided under the law to make an official declaration, after the birth, that, in the sense of the law, she does not want to be mother of the child. All rights and obligations regarding the child are eradicated. The woman is entitled, to that degree to call herself childless" (p. 732). Aside from the prospect of adoption (the possibility of which is questionable at best in Germany), there is, however, no suggestion as to what social measures are to provide for more than basic physical well-being of the unwanted children, whose rights in pregnancy and birth have been guaranteed by the law.

[57] Simson: *loc. cit.,* p. 204.

this latter purpose. Simson reports that in Sweden it is looked upon as "higher law" "that social needs, social evils, and social inadequacies should never make the interruption of pregnancy necessary." [58] That these measures could serve to reduce the need for abortion in Germany, too, would seem to be indicated by the estimates of the Federal Office of Statistics which indicate that for the years 1954-56 approximately 40 % of all legitimate German first children and about 70 % of all children born within a year after the marriage of their parents were conceived out of wedlock.[59] And the number of undiscovered abortions is estimated at about 1:500 or about 1,700,000 a year.[60]

The question of sexual education seems to be a popular issue both with the public and in the schools at present, but the matter of birth control is complicated by the provisions against distribution of, announcement of, or advertisement for "articles intended for indecent purposes" (§ 184.I.2 [formerly I.3] StGB). This provsion—a subheading under the title for obscene writings, pictures, etc.—was, according to Harmsen [61] not originally intended to exclude articles for birth control but was extended in practice to do so. For, whereas birth control itself may not necessarily be considered indecent, articles for use in birth control may be looked upon as generally "suitable for such purposes" and "from experience they are used in that way." [62] RGSt 57, 309 made an exception of those articles designed to protect health, and in 1927 § 184, para. I, 2a [formerly 3a] was added to the law implicitly allowing such articles so long as sold in an inoffensive manner.[63]

During the war years, population and race regenerative considerations led to various police bans on numerous contraceptive devices (except,

---

[58] *Ibid.*, p. 201.

[59] *Ibid.*, *p.* 203. Simson cites the official journal of the *Statistisches Bundesamt, Wirtschaft und Statistik*, 1958, p. 214.

[60] Bernd Wehner: *Die Latenz der Straftaten (Die nicht entdeckte Kriminalität)*, Schriftenreihe des Bundeskriminalamtes 42°°. Bundeskriminalamt, Wiesbaden, 1957/1, p. 91. There is in fact no hard estimate here. Wehner reports estimates between 1:100 and 1:1000. The figure may seem fantastically high by comparison with a frequent estimate of only a million illegal abortions for the United States (see ch. III: A above). But the Breiteneckers (*loc. cit.*, p. 208) cite statistics estimating the number of abortions at a million in 1929-30.

[61] Hans Harmsen: "Mittel zur Geburtenregelung in der Gesetzgebung des Staates, unter besonderer Berucksichtigung des neuen Entwurfes eines Strafgesetzbuches," in F. Bauer et al. (eds.) *Sexualität und Verbrechen, op. cit.*, pp. 175-98.

[62] RGSt 46, 7. See also H. Welzel: *op. cit.*, p. 382.

[63] Harmsen: *loc. cit.*, p. 177.

upon insistence from *Wehrmacht* quarters, for the army's favorite means [64]). The post-war years provided a colorful history of off again/on again use of these Gestapo orders until their specific annullment in 1961 [65]; the EStGB 1962 attempted to regulate the whole matter of admissability and propriety in sale in § 220 (a new formulation of § 184 StGB) and § 221 (a new formulation of § 184.I.2a [formerly 3a] —both to have been included under the general section for "indecency." The AE authors, on the other hand, considered that they could do without provisions regulating obscenity, and, specifically, means of birth control, altogether.[66]

This contrast easily reflects the differences in both public opinion and legal opinion in Germany. Its results are a lingering preoccupation with the need for moral control, pressure for reform, and an ever growing sex consumption industry with barely acceptable sales methods.

The basic conception of the EStGB 1962, one which doubtlessly enjoys considerable support among conservative thinking people, lay in the acceptance of the penal law tradition of guilt and retribution [*Schuld-strafrecht*].[67] For them the acceptance of moral values is a phrase frequently used to mean the literal sense of the maxims of traditional usage. And, in this sense, "indecency" was to the authors of the EStGB 1962, action "where the interest of the one engaged is to arouse or satisfy his own or another's sexual lust." [68] In a very much disputed decision of the BGH, where parents knowingly tolerating pre-marital sexual relations of engaged couples is classed as procuring (*Kuppelei*—lit. coupling)—this interpretation was left untouched in the first reform act, but has been specifically rejected in subsequent legislation—the court recognized that "Moral order [*sittliche Ordnung*] requires in principle that sexual relations take place within the monogamous marriage, because the sense and consequence of those relations is the child." [69] Obviously

---

[64] *Ibid.*, p. 179.

[65] *Ibid.*, p. 184.

[66] J. Baumann *et al.*: *Alternativ-Entwurf eines Strafgesetzbuches, Besonderer Teil: Sexualdelikte* etc., *op. cit.*, p. 41. See also E.-W. Hanack: "Empfiehlt es sich, die Grenzen des Sexualstrafrechts neu zu bestimmen?" Gutachten A, *Verhandlungen des 47. Deutschen Juristentages*, C. H. Beck, Munich, 1968, pp. A 241ff. Hanack, too, sees no need for criminal law provisions since the matter is fairly well covered by the health laws and the articles concerned are often prescribed by doctors.

[67] *BT Drucksache* IV/650 of 4 Oct., 1962. See also in F. Bauer *et al.* (eds.): *op. cit.*, p. 372f.

[68] *Ibid.*, p. 360.

[69] BGHSt 6, 1954, 53f.

where sexual activity is pursued without regard for that "sense and consequence"—and, quite clearly, when exceeding the bounds of "monogamous marriage"—that activity must be, following judicial opinion, of that time, "indecent".

Yet, regardless of "moral law", consistent demand and rate of consumption keeps an active sex industry alive. Sales of items of sex interest in West Germany is largely the business of about 100 special mail order houses. Their correspondents are estimated to number about 10.5 million or one in every 3 or 4 households.[70] Despite past legal reservations, today's market in a randomly selected family magazine includes such items as:

> *Brutale Liebe* [*Brutal Love*] (a book);
> *Entspannungsdragees* [Relaxation Pills];
> *Männer Creme* [Cream for Men];
> *Tempty Lingeri* (sic);
> *99 x Liebe* (photos);
> *Aus Schweden "Lieber John" ein rassiges Liebespaar; zeigt Ihnen die raffinierteste Liebesspiele* [From Sweden *"Dear John"* a racy couple show you the most intriguing love games] (book);
> *Pariser Liebestropfen* Paris Love-Drops;
> *Intime Liebesfreuden* [Intimate Joys] (photos);
> *340 Liebesspiele* [340 Love Games];
> *Der Weg zur vollendeten Büste* [The way to the perfect bust];
> *Stein des Feuers* [Stone of Fire];
> *Nur noch wunschkinder* [Only Wanted Children];
> *Die Liebes Pille* [The Love Pill];
> *Mini Slip mit Rosenduft* [Mini panties with rose perfume];
> *Parade der Gottlosen, der grosse Sex Roman* [*Parade of the Godless*, the great sex novel];
> *Homo Sexualitat, offene Darstellungen der weiblichen und männlichen H.* [open presentation of female and male homosexuality].[71]

But even the privacy of mail order supply is dependent on the whim of the law and its enforcers. Harmsen reports the results of the police interrogation of 34.5 % of the mailing list subscribers of a mail order firm (or about 700 persons). The resulting statistics are interesting from the point of view of critics' opinions about who are thus supplied:

---

[70] Harmsen: *loc. cit.*, p. 194.
[71] *Quick*, 30 Oct., 1968, p. 64.

18 (supposedly)-21:	7 %	Married :	79.2 %
over 60	: 36 %	Single	: 20.8 % [72]
30-50	: 54.6 %		

Despite the often lax appearance the popular magazines and advertisements may give, the law against distribution and advertising of articles of the sex consumption industry is no dead letter—if only irregularly enforced. Clearly, the means for birth control are thus readily available and in use. But perhaps the one persistent difficulty is that the mail order houses provide, through their literature and correspondence advice, the most conspicuous part in sex education for the general public.

(2) *Homosexuality and varieties of Sexual Offenses*

Although not entirely predictable until final passage, a new provision governing male homosexual acts was passed under which acts done in private between consenting adults (without exploitation or compensation) are no longer covered.

As one of the three basic morals issues of the proposed reform, the question of whether voluntary homosexual acts between adults should continue to be prohibited by the law aroused considerable discussion in the journals of the legal, moral theological, and medical professions. The number and extent of these general discussions alone is so great that there is no place here to begin to consider all of them individually. Since this is again only one sub-area of our considerations it may suffice to review only a few attempts at a survey of this literature.[73]

---

[72] Harmsen: *loc. cit.,* p. 195.

[73] To some extent the following, perhaps properly moral-ethical studies, include surveys of especial use here: Hans Bolewski: "Die evangelische Theologie und das Problem der Homosexualität" 19 *Studium Generale,* 368 (1966). (This is perhaps the most dispassionate, and informative of the articles of theologians employed here. Bolewski considers historically the development of this literature in the areas of moral theology, sexology, and sociology, not, however, entirely unmixed with both liberal and Christian moralizing);

Adolph Köberle: "Deutung und Bewertung der Homosexualität in Gespräch der Gegenwart," 6 *Zeitschrift für evangelische Ethik,* 141 (1962). (Very general and hesitant, ending with the remonstrance perhaps more conservative than reform-minded: "It is insupportable to tolerate with great mildness the heterosexual debauches such as at Carnival time as a 'necessary outlet' while the homosexual inclination is condemned as disgusting uncleanness");

Helmut Thielicke: "Erwägungen der evangelisch-theologischen Ethik zum Problem der Homosexualität und ihrer strafrechtlichen Relevanz," 6 *Zeitschrift für evange-*

Perhaps the single most influential contribution to this controversy in Germany—and one mentioned in almost every selection on the subject —is the *Kinsey Report* (1949) [71] which appeared in German translation in 1955. As in English speaking countries, Kinsey's statistics have had great effect. According to Kinsey 37 % of the (American) male population has between puberty and old age had some kind of homosexual experience.[75] (See the discussion of these statistics on page 161f. above.) Depending upon what significance one lends to the statistic of such responses, a popular German young people's magazine, has provided more local figures. It found after a survey in 1950 in West Berlin, Munich, Hamburg, and Stuttgart, that one in every four German city youths reported having engaged in some homosexual practice at one

lische Ethik, 150 (1962); also in F. Bauer *et al.* (eds.): *Sexualität und Verbrechen,* pp. 48-69. (A detailed, somewhat litigious re-examination of the lack of thought on this point in many Protestant ethics texts which simply repeat the established rhetoric. It concludes with a firm proposal to accept the liberal recommendations of the *Griffin Report,* by the English Roman Catholic advisory committee, 1956, the *Wolfenden Report,* of the Departmental Committee appointed by the British Home Minister, 1957, and the Pastoral Letter of the Swedish bishops, 1951);

Olaf Düsterbehn: "Diskussionsbeitrag zum Thema: Homosexualität und ethische Selbstverwirklichung," 6 *Zeitschrift für evangelische Ethik,* 374 (1962) (A critical re-examination of the remarks of the above named authors in the same volume and their authorities, rejecting the romanticization of homosexuality and pointing to the already lax pursual of § 175 StGB, suggesting that it might be as well to drop that provision which "serves rather to soften § 175a, aggravated homosexuality.")

The prevailing German Catholic position has been a conservative adherence to the StGB of 1871 (as amended, 1935) with somewhat reluctant concession to the easing of penalty in EStGB 1962. Cf. Werner Schöllgen: "Sexualität in der katholischen Moral-theologie," in F. Bauer *et al.* (eds.): *op. cit.,* pp. 70-83. (This contribution to an otherwise outspokenly liberal collection of articles, including those of lawyers, medical people, and sociologists, ends with the exclamation: "Everyone is his brothers keeper!") See also two publications of the *Volkswartbund:* K. Panzer: *Der Katholik und die Strafrechts-reform,* and Richard Sturm: *Die Straftaten gegen die Sittlichkeit im Entwurf eines Strafgesetzbuches* (E 1962), n.d.

For a lawyer's survey of legal, medical, and philosophical anthropology work, see: Th. Würtenberger: "Zur Strafbarkeit der Homosexualität," in H. Welzel *et. al.* (eds.): *Festschrift fur Helmuth von Weber zum 70. Geburtstag,* Rohrscheid, Bonn, 1963, pp. 271-92. A more recent historical and legal survey is J. Baumann: *Paragraph 175,* Luchterhand, Neuwied and Berlin, 1968.

[74] A. Kinsey, W. Pomeroy, C. Martin: *Sexual Behavior in the Human Male,* Saunders, Philadelphia, 1949, (*Das sexuelle Verhalten des Mannes,* Berlin & Frankfort/Main, 1955).

[75] *Ibid.,* p. 263.

time or another.[76] A 1966 survey of German students by the Institute for Sexual Research of the University of Hamburg puts the figure at 19 % for men; 4 % for women.[77]

Quite clearly the now extensive collection of statistics and opinion on this subject does not necessarily allow the conclusion of a growth of homosexuality, if one defines that condition as a confirmed inclination as opposed to a single or occasional experience. Nonetheless, under the old law, these instances, which, as the growing mass of social and psychological literature assumes, are supposed to occur among youthful persons, would have been sufficient (if documentable in detail) to satisfy the title and description of the offense.[78] If one of the participants were under 21 at the time, the court could remit punishment for the minor. This exception for those under 21 is still in force (§ 175,3), but the new law, which exempts voluntary acts (without exploitation or compensation) for those over 21, seems to create a safety zone between minors and adults in the ages between 18 and 21 (§ 175,1). Here the law is perhaps not so sure and intends that youthful pursuits should cease, curiously introducing a penalty of five years imprisonment for an act of indecency by a man over 18 with another man under 21.

The nature and extent of this offense has undergone considerable interpretation and redefinition. Jescheck and Sturm [79] give brief sum-

---

[76] Cf. *Wochenend*, 1950 No. 2, cited by U. Beer in: *Geheime Miterzieher der Jugend*, Rau, Düsseldorf, 1960, p. 6f. These results seem to correspond with the findings of numerous German specialists; a discussion of this literature can be found in Wolfgang Hochheimer: "Das Sexualstrafrecht in psychologisch-anthropologischer Sicht," in F. Bauer *et al.* (eds.): *op. cit.*, pp. 84-117 (esp. p. 105). Interesting in this regard, particularly since they were used by the authors of the EStGB 1962 are: *Gutachten und Stellungnahmen zu Fragen der Strafrechtsreform mit ärztlichem Einschlag*, Bundesministerium der Justiz, Bonn, 1958 (multilith).

[77] Based on 3666 replies (831 women; 2835 men) to 6128 questionaires (1502 women; 4626 men) sent to students at 12 (approving) of the 19 schools of higher learning in the Federal Republic. Cf. Hans Giese; G. Schmidt: *Studenten Sexualität: Verhalten und Einstellung*, Rowohlt, Hamburg, 1968, esp. pp. 23ff., 171 ff.

[78] The estimated number of unreported violations (N.B. including those unsuccessfully prosecuted) (*Dunkelziffer*) in the case of § 175 is reported to be 99.80 % of all cases, or, in absolute numbers, approximately 3,850,000, computed on the basis of cases successfully prosecuted. The figures are from Bernd Wehner: *Die Latenz der Straftaten*. (*Die nicht entdeckte Kriminalität*), Schriftenreihe des Bundeskriminalamtes 42°°, Wiesbaden, 1957/1.

[79] Cf. H.-H. Jescheck: "Die Behandlung der männlichen Homosexualität im ausländischen Strafrecht," 19 *Studium Generale*, 332 (1966) p. 333; R. Sturm: *op. cit.*, pp. 42-47.

maries and comparisons of the history of the description under the original text of 1871, the text as extended, 1935, and as it appeared in the EStGB 1962. The provision against simple homosexuality (the original § 175 StGB) was adopted directly from the Prussian StGB of 1851 (although the offense had been dropped in a number of German states prior to 1871) which had taken it from the Prussian *Allgemeines Landrecht* of 1794 and the *Constitutio Criminalis Carolina* (1532) in turn. This provision was directed against "unnatural unchastity between males", and was interpreted [80] to apply to "coition-similar acts", a decision following the customary law understanding according to Jescheck.

Where no other satisfactory means was available, this charge, of an act universally possible, and universally construable, and so far dependent more on popular associations than evidence, was utilized by the Nazis in show trials. The charge was used in the liquidation of opposition groups in the SA leadership, where many charges appear substantiated, although here that fact was ignored until liquidation seemed opportune for other reasons. But it was also employed in the defamation of certain groups in the army and the Catholic church.[81] In this respect they were able to take advantage of a recurrent anxiety in German society, which had been aroused on a number of occasions in the past.[82] In this connection, the provision was extended by a law of June 28th, 1935 to read: "A man who commits indecent acts with another male...." (A good deal of the difference seems, however, to lie in the official interpretation accepted to distinguish between the expressions: *"widernaturliche Unzucht begehen"* rendered as "commit unnatural unchastity" and *"Unzucht treiben"*, "engage in indecent acts").

This addition is certainly a logical extention, once one has decided to legislate in this area at all: "if homosexuality is looked upon as some-

---

[80] Cf. e.g. RGSt 20, 225; 1, 395; 34, 246; 64, 109. See also commentaries e.g. H. Welzel: *Das deutsche Strafrecht*, p. 376.

[81] Despite whatever other deficiencies it may have, William L. Shirer's: *The Rise and Fall of the Third Reich*, Simon & Shuster, New York, 1960, contains one of the best overall surveys of such single significant events during the years of Nazi rule.

[82] Cf. e.g. A. Köberle: *loc. cit.*, p. 144: "Certainly the lesbian woman is out of the question as a mother. And yet, there will always be more than enough women with the longing for a child, and with the desire and the will to become a mother. But what will become of a people in which man lies down with man! Such considerations may have determined Himmler and Hitler to act with the cruelest retribution even to mass executions, when during the Third Reich, and above all during the war, homosexuality in the HJ, SA, and SS began to spread like a plague."

thing that ought to be penalized, then a consistent and practically realizable solution can not consist of only taking in very definite and difficult to prove acts."[83] This wider prohibition seemed capable of encompassing all possible forms of offense, if not to close the gap on puberty. In RGSt. 73, 78 the *Reichsgericht,* furthermore, gave up the restriction that there must be bodily contact. This was left unchanged after 1945, and the interpretation not requiring bodily contact between participants was re-affirmed.[84] Subsequently, the BGH has made the reservation that "committing" indecency (*Unzucht "treiben"*) does assume a certain "length of time" involved and "degree of intensity" of activity.[85] This decision aroused concern, however, that it might in effect restrict interpretation to those cases where there is in fact bodily contact.[86]

One difficulty with the original rule, (pre 1935) as Sturm points out[87] was that if it were intended as much for the protection of minors as against the practice itself, not only were non-coition-similar acts between adults not included, but there was also no special prohibition of acts between adults and minors, insofar as these were not children under 14 (§ 176.I.3), or dependents, or personal charges of the accused (§ 174). For these latter cases, § 175a (aggravated homosexuality) was also introduced in 1935 to cover cases of force, misuse of subordinates and minors, and male prostitution. (Since § 175a has now been eliminated, the latter two offenses are now covered by § 175, 2 and § 175, 3 respectively.)

To accomodate all these considerations and preclude all possible omissions, the EStGB 1962 had been given a broad and intricate design. § 216.1 would return to the legal position of judicial opinion before the act of 1935, prohibiting only "coition-similar acts" between adult males. § 216.2 incorporated the rule of the act of 1935, making the "committing of indecent acts" by a man over 21 with a man under 21 punishable, but precluded the restriction construable in a possible insistence on there having been bodily contact by expressly making indecency for show equally liable. § 216.3 would have carried the guarantees a step further toward closing the gap on puberty by extending

---

[83] H.-H. Jescheck: "Die Behandlung. . . ," *loc. cit.,* p. 333.

[84] Cf. BGHSt 4, 323; 5, 88, 1.

[85] BGHSt 1, 294.

[86] Cf. W. Welzel: *op. cit.,* p. 376. Welzel also cites: R. Maurach: *Deutsches Strafrecht: Bes. Teil,* 3rd ed., C. F. Müller, Karlsruhe, 1959, p. 386; Schmidt-Leichner in *Neue Juristische Wochenschrift* (NJW) 53, 1761; 55, 1600; and A. Bohne in JZ 54, 444.

[87] R. Sturm: *op. cit.,* p. 43.

the prohibition to a man over 18 committing indecent acts with, or before, a man under 21. In the case of a participant under 21, the court might, however, remit punishment.

It is instructive as to the comprehensive coverage of varieties of indecency, which moral legislation can hope to attain, to learn from a complaint against the return to the pre-1935 rule proposed in EStGB § 216,1, that it would have given 65 % less protection. For, according to statistics, coition-similar acts are preferred in only 35 % of the investigated cases.[88]

It is also interesting to note two constitutional decisions made concerning the former law. Reservations made against the old law on the grounds of *Grundgesetz* (GG) Article 2. (1.), "the right of free expression of one's personality" and Article 3: "equality before the law", (notably the equality of the sexes) were rejected.[89] The overwhelming opinion has been that female homosexuality—even in the case of minors—does not constitute a threat.[90] Such is the faith in German motherhood!

Some countries seem to be able to cover the offense with merely a provision concerning outrages against public morals.[91] Yet despite their complexity neither EStGB § 216 or § 217 (aggravated male homosexuality) seemed adequate to cover all possible variations of the crime. They were to be extended by the further provisions: cases of threat (§ 206), use of force (§ 206a), victims unable to resist (§ 208), indecency with children (§ 210), indecency with one's charges (§ 211), indecency before children or one's charges (§ 212), indecency in misuse of subordinates (§ 214), indecency in institutions (§ 215), indecency in public (§ 219), advertising for indecent traffic (§ 222), prostitution in restricted areas (§ 223), and soliciting for indecent purposes (§ 224). It is, of course, conceivable that some of these offenses might also occur with female persons.

The literature on this subject varies from the most vigorous condemnation to complete romanticization. Köberle begins with a discussion of

---

[88] Sturm (*op. cit.*, p. 45) cites R. Grassberger: *Bekämpfung der Sittlichkeitsdelikte*, Bundeskriminalamt, Wiesbaden, 1959, p. 59.

[89] *Entscheidungen des Bundesverfassungsgerichtes* (BVerfG) 10 May, 1957, cf. NJW (1957), p. 865.

[90] Cf. e.g. the "justification" [*Begründung*] to EStGB § 216, in *BT Drucksache* IV/650 of 4 Oct., 1962; also in F. Bauer *et al.* (eds.): *op. cit.*, p. 411. Compare the opinion of A. Köberle cited above n.82.

[91] H.-H. Jescheck: "Die Behandlung. . .," *loc. cit.*

H. Blüher: *Die Rolle der Erotik in der männlichen Gesellschaft* [92] which apparently caused considerable concern in pre-World War I days, describing erotic bases in all the most honored and masculine German traditions. Both Köberle and Thielicke devote much space to Th. Bovet,[93] a Swiss psychiatrist, who suggests that "homophilia is not necessarily detrimental" but can be "just another form of expression". Three other major foreign contributions to the discussion seem to have had considerable effect: the *Wolfenden Report* (of 1957), the *Griffin Report* (of the English Roman Catholic advisory committee, 1956), and a pastoral letter of the Swedish bishops (1951), all of which assume more-or-less liberal positions.

Thielicke describes the other pole from the often not too analytical rhetoric of established Protestant ethics texts: "weak-charactered, unstable homosexuals were preferred for all sorts of treasons" (W. Becker [94]); "psychopathic natures, schizophrenics, weak and underdeveloped, infantile types" (H. van Oyen [95]); "pathological infantility; plain organ stimulation without sexual encounter" (O. A. Piper [96]); "sickness; perversion; decadence; decay" (Karl Barth [97]). He tops off the catalogue of tabus with the results of homosexuality as seen by the 17th century Lutheran Church and criminal lawyer Benedikt Carpzow: "earthquakes, famine, plague, saracens, floods, and very fat, insatiable burrowing mice." [98]

H.-J. Schoeps [99] considers the basis for this attitude insofar as it may be considered to be derived from Biblical sources.[100] These pronouncements are put by Schoeps into the context of other ritual laws [101]—all

---

[92] Diederichs, Jena, 1917/19; reprinted 1961.

[93] *Sinnerfülltes Anders-sein: Seelsorgerliche Gespräche mit Homophilen*, Tübingen, 1959.

[94] *Informationsblatt* 17 1954 pp. 268ff.

[95] *Liebe und Ehe*, Basel, p. 132.

[96] *Die Geschlechter: Ihr Sinn und ihr Geheimnis in biblischer Sicht*, 1954, p. 274.

[97] *Kirchliche Dogmatik*, Vol. II, 4, p. 184f.

[98] In *Practica Rerum Criminalium*, quoted by Thielicke, *loc. cit.*, p. 155.

[99] H.-J. Schoeps: "Homosexualität und Bibel," *Zeitschrift für evangelische Ethik*, 369 (1962).

[100] Principally two: Lev. 18, 22; 20, 13—which speak of a "crime worthy of death"; 1 Cor. 6, 9f—which speaks of "grounds for exclusion from the Kingdom of God."

[101] Cf. e.g. Schoeps, *loc. cit.*, p. 370f.: "All these for us often no longer clearly understandable legal stipulations intend to prevent the arising of *tumah* (ritual impurity). This occurs primarily through *aboda sara* (idolatry, or turning away to serve foreign gods). . . . On this account the Thora declares even that impure which

designed, he demonstrates on the basis of recent biblical scholarship, to have to do with a rejection of practices associated with various Near Eastern religious cults, their supposed profligacy, impurity, and idolatry. Specifically, the practice of the keeping of hierodules, servants of temple cults employed in a kind of sacral pederasty, is intended. Again on the basis of recent studies, Schoeps contends that Paul, too, must be understood in context of Hellenistic Judaism reacting against the thousand hierodules in the city of Corinth. Where there is the story of love between men of the Bible, he reminds us, the Bible is neutral.[102]

Yet, while this article is an interesting contribution to the study of the history and philosophy of religion, it can go only very little way to explaining the historical development of the practical Christian moral-ethical outlook. It is a defensible argument that to some extent Christian moralism may originally have been based on a misinterpretation of the scripture as read, without the benefit of the comparative religionist's gloss. But although moral instruction refers to the text of scripture, moral theology is a much vaster system. Although theology is also based on the texts, it explains them in terms of the purposiveness and design of the whole scheme of natural order. According to doctrine, Christian

---

is considered pure in foreign cults .... Even the declarations of impurity in the sexual sphere, which lay especially under the domination of demons, are always understandable as anti-heathen protests .... This is, furthermore, the same for the dietary laws .... In short, it is not at all a matter of ethical but rather of cult-ritual regulations, whose background has only become clear in the last decades." (N.B. Schoeps says "one can always suspect a connection with foreign cults by all things labeled impure." "... not at all a matter of ethical, but rather of cult-ritual regulations" may well go too far. The prohibition against eating the "life with the flesh" shows, for example, ethical as well as formal ritual reservation.) He also quotes Max Weber: "The entire regulation of the sexual sphere took its lasting character in Judaism from the struggle against the Baals .... All specifically Israelite regulations of sexual matters has not an ethical but rather a ritual character." (*Gesammelte Aufsätze zur Religionssoziologie*, Vol. III "Das antike Judentum", 3rd photo-offset ed. of the 1920 ed., Mohr (Siebeck), Tübingen, 1963, p. 203f.)

[102] He cites 1 Sam. 20,30; 2 Sam. 1, 26: "I am distressed for thee, my brother Jonathan; Very pleasant hast thou been unto me: Thy love to me was wonderful, Passing the love of women." Bolewski (*loc. cit.*) adds Philemon 7 (Paul to Philemon): "For I had much joy and comfort in thy love, because the hearts of the saints have been refreshed through thee, brother." and Pilemon 12-13 (Paul on Onesimus): "... my very heart: whom I would fain have kept with me...." (Bolewski suggests that the differentiation of *eros* and *agape* arose only after long reflection and deprives each of its content of the other.)

theology is not only natural, but historical, this is to say not only is everything laid out according to plan, but the plan also realizes itself in an orderly manner, for the express purpose of attaining specific goals.

To put it simply, traditional Christian moral theology is laid down to provide for all phases of natural and social behavior. The measure of the naturalness of any practice is the degree to which it realizes the ambition or goal of its function. If one recognizes as the natural ambition of sexual relationships that which they have been naturally provided to achieve, i.e. setting forth the line of human life, then any relationship which is not intended to achieve this natural ambition is in danger of contravening the natural moral order. This describes an unnatural union when the parties to such a relationship are not those commonly capable between them of procuring issue. Yet even a union which is natural and solemnized may be immoral if any step is taken to inhibit what may be looked upon as its natural consequences.[103]

Yet despite the expansiveness of this confrontation, it seems that even in Germany this question may soon have only historical interest in the general discussion of the role of social ethics in the law. The general tendency of the post cold war years seems to have been away from many varieties of established and legalistic moralism. This popular tendency has not been without its echo in the medical, moral theological, and legal literature.[104] Most recently, Professor E.-W. Hanack of Heidelberg has summed up the discussion in his position paper for the 1968, 47th *Deutscher Juristentag* (DJT):

Last but not least the discussion which ensued as a result of the EStGB 1962 has made clear that almost everybody is convinced that non-aggravated homosexual acts between adults do not represent a legal interest that should be protected by means

---

[103] This seems to be the sense of the *Encyclica Humanae Vitae* of Pope Paul VI: (issued 29 July, 1968, at the Vatican): ". . . This love is fecund for it is not exhausted by the communion between husband and wife, but is destined to continue, raising up new lives . . . . In the task of transmitting life, therefore, they are not free to proceed completely at will, as if they could determine in a wholly autonomous way the honest path to follow; but they must conform their activity to the creative intention of God, expressed in the very nature of marriage and of its acts, and manifested by the constant teaching of the Church." translated as "Of Human Life" by *Our Sunday Visitor*, Huntington, Ind. (II.2.10).

Although several major Protestant denominations and many Catholic laymen and clergymen have recently taken a more individualistic approach to "responsible parenthood", the *Encyclica* is essentially consistent with what both Catholic and Protestant teaching has been in the recent past.

[104] See note 73 above.

of the criminal code. It is interesting that this consensus of opinion has developed although allegedly "by far the overwhelming attitude of the German people" regards the homosexual relationship "as a disreputable misguided behavior" which is capable of "breaking down" character and "destroying moral sensibility" [cf. official explanation of the draft, p. 376]. Even today the ever renewed attempts to justify prosecuting these acts under the law are ultimately traceable to irrational points of departure.[105]

A large majority of the criminal law section of the DJT voted to recommend elimination of § 175 StGB and a number of other sexual moral prohibitions. The "special part" of the AE dealing with sexual offenses which appeared in time for the September, 1968 meeting of the DJT eliminated the older titles and provided (AE § B8) penalties only for homosexual acts "of some intensity" with juveniles (male) between 14 and 18.[106] Ultimate elimination of the provision, however, proved, perhaps, more a by-product of the "grand coalition" of the conservative Christian Democrats (CDU) and the socialist SPD. Federal President Gustav Heinemann (SPD), who was Justice Minister at that time, had said in April, 1967 that he would again submit the EStGB 1962 as it stood, for consideration in the continued efforts at reform of the criminal law, because there was no time to rework the whole draft before it was to be presented. Instead, he would urge certain changes in committee.[107]

Here again, however, the motivation is as interesting as the act itself, for socialists are traditionally as attached to the notion of a purposive, goal-directed society as the staunchest conservative. Thus elimination of the provision would rest not upon the free discrimination of the *Wolfenden Report* that "there must remain a realm of private morality and immorality which is in brief and crude terms, not the law's business." [108] The final argument of the moral-legal social conservative is that the positive law has also the "power to strengthen morals" ["*sittenbildende Kraft*"].[109] This is of course one of the essential premises of those who believe that the positive law is the concrete affirmation

---

[105] E.-W. Hanack: *loc. cit.*, p. A 214 (§ 331).

[106] J. Baumann *et al.*: AE, *op. cit.*, *Bes. Teil*, "Sexualdelikte etc." p. 34.

[107] Gustav Heinemann in "Schuld ohne Strafe? *Spiegel*-Gespräch mit Bundesjustizminister Dr. Dr. Gustav W. Heinemann," *Der Spiegel*, 10 April, 1967, p. 44f. N.B. compare similar statements by Max Güde (CDU), Chairman of the Bundestag Committee on Criminal Law Reform, in "Man darf den Souverän nicht reizen," *Der Spiegel*, 16 Sept., 1968, pp. 59-64.

[108] *Wolfenden Report*, Section 61.

[109] Cf. e.g. the "justification" [*Begründung*] to EStGB § 216 (compare note 17 above) in F. Bauer *et al.* (eds.): *op. cit.*, p. 411.

of the highest social moral ideals of a people. Thus, in a final unsuccessful gesture, Professor Jescheck proposed a last minute compromise to those arguing the irrelevance for the law of private acts between consenting adults: "prosecution would be made dependent on the existence of a special public interest," but the principle of the prohibition and penalties for simple homosexuality would remain.[110] Understandably in the land where the law is expected to account for every conceivable possibility, and where from time to time it is accorded a "power to strenghten morals", the grounds for excluding any aspect of human behavior from legal supervision would still be put in more positive—even explicitly moral legal—terms: "One ought to remove the stigma of the despised from people whose differentness has no corrupting influence." [111] The way to reform among moralists, it seems, is not to question the principle, but to put another in its place.

(3) *Adultery*

Adultery belongs, according to traditional Jewish law, alongside murder and idolatry, to three fundamental prohibitions. The rabbis were ready in case of extreme necessity to permit the contravention of any other law of God insofar as it was not necessary to take a life, to commit adultery (or incest), or to practice idolatry.[112]

Modern popular morals seem to make far less of the free exchange of sexual partners, even so far as the bounds of marriage are concerned.[113]

---

[110] Cf. H.-H. Jescheck: "Zur strafrechtlichen Behandlung der einfachen Homosexualität," in Hans Giese (ed.): *Zur Strafrechtsreform: Symposion der Deutschen Gesellschaft für Sexualforschung auf Anlass des 70. Geburtstages von Herrn Prof. Dr. Dr. h.c. H. Burger-Prinz, Beiträge zur Sexualforschung*, Fasc, 43, 1968, (pp. 45-52) p. 51.

[111] G. Heinemann: "Grundgesetz und Strafrechtsreform," *loc. cit.*, offprint, p. 5.

[112] I. Epstein (ed.): *The Babylonian Talmud*, Soncino Pr., London, 1935 (cf. also L. Goldschmidt (transl.): *Der Babylonische Talmud*, Jüdischer Verlag, Berlin, 1933, Vol. VIII.7).

Sanhedrin 74a: "... in every other law of the Torah, if a man is commanded: 'transgress and suffer not death' he may transgress and not suffer death, excepting idolatry, incest [which includes adultery], and murder...."

Religious sanctions against adultery are based generally upon the following prohibitions: 7th Commandment, Ex. 20, 14; death penalty for: Lev. 20,10; Deut. 22,22; fornication forbidden: I Cor. 10,8; I Thess. 4,3.

[113] Two anthropological sources may be useful in examining attitudes towards adultery: Jack Goody (ed.): *Incest and Adultery*, Cambridge Papers in Social Anthropology, C.U.P., Cambridge; a book by an American anthropologist purports

But, in countries with criminal codes which reflect more popular conscience than popular fashion, the title has been preserved. Within the United States, a large number of states list the offense. Yet whereas some states make even a single act punishable, some others do so only if the adultery is open, notorious, or continuous.[114] For the most part, however, the days of the *Scarlet Letter* are long past in America, and the crime of adultery, like many other sexual offenses listed in former days, is now pretty much dead letter.[115]

The average German is probably far more conscious of his (or her!) "rights", however. For, while in the United States outwardly unsystematic and outdated state codes often fill whole walls in libraries or lawyers' offices, handy paperback editions of the rent laws, business laws, and the criminal code are available in any German Woolworth's. And, the adultery provision (§ 172 StGB)—now repealed—did in fact play a special nuisance role in the German practice. The injured party in a divorce proceeding, based on adultery, could (until the law's recent repeal) if successful in the divorce, subsequently issue a complaint against the offending party and/or correspondent; conviction could carry a prison sentence of up to 6 months (in practice, usually a fine). To the dismay of many a neglected wife, the complaint was possible only after the divorce, and then only "if the marriage had been dissolved on these grounds."

The peculiarity of the German statute had been that there was no legal recourse (except divorce) so long as the marriage lasted, and prosecution after divorce was only possible upon the complaint of the injured party. The legal basis for this provision was the theory that the legal interest here protected was not the claim of any individual to the

---

to make the same kind of study of "wife-swapping" among Middle Americans; Gilbert Bartell: *Group Sex*, Widen, New York, 1971.

[114] Cf. e.g. American Law Institute (ALI): *Model Penal Code*, Tentative Draft No. 4, Philadelphia, 1955, pp. 204-10.

[115] H.L.A. Hart remarks on the difficulty of ascertaining the extent of enforcement exactly, because annual criminal statistics often do not break down figures beyond two heads: "rape", and "other sexual offenses". He notes that as late as 1954: "normal" enforcement of the sex laws is reported in Boston, including, in 1948, 242 *arrests* for adultery (cf. ALI; *op. cit.*, *p. 205*, n. 16—cited from Plowscowe: *Sex and the Law*, 1951, p. 157). If this figure is also indicative of *convictions*, then the number is, indeed, far larger than the figures for all of West Germany for any time in recent years (cf. *Veröffentlichungen des Statistischen Bundesamtes*, 1954-68)! (Cf. H.L.A. Hart: *Law, Liberty, and Morality*, O.U.P., London, 1963, p. 27.)

fidelity of his spouse. Rather the legal interest lay in the claim of society to upholding the social, ethical value of the institution of marriage itself.[116] The difficulty with this notion was that here the initiative for filing the charge that was to protect the interest of society lay solely with the individual, and was dependent entirely on his, or her, willingness to do so. Obviously it is too much to oblige the injured party of such a divorce proceeding to invite a further public examination of the private affairs of a marriage. Yet, on the other hand, the option to file the charge—the threat to base the divorce proceedings on adultery; and/or to file a charge against the offender (and correspondent) afterwards—was the perfect weapon in the hands of the "injured" spouse with ambitions for a very favorable divorce settlement, or for fixing the extent of custody of the children.

A plain fault of this provision was that for the most part the filing of a charge was a matter of pure chance and the good will or sensibilities of the "injured" party, who may well have driven the guilty spouse to outside relations. Yet, with only little change in the formulation, the substance of the statute (§ 172 StGB) was carried over into the draft code (EStGB 1962 § 193); but here the maximum penalty was to be raised from 6 months in prison (*Gefängnis*), to one year.[117] "I consider that grotesque," the then Justice Minister Heinemann remarked to the *Spiegel* interviewers, as he prepared to lead the coalition government's new presentation of the draft code.

In 1964, 123 persons were sentenced for adultery; of those, 101 only to fines. The remaining 22 were given sentences of up to three months. And these sentences were mostly set out to probation.[118]

True the number of sentences in the last few years rarely approached 200. But even for the 123, the matter was of concern, and there was no

---

[116] Cf. e.g. Welzel: *Das deutsche Strafrecht,* p. 362.

[117] The logic behind this move is possibly just that which Lackner warns against in Baumann's counter draft StGB (esp. GE § 37 I): where the possibility exists to substitute a fine for a short term prison sentence, the objection that everything "can be taken care of with money" would probably drive the courts into giving longer prison terms in the case of minor crimes, where the moral objection is too great to allow the offender to get away by writing a check. Adultery is apparently such a moral offense to many, including a majority of 11 to 9 of the *Grosse Straf-rechtskommission.* (Cf. Lackner: "Der Allgemeine Teil des künftigen Strafgesetz-buches in der Auseinandersetzung," 18 JZ, (1963), p. 619.)

[118] Cf. in "Schuld ohne Strafe?" *Der Spiegel, loc. cit.,* p. 49; also in "Grundgesetz und Strafrechtsreform," *loc. cit.,* offprint p. 4.

indication that their offenses were any worse than those which went unpunished. The fact that fines or probation were given instead of prison sentences was certainly a comfort to those who managed it. But simply to be entered into the registers as a first offender may carry as far reaching an effect in German society. The "justification" for the proposed draft (EStGB § 193) recognized the opportunity for revenge and extortion arising under this provision but rejected the idea that this misuse—or even lack of use of the paragraph—were sufficient grounds to remove the title. The essential meaning of the prohibition, it was said, lies in its "morals-forming [*sittenprägende*] and morals-conserving [*sittenerhaltende*] effect" and "in it the dedication of the state to the institution of marriage as one of the fundamental bases of our society is expressed."[119] The "justification" continues:

> in a time when the attitudes towards the relationships between the sexes are being relaxed in many ways, reduction of the penal law protections would not be understood among large sections of the people and would be misunderstood by others that the state no longer attaches the same importance to marriage as before.

On this count, however, Else Koffka (herself a member of The *Große Strafrechtskommission* appropriately commented that whereas very few people would ever hear of an adultery trial, divorce trials are both common and their results widely known among families and friends. These proceedings, then, for divorce, support, and custody of children should be sufficient to indicate the positive "interest of the state" in institutions of marriage and family.[120]

The Fundamental Law of the Federal Republic provides for "the special protection of marriage and family" (Art. 6(1) GG). Surely the initiative for incorporating these guarantees in the constitution proceeded more from sectarian social theory than political or legal necessity. Similarly the adultery statute testifies more to the juristic and theoretical completeness of the traditional social outlook embodied in the articles constituting the new republic than it does to the need or desire of the lawgivers to pursue the prosecution of adultery as such. Yet, with this theoretical completeness in mind, supporters of the EStGB 1962 considered that elimination of the title would be misunderstood, and inconsistent with Article 6(1) GG. The paradox of the supporters position,

[119] *BT Drucksache*, IV/650 of 4 Oct., 1962 ("EStGB 1962" § 193). See also in F. Bauer *et al.* (eds.): *Sexualität und Verbrechen*, p. 393.

[120] E. Koffka: "Der Ehebruch in der Strafrechtsreform," in F. Bauer *et al.* (eds.): *op. cit.*, (pp. 144-48) p. 147f.

in purely legal terms, was that they had no illusions about enforcement of the provision, and did not even necessarily recommend filing charges, where possible. On the contrary, they preferred to look at the provision as a "minimum social ethical obligation" designed to "influence and support the general conviction." [121] In other words positive law might be and should be used to mobilize the only real power the rabbis ever had to enforce the prohibition of adultery, universal disapproval. The question remains, however, whether positive law has the power to keep tradition alive, where the people do not care to shoulder the burden themselves.[122] And, if it did, would a year in prison, twice the previous maximum penalty, be a suitable form of enforcement for the random selection of offenders the law had been seen to effect. The opinion that elimination of the adultery provision would be equivalent to desertion of Art. 6 (1) GG seems exaggerated in comparison with the extent of existing marriage and family law.

The AE eliminated the title.[123] And the then Justice Minister Heinemann (SPD) and the Chairman of the Special Committee for Criminal Law Reform in the Bundestag, Max Güde (CDU) had both indicated that the title ought to be, or would be dropped before the draft were presented to the full house.[124] And indeed, on October 30, 1968, the Committee on Criminal Law Reform voted to drop the adultery provision from the government's draft code.

The dispute over the admissability of artificial insemination is, however, an extention of this same problem. But, a law regulating this area is yet to be passed. § 203 of the EStGB 1962 would have introduced penalties for anyone who performed heterologous artificial insemination (up to three years in prison), and the woman who permitted it to be done (up to a year in prison or confinement). The "justification" for this new

---

[121] Cf. e.g. K. Lackner: "Für und Wider die Strafbarkeit des Ehebruchs," *Zeitschrift für das gesamte Familienrecht,* 411 (1962), p. 413.

[122] An interesting observation is H. Popitz's: "Even the 'preventive' function of the penalty can only be retained as long as the 'general prevention' of the undiscovered number of violations [*Dunkelziffer*] remains intact." ("Über die Präventivwirking des Nichtwissens: Dunkelziffer, Norm und Strafe," in series *Recht und Staat,* Fasc. 350 (1968), p. 20. See also in University of Freiburg i. Br., Rechts- und Staatswissenschaftliche Fakultät: *Zur Einheit der Rechts- und Staatswissenschaften,* C.F. Müller, Karlsruhe, 1967.)

[123] Cf. J. Baumann *et al.*: AE, *op. cit.,; Bes. Teil:* "Sexualdelikte etc.," p. 60f.

[124] Cf. G. Heinemann: "Grundgesetz und Strafrechtsreform," *loc. cit.,* offprint, p. 4f.; cf. also Max Güde in: "Man darf den Souverän nicht reizen," *Der Spiegel, loc. cit.,* p. 64.

title showed the considerable concern which the subject aroused in Germany in the years of *Große Strafrechtskommission*.[125] The argument has subsided in the intervening years, and it is widely assumed that, despite past fears, the practice is not very widespread—partly, however, this may be a result of rejection of the procedure on the part of the doctors.[126] The Catholic Church and some Protestant churches have opposed heterologous artificial insemination.[127] It is curious that, despite the doctrine of the sin of lust, Catholic and some Protestant authorities have rejected homologous artificial insemination as well.[128]

In any case, the statements of the then Justice Minister Heinemann and Representative Güde, cited above, had indicated that this new section, would probably be dropped, too, before the draft was presented.[129] It would not be unexpected, however, if the same arguments were to be brought up again, when and if the Bundestag attempts to regulate this area.

---

[125] *BT Drucksache* IV/650 of 4 Oct. 1962. Also in F. Bauer *et al.* (eds.): *op. cit.,* pp. 393-98.

[126] *Ibid.;* Bauer *et. al.,* p. 397f.: "The 62nd German Physicians Congress [*Deutscher Ärztetag*] 1959 rejected heterolog insemination on moral grounds. . . ." The German Women Physicians Union [*Deutscher Ärztinnenbund*] and the German Society for Psychotherapy and Depth Psychology [*Deutsche Gesellschaft für Psychotherapie und Tiefenpsychologie*] favored legal prohibition as well.

[127] See references to a Church of England commission (1948), Bishop Dibelius (1949), Präses Beckmann, the Family Law Commission of the Protestant Church in Germany, and Pope Pius XII (1949) in K. Panzer: *Der Katholik und die Strafrechtsreform,* p. 78f.

[128] *Ibid.,* p. 78f.

[129] Güde is also cited by Panzer as the author of the proposals of the Catholic *Arbeitskreis für Strafrecht* (which are essentially in favor of the EStGB 1962 provisions): *Ibid.,* p. 72.

CHAPTER VI

CONCLUSIONS ON THE ROLE OF FUNCTION AND IDEAL IN MAKING THE LAW

A. SOCIAL ETHICS IN THE LAW

In a casual remark on the subject of law and ethics, a distinguished specialist in comparative law recently observed:

To be naive and optimistic it might seem likely that customs and law should rest upon a philosophical basis—but the lawyer knows better, and even ordinary intelligence indicates that people's wants shape their ideas, like the feet determine the size of the shoes.

The common law tradition, like the early Roman law tradition before it, afforded perhaps the first real basis for the "behaviorial" form of social studies in the prevailing tradition of "finding the law". Unlike many other legal and political theories, particularly where, in Radbruch's terms: "... private law appears only as private initiative ... in the midst of an all-embracing public law, ..." [1] the common law countries still see themselves rightly or wrongly in the tradition described by Oliver Wendell Holmes where, it is thought: "The life of the law has not been logic; it has been experience." [2]

Yet, however suitable this attitude may seem for the interpretation of most of the precedents of the common law tradition and in the anthropological study of customary law. It is problematical to what degree this attitude can be maintained for many of the concepts of

---

[1] Radbruch: *Rechtsphilosophie,* p. 226f. See discussion in Chapter V.

[2] O. W. Holmes: *The Common Law,* 1887, p. 1; see also pp. 1-5. For a more recent discussion of legal positivism and moral purposiveness see e.g.: Lon Fuller: "Human Purpose and Natural Law," 53 *Journal of Philosophy,* (1953), H.L.A. Hart: "Positivism and the Separation of Law and Morals," 71 *Harvard Law Rev.* 593 (1958), Lon Fuller: "Positivism and Fidelity to Law—A Reply to Professor Hart," 71 *Harvard Law Rev.* 630 (1958).

legislated law, or even at times the personal decisions of judges, or societies which establish custom for themselves, collectively.[3] Without adopting any kind of philosophical determinism, it seems proper to assume that specific legislation as distinct from a living-law tradition— although sometimes that too—will generally be the product of a particular outlook on an issue. How much more, then, can the legislation of an entire code reflect the outlooks of its authors, as well as the needs of the moment.

B.　POLITICS IN THE FORMATION OF THE LAW

Politics is not infrequently as much the meeting place for the contention of political, social, and legal philosophies as it is the common ground for practical trading and the attainment of consensus or consent. In the United States, although there have been occasional political, ideological scares, such as Jacobinism, Communism, and even the John Birch Society, party politics has mostly been a matter of division over the issues or the personalities, rather than a confrontation of basically opposing political philosophies. It is understandable, therefore, that with the optimism that brought a thaw in the cold-war and prior to the slogans of "black power" and the "student revolt" at home, Americans should have agreed with Bell that we had indeed reached "the end of ideology".[4] In other parts of the world, this does not necessarily seem to have been the case.

Instead, the historical Western ideological religious denominational outlooks seem very much alive, in the law as well as in politics. But, it is in the law that the peculiarities of such points of view may have their lasting effect despite the limited time that any particular philosophy may itself endure, and despite the apparent reverses that practical politics bring about in government policies.

---

[3] For a comment on the question of personal outlook and lack of uniformity in decisions and sentencing, see e.g.: Wesley A. Sturges in 40 *Harv. L. Rev.* 513 (1927): "One learns from the reports each day that the courts are not ordinary slot machines, whether or not we welcome a given decision. Experience is nursing a notion that the courts are judges and that the judges have pleasures, pains, and other behavior complexes, frequently called emotions, like other human beings."

[4] Cf. Daniel Bell: *The End of Ideology. On the Exhausting of Political Ideas in the Fifties,* Rev. ed., Free Pr., New York, 1966.

C. PUBLIC CONSCIENCE: REASON AND RHETORIC

The temptation in legislating, as suggested at the outset, is that we may legislate not only to provide for a "public need", we may also legislate to provide for the way things "ought to be". To some extent the deliberate choice is inevitable. Given the task of re-writing the criminal code, for example, there must be some design from the moment we decide what purpose is to be served by the penalties. For that matter, it is not only a question of providing a design for society, but also one of what concept we have of society as it is or as it "ought to be". The legal moralists claim that the law has not only to provide penalties for crime but also to insure a "social-ethical minimum". Having discussed the question of whether it is the proper province of the law to undertake this mission, it may be profitable to consider one opinion as to what sociological effect it may have.

Professor Heinrich Popitz has seen a certain success in legal moralism, not because it makes people more moral, necessarily, but rather in its enabling them to lay claim to a higher morality than they may actually follow. And, so long as the written law is not too strictly enforced, it can satisfy people that they are at least respectably moral without their having to justify the aspiration too literally with their own private behavior. The key to Popitz's observations is the projection of unreported crime (*Dunkelziffer*), in which, unlike their official compilers, he is able to take some comfort:

Let us remember yet another phenomenon of the conscious or half-conscious recognition of the use of the number of unreported crimes [*Dunkelziffer*]. It is a part of the wisdom, especially of "good society", that they reckon the *discovery* of the wrongdoer, above all one from their ranks, as an *additional guilt*— or even as the guilt itself.... what is scandalous is less the violation of the norm than the scandal (itself).... The penalty can retain its social effectiveness only as long as the majority do *not* get what they deserve. Even the "preventive" function of the penalty can only be retained as long as the "general prevention" of the number of unreported crimes [*Dunkelziffer*] remains intact.[5]

Mr. Popitz argues, in a way that may seem curiously circular to the "common sense" logic of the good up-standing citizen, not that law has ceased to be meaningful in terms of its underlying moral-ethical content but rather that the means of satisfying conscience lies in declaring

[5] H. Popitz: "Über die Präventivwirkung des Nichtwissens:... Dunkelziffer, Norm, und Strafe," in *Recht und Staat* no. 350 (1968), p. 14.

what the law is to be, not in following the letter of it. It is not the question here that the philosophy which designed that moral-ethical code no longer is prevalent, or is not relevant to the present day. Here, he maintains, is the real "preventive effect" of the law, the "preventive effect" of ignorance of the violation of the law. That is to say that the "preventive effect" does not lie in the threat of punishment, but rather in the acknowledgement of the legal, social-moral "norm", so long as one can occasionally get away with violation of that "norm".

When your neighbor to the right and to the left is punished, the punishment loses its moral weight. Something which happens to everyone in turn is regarded as indiscriminate. Even the penalty can exhaust itself. If the norm is not sanctioned any more, or too seldom, it loses its teeth; but if they have to bite continually, the teeth will become dull. Even the practical disadvantage which the penalty brings is weakened to the degree that it becomes general. But not only does the sanction lose its weight if your neighbor to the right and to the left is punished, it becomes public—indeed singularly obvious—that your neighbor is not keeping the norm either[6]

This is not intended to suggest—at least on the part of the present authors—that it is good and proper to use the law as the last resort of moral remonstrance. Nonetheless, there may be a certain sociological realism in the observation: the good upstanding citizen may have genuine qualms without permitting abortion, but when his self-respect, or that of his name or family is involved, he may be moved to procure one.[7] Obviously the theory can apply only to the side of criminal legislation used to uphold traditional or sectarian morals codes.

What we observe then is neither that the law is alone the shoe to the foot of necessity, nor that it is an easily tractable medium for moral-ethical aspiration, or perhaps even for political or philosophical design. Yet, certainly it has elements of all these things in it, including apparently, some non-rational impulse, and some good effects for the wrong reasons. The best intentions of moral legislators or social rationalists seems to offer no guarantee against dilution by practice already current. Obviously some standards are necessary if only to regulate traffic. But what conceit to ignore the existing standards the lawyer ostensibly sets

---

[6] *Ibid.*, p. 17.

[7] *Ibid.*, p. 22-28, table 1; p. 21, notes. In the case of abortion, Popitz cites a *Dunkelziffer* of 99.80 % (i.e. it is assumed that only about 0.2 % of all cases in the Federal Republic are discovered) or approximately 1,797,000 cases. He attributes this figure to B. Wehner: *Die Latenz der Straftaten (Die nicht entdeckte Kriminalität)*, Schriftenreihe des Bundeskriminalamtes 42°°, Wiesbaden, 1957/1, p. 91.

out "to find". One solution to the complication of the best of legal designs is to design as little as necessary. In that way, the law serves as a device for the security of life, property, and interests. The place for philosophy, ethics, and politics is, then, still associated with laws, but in addition to them, to recognize the place for them, and to apply them with justice, "which if a man do, he shall live by them." [8]

[8] Leviticus 18.5. "The Rabbis take the words 'he shall live by them', to mean that God's commandments are to be a means of life and not of destruction . . . ." (*Pentatench and Haftorahs*, ed. by Hertz, Soncino Pr., London, 1952, p. 489).

A BRIEF BIBLIOGRAPHY OF SOURCES
ON THE GERMAN CRIMINAL LAW IN ENGLISH

TEXTS AND REFERENCE MATERIALS

The German Criminal Code, transl. by G.O.W. Mueller and Th. Buergenthal, Rothman, S. Hackensack, N.J.; Sweet and Maxwell, London, 1961.

The German Code of Criminal Procedure, transl. by H. Niebler, Rothman, S. Hackensack, N.J.; Sweet and Maxwell, London, 1965.

The German Draft Penal Code—E 1962, transl. by N. Ross, Rothman, S. Hackensack, N.J.; Sweet and Maxwell, London, 1966.

Great Britain, Foreign Office (E.J. Cohn et al.): *Manual of German Law,* H.M.S.O., London, 1952, Vol. II.

Gesellschaft für Rechtsvergleichung: *Bibliographie des Deutschen Rechts* (in English and German), Müller, Karlsruhe; Rothman, S. Hackensack, N.J., 1964.

Robert Herbst: *Wörterbuch der Handels-, Finanz- und Rechtssprache* (German, French, and English), Thali, Lucern, 1959.

Hans Schneider: *Bibliographie zum öffentlichen Recht in der BRD / A Reference Guide to the Public Law of the Federal Republic of Germany,* Beck, Munich, 1960.

W. Müller-Freienfels; N.S. Marsh: "German Law," in *Encyclopedia Britannica* (1966), Vol. 10, pp. 252-57.

M. Rheinstein: "Approach to German Law," 34 *Indiana Law Journal* 546 (1959).

ARTICLES AND BOOKS

G. Casper and H. Zeisel: "Lay Judges in the German Criminal Courts," 1 *Journal of Legal Studies* 135 (1972).

W. Clemens: "The Exclusionary Rule under Foreign Law, Germany," 52 *Journal of Criminal Law, Criminology, and Police Science* 277 (1961).

G. Dietze: "America and Europe—Decline and Emergence of Judicial Review," 44 *Va. Law Rev.* 1233 (1958).

—: "Judicial Review in Europe," 55 *Mich. Law Rev.* 539 (1957).

H.-H. Jescheck: "The Discretionary Powers of the Prosecuting Attorney in West Germany," 18 *American Journal of Comparative Law* 508 (1970).

—: "German Criminal Law Reform: Its Development and Cultural Background," in G.O.W. Mueller (ed.): *Essays in Criminal Science*, Rothman, S. Hackensack, N.J.; Sweet and Maxwell, London, 1961.

—: *Penal Law and its Application in the Soviet Occupied Zone of Germany*, Mohr, Tübingen, 1965.

—: "Principles of German Criminal Procedure in Comparison with American Law," 56 *Virginia Law Rev.* 239 (1970).

Hermann Mannheim: "Comparative Sentencing Practice," 23 *Law and Contemporary Problems* 557 (1958).

E. McWhinney: *Constitutionalism in Germany and the Federal Constitutional Court*, A.W. Sythoff, Leyden, 1962.

G.O.W. Mueller: "The German Draft Criminal Code 1960: An Evaluation in Terms of American Criminal Law," 25 *Univ. of Illinois Law Forum* 25 (1961).

H. Nagel: "Judicial Review in Germany," in H. Yntema (ed.): *American Journal of Comparative Law Reader*, Oceana, Dobbs Ferry, N.Y., 1966 (3 *Am. J. of Comp. Law* 233 [1954]).

"Note: Preventive Detention: A Comparison of European and United States Measures," 4 *N.Y.U. Journal of International Law and Politics* 289 (1971).

H.G. Rupp: "Judicial Review in the Federal Republic of Germany," H. Yntema (ed.): *American Journal of Comparative Law Reader*, Oceana, Dobbs Ferry, N.Y., 1966 (9 *Am. J. of Comp. Law* 29 (1960)).

Horst Schroeder: "German Criminal Law and its Reform," 4 *Duquesne Univ. Law Rev.* 97 (1965).

E.H. Schwenck: "Criminal Codification and General Principles of Criminal Law in Germany and the United States: A Comparative Study," 15 *Tulane Law Rev.* (1941).

H.-J. Wolff; B. Shartel: "Criminal Justice in Germany," 42 *Michigan Law Rev.* 1067 (1944).

Th. Würtenberger: "The Reform of the Execution of Penal Sentences in Germany and the Constitutional State," 13 *Universitas* (A German Review of the Arts and Sciences, English ed.) 95 (1970).

A NOTE ON THE U.S. SUPREME COURT'S DECISIONS
ON ABORTION

In two decisions striking down most state laws prohibiting abortion, the United States Supreme Court dramatically changed the character of American law in this area.[1] On January 22, 1973 (this book was already in the press), the Supreme Court struck down the Texas statutes [2] which made it a crime "to procure an abortion", or attempt one, except on "medical advice for the purpose of saving the life of the mother." [3] The Court, furthermore, provided specific guidelines regulating lawmaking in this area:

(a) For the stage prior to approximately the end of the first trimester, the abortion decision and its effectuation must be left to the medical judgment of the pregnant woman's attending physician.
(b) For the stage subsequent to approximately the end of the first trimester, the State, in promoting its interest in the health of the mother, may, if it chooses, regulate the abortion procedure in ways that are reasonably related to maternal health.
(c) For the stage subsequent to viability the State, in promoting its interest in the potentiality of human life, may, if it chooses, regulate, and even proscribe, abortion where it is necessary, in appropriate medical judgment, for the preservation of the life or health of the mother.[4]

In effect, this ruling makes abortion a private matter during the first three months of pregnancy; and the state can only regulate the conditions under which an abortion is procured. For the remaining six months of pregnancy, regulation to prevent possible danger to the mother's health is permitted. But legislation specifically to protect the potential life of the unborn child is allowed only once the foetus is considered viable, or capable of survival outside the womb.

This decision rests on the rights of privacy and personal liberty the Court sees arising from the Ninth and Fourteenth Amendments. In

[1] *Roe v. Wade,* 41 *LW* 4213 (1973), and *Doe v. Bolton,* 41 *LW* 4233 (1973).
[2] *Texas Penal Code* §§ 1191-94, 96.
[3] *Ibid.* § 1196.
[4] 41 *LW* 4213 (1973), at 4229.

concluding that no compelling state interest exists during the first three months of pregnancy, the Court points out that a prohibition against abortion has not existed continuously from ancient times, and traces the uneven course of the development of this prohibition in the common law until passage of most of the abortion laws in the United States late in the nineteenth century. More recent liberalization of attitude on the subject by the American Medical Association, the American Public Health Association, and the American Bar Association is emphasized.

Turning to the reasons for the prohibition in this area advanced by the proponents of the status quo: the desire to curb sexual promiscuity by this means is dismissed as frivolous; and the current safety of surgical procedures within the first three months of pregnancy (when performed by a qualified physician under appropriate conditions) is considered adequate to eliminate the necessity for the state to act to protect the health of the mother. But the heart of the anti-abortion argument has always been that the state must assert its right to protect the potential life of the unborn child as much as the rights of the pregnant woman alone. The Court rejects this position, finding no adequate historical or legal basis for extending the right of legal "personhood" to the unborn child, until it is capable of surviving outside the womb. The Court also recognizes arguments favoring the mother's exercise of discretion in this matter: the mental and physical strain of child-bearing and child care, the stress on a family of an unwanted child, and the stigma attaching to the lot of an unwed mother.

"We need to resolve the difficult question of when life begins," the Court maintains, "When those trained in the respective disciplines of medicine, philosophy, and theology are unable to arrive at any consensus, the judiciary is not at this point in the development of man's knowledge in a position to speculate as to the answer." [5] Instead, the civil rights of the unborn child are seen by the Court to be vested only once "constitutional personhood" can be recognized. The Court states that a "person", in the sense of the Fourteenth Amendment, apparently did not originally include the unborn.[6] It points out that if the foetus is a "person" from conception, allowing it to be aborted to save the life of the mother places one life above another.[7] "Conception is," it

---

[5] *Ibid.*, at 4227.

[6] *Ibid.* n. 54.

[7] *Ibid.* This dilemma is still not resolved when one considers the preference the Court continues to recognize for the life of the mother.

emphasizes, "a 'process' over time." [8] The point of viability, that is once life can be sustained outside the mother's womb, is, it considers, more likely an acceptable time for constitutional rights to attach.[9] The Court adopts that time—after six months of pregnancy—as the earliest that regulation of abortion in the form of outright prohibition may begin.

This decision is a striking one, not only because of the sweeping consequences it has for most states, and despite the reputed conservatism of the new appointees to the Court, but also because of the role the Court continues to play in American social and political processes: it is able to act on controversial questions of law when the legislatures cannot or will not act on the controversial legislative issues. In this manner, it relieves one kind of build-up of social and political pressure through changes in the interpretation of law at times when most legislatures prefer to ignore the problems or heed them much more slowly. On the other hand, there is a serious question as to whether the Court is not also legislating by such radical new interpretation. One can readily sympathize with the Court's rejection of responsibility for determining the moment when life begins. But in the words of Mr. Justice White's dissenting opinion, the Court seems to have gone beyond interpretation in asserting:

... a constitutional barrier to state efforts to protect life and investing mothers and doctors with the constitutionally protected right to exterminate it.[9]

—or "terminate", that is, the potential future life of what is not yet a "constitutional person". As much as we may welcome an unexpected decision in this area on social grounds, many legal and moral questions still remain: Is the "right of privacy" an appropriate basis for a decision of this nature? Do fathers have any less a right than doctors and mothers? Why should the Court adopt the point of "viability", which is only medically relevant to the potential ability of the foetus to survive outside the mother's womb, to fix the time that legal "personhood" attaches, when both historical moral and legal precedent prefers the time of "animation" or "quickening"? Does an unborn "constitutional person" have a right to protection of his life only if the state chooses to prohibit abortion in the third trimester?

[8] *Ibid.*, at 4228.
[9] 41 *LW* 4233 (1973), at 4246.

INDEX OF PERSONS